Cinema's Missing Children

Cinema's Missing Children

Emma Wilson

WALLFLOWER PRESS
LONDON & NEW YORK

First published in Great Britain in 2003 by Wallflower Press
5 Pond Street, London NW3 2PN
www.wallflowerpress.co.uk

A catalogue for this book is available from the British Library

ISBN 1-903364-50-7 (paperback)
ISBN 1-903364-51-5 (hardback)

Printed in Great Britain by Antony Rowe, Chippenham, Wiltshire

CONTENTS

LIST OF ILLUSTRATIONS

ACKNOWLEDGEMENTS

This book was completed during research leave supported by a grant from the Arts and Humanities Research Board; I would like to record my thanks for this. Thanks are due, too, to the French Department in Cambridge for allowing me time away from teaching and for providing a strong research culture. I am deeply grateful to Jill Forbes and to Michael Sheringham for their support of and interest in this project, and to Geoffrey Nowell-Smith for his generous and acute comments on the first draft of the book. Yoram Allon has been an enthusiastic and thoughtful editor; I am indebted to him, to Del Cullen, and others at Wallflower Press. I would also like to thank Elza Adamowicz, Ian Christie, Sarah Cooper, Martin Crowley, Miranda Griffin, Nick Hammond, Susan Hayward, Sarah Kay, Phil Powrie, Kathryn Robson, Jackie Stacey, Heather Williams-Elder and, especially, Josephine Lloyd and Jacqueline Wilson. This book is dedicated to Harry Aitken.

Sections from *Cinema's Missing Children* appear elsewhere in a slightly different form: '*Three Colours: Blue*: Kieślowski, colour and the postmodern subject', *Screen*, 39, 4 (Winter 1998); 'Isabel's Child: *The Portrait of a Lady*', *Film Studies*, 3 (Spring 2002); 'Uncanny Families: *Olivier, Olivier*', *Studies in French Cinema*, 3 (2002). I am grateful to the editors of these journals for permission to draw on this material here.

INTRODUCTION

Cinema's Missing Children

In Bruno Dumont's 1999 film *L'Humanité*, a detective, Pharaon de Winter, investigates the murder of a local young girl. In one scene he catches the school bus the girl took on her last afternoon. The camera watches two little girls coming down the aisle of the bus to get off at the final stop. Pharaon follows them up a path in the flat green landscape and we watch them disappear around the corner of the road. The film watches their vanishing point before Pharaon turns to look into the grasses in the surrounding fields, grassland where the child's brutalised body, like a pale contorted doll, has been found in shock scenes earlier in the film. *L'Humanité*, and its detective, revisit the time and space at which the child went missing. This act of physical and mental rehearsal is a means of attempting to forestall and deny the loss of the child, to revisit a scene from before her loss, a scene in which she is always already missing. Mourning the child, attempting to trace the culprit, become bound up with a process of return, return to a more universal space of nostalgia and prescient fear. *L'Humanité* looks beyond the specific details of its own case history to reflect on a subject which has come to preoccupy independent and art cinema of the last decade: the missing child.

In their treatment of the subject of the missing child, the films discussed here work, like *L'Humanité*, as so many attempts to recall and remember the lost child, to revisit the site of loss and sift through its evidence and debris. As such they raise new questions about cinema as a medium of social and psychological engagement, about emotional extremes and the limits of representation.

1

Cinema's Missing Children contends that one of the central fears and compulsions explored in recent independent and art cinema is the death or loss of a child. Using the term 'missing children', and 'the missing child', I draw together a number of different threats to children and experiences of loss, abuse, murder, sickness and death. Personal loss, individual horror and mourning intersect in a network of films haunted by the spectre of children at risk from abuse, abduction, accident and illness. The issue of the missing child enables films to mobilise questions about the protection and innocence of childhood, about parenthood and the family, about the past (as childhood is constructed in retrospect as nostalgic space of safety) and about the future (as fears for children reflect anxiety about the inheritance left to future generations). As these particular issues doubtless indicate, this study takes as its focus only the topos of the missing child in a first world, Western context, and contends more with the psychology than the politics of threats to children.

In this specific context (as in others) the topic of the missing child is, of course, not new or singular to the last decade. In his sociological study, *Threatened Children: Rhetoric and Concern about Child-Victims*, published in 1990, Joel Best looks at the emergence of the issue in American culture and society. He argues: 'The recent wave of public concern over threats to children began with the discovery of the battered-child syndrome in the 1960s, spread during the 1970s through campaigns against sexual abuse, adolescent prostitution, child pornography and child snatching, and peaked with the missing-child movement in the 1980s' (1990: 176).[1] He analyses the occurrence of missing child stories on network news and in popular culture, in the form of genre film, popular fiction and urban myths, suggesting that 'by the mid-1980s, the missing-children problem had achieved extraordinary visibility. Americans saw photographs of missing children on milk cartons and grocery bags, billboards and televised public service messages' (1990: 22). The perspective of the next decade would seem at a glance to show that the problem, and its visibility, did not peak at the end of the 1980s as Best tentatively predicts, and indeed the problem has more recently been given new urgency in increasing concerns about paedophile rings and the internet, and in high profile cases of abuse and murder, witnessed in the US in the death of JonBenet Ramsay, for example, and in Europe in the Dutroux affair in the 1990s.[2] In the US, organisations such as the National Center for Missing and Exploited Children and the North American Missing Children Association are still doing essential work.[3] In France, APEV, the Association des Parents d'Enfants Victimes, still displays images of missing children in post offices.[4] Interpol currently has a database of missing and abducted children from its 178 member countries.[5] While these registers of missing children commonly include children who are victims of parental custody wrangles, teenage runaways and voluntarily missing adults listed by their parents, their existence and charting of unexplained disappearances, nevertheless, heightens awareness of the continued victimisation of children.

Although this historical perspective, and concerns about real children, must always haunt such an exploration, it is not my aim to try to say anything about true stories or about the lived horror of losing a child. These issues by necessity outreach the bounds of my study.[6] My interest, more narrowly, is in the treatment of the topic in recent cinema, and in particular in the ways in which films have sought to offer new more or less adequate modes of response to the fear or experience of losing a child. Best briefly explores the representation of the subject in film, but limits his enquiry to popular film, looking in particular at the emergence of horror as a genre in tandem with the increasing visibility of the child-victim. He argues: 'During the 1980s, popular culture frequently depicted threats to children, but it portrayed these problems in ways that fit existing entertainment formulas' (1990: 19). While the topic of missing children and child-victims continues to hold favour in popular film and fiction, of different and critical interest is a body of work that has emerged in independent and art cinema, in the work of directors such as Atom Egoyan, Pedro Almodóvar, Todd Solondz and others. What their work does, precisely, is refuse to fit existing entertainment formulas in both their manipulation of film form and in their treatment of the missing child as subject. In contrast to Hollywood in particular, the avoidance of sentiment in the treatment of this subject is seen as paramount, as witnessed in the words of a number of the directors discussed below. Further, the freedom of self-expression, beyond censorious production company constraints, is significant. A film such as *Happiness*, dropped by its production company, bears witness to the ways in which the work studied here outstrips Hollywood and mainstream conventions in both choice of subject matter and in its treatment.

Genre cinema and other popular forms function as important indices of our cultural climate and our understanding of gender, race, sexuality and other social and cultural determinants (as the work of Carol Clover and many others has indicated). Yet complementary to the study of such forms might be a renewed engagement with the ways in which independent and art cinema, too, hold singular diagnostic and interrogative power. Of course, specific distinctions between genre/Hollywood cinema on the one hand and independent/art cinema on the other are increasingly difficult to sustain and may be unhelpful in thematic approaches to cinema. The theme of the missing child is important, for example, in a box-office success such as *Minority Report* (2002). Spielberg, as elsewhere in his cinema, explores the theme of the missing child and of lost innocence in new and compulsive forms (and with particular pictorial resonance in the massive collage of photographs in *Minority Report*). Like the popular (independent) film, *In the Bedroom* (2001), or indeed *The Pledge* (2001), however, *Minority Report* makes use of the drama of the murdered child to explore the desire for recrimination and revenge. Such films explore possibilities of action rather than reflection, even if they show the mental and moral problems such action creates. Indeed in *Minority Report*, the loss of the child, which pre-dates the film's narrative, is a trigger to action but not a subject of investigation in its own right. In the sentimentality of the ending the lost child seems economically replaced where we see John Anderton back together with his now pregnant wife.

By contrast, and certainly with exceptions, many independent and art films can be seen at their best to conjure the fears and phantoms of our culture in ways which offer no easy solutions or redemptive closure. This indeed is one of the key links between discussions in the chapters of this volume. Such refusal of (re)solution and often of action opens a space for reflection and imaginative, emotive viewing. It also suggests a mode of respect and reckoning with the difficulty of the subject treated. In this respect, I argue that the films under discussion offer engaged means of thinking through and responding to the topic of the missing child. I do not look at independent and art cinema independently of other more popular films and art forms, but I do argue for the specificity and importance of such films' treatment of emotive and excessive subjects. Further, while independent films may bring a new seriousness to the treatment of the subject of the missing child, as feature films they do not perhaps have the same responsibility to their subject as documentary film or news footage, offering possibilities of more creative, risky or amoral interrogations of loss and survival.

A number of questions central to my project, about the loss of a child, about parental guilt, testimony and survival can be raised by returning to a much-referenced extract from Freud: the dream of the burning child. I will briefly sketch out the dream and some of its key interpretations before relating them specifically to missing child film.

The dream of the burning child is found in the seventh chapter of *The Interpretation of Dreams*. Freud introduces it as a model dream, told to him by a woman patient, who had herself heard it in a lecture on dreams. Freud narrates the dream as follows:

A father had been watching beside his child's sick-bed for days and nights on end. After the child had died, he went into the next room to lie down, but left the door open so that he could see from his bedroom into the room in which his child's body was laid out, with tall candles standing round it. An old man had been engaged to keep watch over it, and sat beside the body murmuring prayers. After a few hours' sleep, the father had a dream that *his child was standing beside his bed, caught him by the arm and whispered to him reproachfully: 'Father, don't you see I'm burning?'* He woke up, noticed a bright glare of light from the next room, hurried into it and found the old watchman had dropped off to sleep and that the wrappings and one of the arms of his beloved child's dead body had been burned by a lighted candle that had fallen on them. (Freud 1985a: 652)

Freud invites us to wonder why the dream occurred, in circumstances in which the most rapid awakening was called for. The first answer he provides, in line with one of the general theses of *The Interpretation of Dreams*, was that the dream contained the fulfilment of a wish to deny the child's death. He writes: 'For the sake of the fulfilment of this wish the father prolonged his sleep by one moment. The dream was preferred to a waking reflection because it was able to show the child as once more alive' (1985a: 653).

Lacan returns to the dream of the burning child in his Seminar 11, with a reading which departs radically from Freud's interpretation. Lacan questions: '*What is it that wakes the sleeper*? Is it not, *in* the dream, another reality?' (1994: 58). Lacan finds in the dream, a horrifying encounter with the Real:

For it is not that, in the dream, [the father] persuades himself that the son is still alive. But the terrible vision of the dead son taking the father by the arm designates a beyond that makes itself heard in the dream. Desire manifests itself in the dream by the loss expressed in an image at the most cruel point of the object. It is only in the dream that this truly unique encounter can occur. (1994: 59)

Slavoj Žižek, glossing Lacan, explains his reading:

First [the subject] constructs a dream, a story which enables him to prolong his sleep, to avoid awakening into reality. But the thing that he encounters in the dream, the reality of his desire, the Lacanian Real – in our case, the reality of the child's reproach to his father, 'Can't you see that I am burning?', implying the father's fundamental guilt – is more terrifying than so-called external reality itself, and that is why he awakens: to escape the Real of his desire, which announces itself in the terrifying dream. He escapes into so-called reality to be able to continue to sleep, to maintain his blindness, to elude awakening into the real of his desire. (1989: 45)

For Žižek, the encounter with the Real is bound up with an (excessive) realisation of parental guilt. This is the horror encountered in the dream from which the father escapes in waking.

Cathy Caruth makes a further important reading of the dream. She argues that for Lacan: 'It is *the dream itself … that wakes the sleeper*, and it is in this paradoxical awakening – an awakening not to, but against, the very wishes of consciousness – that the dreamer confronts the reality of a death from which he cannot turn away' (1996: 99). She continues: 'For if the dreamer's awakening can be seen as a response to the words, to the address of the child, within the dream, then the awakening represents a paradox about the necessity and impossibility of confronting death. Waking up in order to see, the father discovers that he has once again *seen too late* to prevent the burning' (1996: 100). Caruth's thinking on traumatic response is governed, however, by a profound concern for the possibility of survival. For Caruth: 'It is precisely the dead child, the child in its irreducible inaccessibility and otherness, who says to the father: *wake up, leave me, survive*; *survive to tell the story of my burning*' (1996: 105). The imperative to survive in order to testify is Caruth's supplement to the narrative. Her prose testifies to her sense of the dream, and its address to the father, as imperative. Lacan's observation, 'for no one can say what the death of a child is, except the father *qua* father' (1994: 59), is glossed by Caruth as: 'The father must receive the dead child's words' (1996: 106). Her move into a reading of the dream which privileges the imperative of a speaking that awakens others is, though ethically motivated, open to question.

Caruth's reading is at odds with Žižek's. This she acknowledges in a footnote, where she writes: 'Slavoj Žižek suggests that the awakening in Lacan's reading of the dream is the precise reversal of the usual understanding of dream as fiction and of awakening as reality: he argues that the awakening of the father in Lacan's reading is an "escape" from the real into ideology' (1996: 142). Disagreeing with Žižek, she speaks of 'the difficulty of accepting that awakening to a child's dead corpse could ever be understood as an escape' (*Ibid.*). For me, the brilliance of Žižek's reading is that it hazards an interpretation of the (missed) encounter with the Real: at its heart, Žižek suggests, is the father's impossible, tortured guilt in response to his child's suffering and death. This is what is worse than awakening to the knowledge of the child's death.

The dream of the burning child, and its interpretations, anticipate on several levels the concerns of this study. In the first place the manifest content of the dream of the burning child predetermines its relevance to a study of ways of contending with the loss of children. More than the commentators above, I am interested in the dream literally because it is about the death of a child, about hesitance in facing and accepting that death, about parental responsibility and guilt, about the impossibility of representation of such experience.

To return, then, to the wish-fulfilment thesis in which the dream offers a reparative glimpse of the child still living, a moving, speaking subject. Freud's first interpretation itself draws on the hesitation between life and death, seeing in the dream a denial of the knowledge of the child's death. In this respect, it bears comparison with other representations of parental experience of attending a child's death bed and contending with the illusory, desperate wish for the dead child's animation. Consider for example a description, contemporary to Freud, from Stefan Zweig's *Twenty-Four Hours in the Life of a Woman*:

> There he lies, my darling boy, in his narrow cot, just as he died. Only his eyes have been closed, his wise, dark eyes; and his hands have been crossed over his breast. Four candles are burning, one at each corner of the bed. I cannot bear to look, I cannot bear to move; for when the candles flicker, shadows chase one another over his face and his closed lips. It looks as if his features stirred, and I could almost fancy that he is not dead after all, that he will awake and with his clear voice will say something childishly loving. But I know that he is dead. (1999: 10)

In this extract, as in the tradition of funerary photography, the corpse is seen as sleeping, as not quite yet dead. Here there are candles, as in the dream of the burning child, and it is their light, their burning flames, which offer the illusion of animation, of visual movement. The child's animation is a visual delusion and hallucinatory, rather than oneiric as in Freud. The scene seems protocinematic in its visual detail. While Zweig looks forward to the lighting and *mise-en-scène* of cinema, film itself has proved a privileged medium for the exploration of the hesitation between life and death, of phantoms, of the living dead, of wish-fulfilling animation, visual memories and hallucinations.

Freud's account of the dream itself may be usefully reconsidered for its protocinematic qualities. Freud attends to details of space and light: the proximity of the rooms where the child lies and where the father sleeps, with an open door between them, the tall candles around the child's body, the bright glare of light from the child's room. The father is called to see a visual spectacle of the child on fire. Where troubled vision and hallucination can offer the illusion of animation, vision is also shown in Freud as an acute form of witnessing. The father is called to see the child's annihilation a second time in the burning of his body. The candles which might offer the illusion of animation (as in Zweig) consume the flesh which seems still horribly sensate.

The burning of the child's flesh illustrates another way in which doubts over life and death remain, this time through affect, rather than (as in Zweig) through visual hallucination. The child's body is still vulnerable and friable, though dead: in this sense the father is still conscious, in some senses, of the child as suffering subject. The repetition of the child's bodily trauma (the burning candle echoing the fever which has killed the child), and of the father's recognition of loss, accumulates pathos; the child's body, though inanimate, still calls for protection and repair. Such intense investment in the fate of the child's body has been witnessed recently in the UK scandal about the retention of children's organs after post mortems. The fantasy of the intact body of the child seems to stand as some small defence against the knowledge of the child's loss. In the dream of the burning child the father is brought to confront a further horror of the wish to see the child alive again: if he is alive, the child can still die.

In discussions of the films which follow I will examine ways in which the fantasy of the lost child's animation and continued existence is crucial to the genre of the missing child film. More than offer reparative illusion however, film itself will be seen to offer a material form in which doubts about the return, the reanimation, the fantasy, the phantom of the missing child, can be tested, played out or dismissed. Such mourning rituals frequently depend on disavowal, a disavowal which cinema as medium at once of photographic realism and reparative, commemorative, knowing illusion, seems particularly apt to represent. Indeed the space and light which are the visual matter of cinema of the mind, dream and psyche recall the literal *mise-en-scène* of Freud's dream of the burning child.

Yet the films under discussion will only offer a cautious engagement with wish-fulfilment; at no point do they suggest that dream, hallucination, or cinematic illusion can offer relief, repair or exit from the horror of the loss of a child. Instead cinema is seen as a medium in which to play out such losses, to debate their meanings and to offer them cultural significance. While I have perpetuated the Freudian notion of wish-fulfilment, above, there is no sense in which I see the cinema of missing children as escapist. On the contrary it calls attention very forcefully to these losses as inescapable, whilst revealing too the pathos of the wishes and dreams, rituals and hallucinations of those in the process of mourning. The wish to see the child alive carries its own terrors of the child's continued suffering. In the Zweig text, notably, the mother narrates: 'I cannot bear to look, I cannot bear to move.' The illusion of the child's animation would be too terrible if it then had, once again, to be relinquished. In this sense, we come closer to Lacan and Žižek's rereadings of the dream; waking to find the child really dead is seen as a form of escape.

For Lacan, as we have seen, the father's encounter with the dead child in the dream is a (missed) encounter with the Real, with fear, suffering and sensation beyond language. I am interested in what is at stake in this instant of fusion between the Real and the encounter with the dead child. Can this bear on other instances of the child as dead, endangered, under threat or erasure in dreams, in film, in images? How far does the dead child, and the apprehension of a child's suffering or loss, stand as a form of an ineffable or absolute, of the Real fissuring representation?

For Žižek, the encounter with the Real in the dream is embodied in the child's reproach to the father, implying the father's guilt. This has particular resonance for the missing child film, which has made one of its points of exploration the guilt and (excessive) responsibility of the grieving parent. The missing child topos offers a form and focus for an unsettling of the foundations of parenthood. Indeed the films in question work to explore both maternity and paternity in relation to the missing child. Maternity is seen as experience of loss, of loss of the child who grows up, and more monstrously loss of the child who disappears or dies. Paternity is seen to be sometimes disquietingly bound up with questions of abuse, as the figure of the Father of Enjoyment infiltrates art cinema. Several films under discussion confront sexual abuse in the family context, exploring the sexualisation of children as an excessive, distorted image of normative processes of separation, initiation and the acquisition of sexual knowledge. Guilt, protection and abuse, so enmeshed as at times to be indivisible, form the fabric of much of these films. Their aim appears not to be to order or organise experience, to establish values or rules, but rather to represent and respond to its mess and pain. This levelling, and suspension of judgement, may be disturbing in a territory where views on right and wrong have tended to be entrenched and absolute. My aim is by no means to correlate the experiences of the bereaved parent and the abuser; to many this would seem obscene. Rather I want to look at the ways in which adults, loving parents and criminals alike, contend with an image of the missing child, with the child hopelessly (or viciously) idealised, of the child whose development in time and memory has been arrested.

Through my readings of these missing child films, I tend to see the encounter with the Real, the loss of the child, as irreparable damage, as irrecoverable horror: horror which cannot be recovered in memory or representation, horror from which there is no absolute recovery. I want to register then my hesitant acceptance of Caruth's reading of the dream of the burning child as narrative of possible (if belated) survival. Possibilities of survival remain tentative. While a number of different creative methods are used for distraction and for commemoration, it is open to debate whether the bereaved in these films find expression or relief in testifying to the life or suffering of the child. The losses pictured cannot be made sense of or adequately encompassed in narrative or other testimonial forms. These losses are relived, denied, obliterated, fictionalised without repair. The missing children are angelised, idealised, embalmed in memory and, in more lurid examples, fragilised, sexualised and even set in formaldehyde. This is the sickening, surplus horror of the love of children. Child death insists without sense, without taste, without place in representation. It is unnatural and unredeemable.

The aim of the films under discussion appears to be to stage an encounter with both the real and the Real: to bring cinema into contact with one of the most urgent emotional subjects, and to respond to that issue by showing its losses as annihilating, immense and nonsensical. Such a remit seems to bring risks of sensationalism: the missing child film as an ultimate in psychic violence and horror. Such exploitation is avoided in these films in their respective, engaged attempts to challenge the inadequacy of art forms in the face of trauma and suffering. Cinema as art form, as mode of commemoration and response, is interrogated and transformed in each of the films under discussion. I should clarify, indeed, that this artistic engagement and self-reflexivity, where an excessive subject calls for new modes of showing and seeing, has been an important criterion in my choice of films. These films not only take missing children as their subject (as do many other mainstream works), they also make of that encounter with the child as missing or endangered a tear or fissure in their film-making art such that new ways of seeing may briefly be glimpsed. Film at its most devastating is not escape from reality, but an encounter with the Real we seek to leave behind in the movie-theatre. In this sense, returning to Lacan, I see these films working as dreams which wake the sleeper.

Cinema's Missing Children presents discussion of a series of films made since 1990: *Three Colours: Blue* (1993), *Exotica* (1994), *Happiness* (1998), *Olivier, Olivier* (1992), *All About My Mother* (1999), *The Portrait of a Lady* (1996), *Jude* (1995), *Ratcatcher* (1999), various Dogme films, and *The Son's Room* (2001). A number of other films – *La Classe de neige* (1998), *The Lost Son* (1998), *L'Humanité* (1999), *The Five Senses* (2000) – vied for inclusion. The choice of my corpus of films testifies, however, to a more abiding concern with questions of childhood, loss, abuse or mourning in the work of the directors selected. In the case of *Happiness*, there is no actual missing child; yet in its exploration of child abuse and paedophilia, the film is key to current debates about the family and children at risk. Further, Solondz's works, and those of others, encourage viewers to consider whether the topos of the missing child can and should also encompass the question of the destruction of childhood by abuse. Although in the other films discussed here there are, literally, missing or mourned children, throughout the study I hope to retain some elasticity in exploring the ways in which this topos touches on broader issues about abuse, loss and nostalgia. A number of the films directly confront material in a contemporary context, while others use a contemporary frame in which to view earlier child deaths (notably those of the nineteenth and early twentieth century).

While each film raises a distinct set of issues, allowing each chapter to stand alone, a number of themes will re-emerge at various points in discussion. The ordering of the films here runs from intrauterine relations and birth in *Three Colours: Blue*, through burial and exorcism in *The Kingdom* (1994), to some hesitant sense of future survival in *The Son's Room*. Yet this illusory cycle partly undermines my sense that each of the films discussed represents a new experiment in representing loss or personal horror and its management. I do not wish to imply any sense of progress in treating the subject; only perhaps a limited optimism in cinema as medium witnessed in the engaged return to this excessive subject. My aim here is to pay close attention to the films themselves, to look at their sentient and expressive details and to consider the possibilities they offer for response.

While the films discussed all date from the last decade, missing children have appeared and disappeared in earlier art cinema, as cross-references throughout the study will indicate. Emblematic of the subject and its representation is *Don't Look Now* (1973), where the figuring of the dead child is bound up with the aesthetic of the film, its return to shapes and liquid forms, seepage and bleeding of colour. *Don't Look Now* anticipates, indeed, the type of experimentation with representation of the subject of the missing child which I find pursued throughout the films studied here. However, while looking at the ways in which these films change cinema as medium, I also want to consider the changes wrought in the general context and forms of representation of childhood in the decades since *Don't Look Now*.

In *The Queen of America goes to Washington City*, Lauren Berlant considers the ways in which new means of representation work to reconstitute the family, the way it is constructed and recorded. She writes, for example, that 'the video camera is a direct extension of the portable camera, whose mass production reconstructed childhood and domestic memory' (1997: 142–3).[7] Berlant links this imbrication of technology and domestic memory to nostalgia and fantasies of the family, arguing: 'The nostalgic energy for a family that does not yet exist and has never existed enables the new reproductive technologies – which now include cinema and television – to exploit commodity identification for the purpose of promoting "family values"' (1997: 140). She looks further at the development of the sonogram

Figure 1 *Don't Look Now*

and the foetal photograph, arguing that foetuses become subjects, innocent and incipient Americans, by virtue of being photographed. She concludes: 'most important, the fetal/infantile person is a *stand-in* for a complicated and contradictory set of anxieties and desires about national identity' (1997: 6). Berlant's comments draw attention to the value which is increasingly given to the (imagined) figure of the child in contemporary culture. She sees this over-investment in fantasies of innocence produced or propagated by the new forms through which the child, incipient or actual, is represented.

The missing child topos is, in some senses, always already photographic. News reports and public information invariably figure an image of the missing child, a family snapshot or school photograph. This painful visual motif is adopted too in documentary and feature film-making. The pathos of the image of the missing or dead child is witnessed, for example, in Spike Lee's use of photographs and images of grave stones in his documentary about the bombing of the Baptist church in Birmingham, Alabama: *Four Little Girls* (1997). Images of missing children on milk cartons are glimpsed in *The Lost Boys* (1987). Looking back to earlier films we see a photograph of a missing girl circulating in *The Wicker Man* (1973), while missing girls are imaged in a searing close-up of a poster in *Picnic at Hanging Rock* (1975). If photography is always already linked with the genre, the films which make up the basis of this study work more broadly to make self-conscious use of some of the medical and domestic devices to which Berlant draws attention: the sonogram image, the family photograph, home movie and video footage.

A literal sonogram (or ultrasound) image, and its link to a more general exploration of colour as a means of recalling intra-uterine symbiosis, are found in *Three Colours: Blue*, as discussed in chapter one. Family snapshots appear in *Happiness* and a photograph as fetish in *All About My Mother*. Considering the broader aesthetic of the films under discussion, (nineteenth-century) funerary photographs and photographs of children (in particular those of Sally Mann) are possible points of reference in *Jude* and *Ratcatcher* respectively. Video footage is key to processes of recall and mourning in *Exotica*, while a home movie aesthetic is seen to be adapted, and disrupted, in the Dogme films discussed. Investment in the uses and abuses of these media is very different in the films studied here from that of the dominant US culture Berlant works to analyse. Indeed the films under analysis take the motifs and modes of representation of childhood and the family of dominant culture, and insert them creatively in their art in order to renew cinema as art form and interrogate the nostalgic values they embody. Key to this interrogation is a knowing, and melancholic, recognition of the inter-relation between childhood, loss and representation.

Emblematic of this interrelation is the use of home movie footage in Derek Jarman's *The Last of England* (1987) where we see a delicate child in a flower garden with his sister. Such images always already speak of loss, I think, as well as nostalgia, heightened in particular here in the knowledge of adult mortality. A similar effect is achieved more directly in the closing moments of *Philadelphia* (1993) where the dead protagonist is recalled, emotively, in home movie footage of his childhood. Home movies conjure a past that is now missing, that is restored as illusion in hesitant moving forms. Cinema more generally has been recognised as melancholic medium, as one which depends on loss and temporal *décalage*, as Bazin, Metz, Barthes and others have identified. What missing children films do, however, is to confront the connection between this quality of the medium, this imbrication of cinema with memory and loss, and the specific subject of childhood.

Berlant shows a society impelled by the force of nostalgic energy, drawing on representations of children in order to shore up a fantasy of the family and family values. It is instructive to remember, though, as Svetlana Boym reminds us in *The Future of Nostalgia*, that there are two kinds of nostalgia: 'Restorative nostalgia stresses *nostos* [return home] and attempts a transhistorical reconstruction of the lost home. Reflective nostalgia thrives in *algia* [longing], the longing itself, and delays the homecoming – wistfully, ironically, desperately' (2000: xviii). Where the nostalgia Berlant analyses may be seen as restorative nostalgia (Boym herself links such nostalgia to recent religious and national revivals), the nostalgia of the films investigated here is, by contrast, reflective, wistful and desperate. The missing child, lost or dead, as topos, offers an ironic and painful contrast to the championing of family values of restorative nostalgia.

Certainly both investments in childhood, the restorative and the reflective/melancholic, are haunted by certain angelic illusions of the child, fantasies of childhood recalled. The difference between the two lies in the belief (or lack thereof) in the possibility of restoration, the return of the missing child, the re-instatement of a system of family values. The films discussed below are cautious and doubtful about this possibility. Rather than working to be reparative or restorative, their motivation is to find an (adequate) means to lament and mourn missing children and childhood as missing. This leads to experimentation with film art, self-conscious manipulation of the melancholic and illusory properties of cinema (as seen, say, in the visual illusions and restorative hallucinations of *All About My Mother*, *Olivier, Olivier* and *The Son's Room*, in the self-conscious experimentation with period and heritage forms in *Jude* and *The Portrait of a Lady*). Film is used as medium in which to contest abuse, suffering and the misplacement of children. It is used as medium in which to record the disrupted temporality, physical and mental horror of mourning a lost child.

Questions may arise about whether such a subject should be represented at all, whether any representation runs the risk of aestheticisation and exploitation. Indeed questions of the avoidance or elision of representation arise in chapter one on *Three Colours: Blue*, chapter three on *Happiness* and chapter seven on *The Portrait of a Lady*. While being wary of the risks of exploitation, I remain committed to a view that cinema can and should intervene in such personal and social questions. The beauty and order of film-making art may always fall short of the emotion and pain of lived experience. Recognising this need not remove the possibility of film as an act of commemoration, as a creative response to experience, as a means vicariously to intimate something of emotion and sensation always beyond the viewer's reach. In her extraordinarily rich *Quoting Caravaggio*, Mieke Bal looks at the photographs of Andres Serrano, in particular a photograph of 1992, *The Morgue (Child Abuse)*, where we see an image of a child's angelic face in a white shroud. Bal argues: 'the image's beauty pays homage to the child it mourns, transfiguring its abject state of dead body and discarded subject into a sacrificial presence. But this is a sacrifice that does not redeem; it aims to effectuate change, not to overcome, for the visual presence of the dead child insists that abuse cannot be redeemed' (1999: 70–1). I would borrow her words to speak of the representations of missing children studied here; the undoubted visual beauty of some of the films studied, and of their mourned

14

and mourning subjects, comes as a stringent call for change, as a tribute and as witness to the impossibility of redemption (or cure). Arguably this beauty also risks working insidiously to make the (suffering) child desirable. More than Serrano, however, and with the aid of narrative progression as well as visual framing, the films under discussion also work to consider the risks of beauty, suffering and abuse in representation. As will be seen in particular in discussion in chapters two and three, on *Exotica* and *Happiness* respectively, these films work to run risks in order then to be more thoroughly inoculated against the desires they represent.

Bal links the beauty of the Serrano image to nostalgia; for her, nostalgia is defined 'as a longing for a past that never existed; a past is called upon to provide what the present lacks' (1999: 72). She argues that 'taking nostalgia seriously is as important as accepting and seriously studying other forms of "popular" culture' (1999: 73). The missing child is arguably a nostalgic, even sentimental or maudlin subject. The topos, intensely emotive, inherits some of the forms of melodrama or the women's film. Following Bal's defence of nostalgia, I suggest that the topos of the missing child too deserves to be taken seriously. Its treatment across a range of art movies, demonstrates the ways in which art cinema can be cross-fertilised by the concerns of popular art forms – here horror and melodrama – and by the news media, and bring forth new, hybrid, and eviscerating representations.

Cinema has long been concerned with the lady who vanishes. It may be time to register a shift in this cultural obsession. In contemporary film, increasingly, the lost object of desire, origin and vanishing point is the missing child.

CHAPTER ONE

Kieślowski's Lost Daughter:
Three Colours: Blue

Three Colours: Blue (1993), the first part of Krzysztof Kieślowski's trilogy, makes trauma and loss, both public and personal, its central subject. Julie, the main protagonist, loses her husband and small daughter in a car crash whose impact reverberates from the first minutes of the film. Julie's distress and subsequent survival in denial, as she attempts to dispossess her past, are Kieślowski's focus. The film offers a charged analysis of a terrorised and numbed survival, of the isolation of the trauma victim and of the gradual rediscovery of relationality. In this way, the film's relations to the cultural and psychological concerns of the last decade, and to the other films studied here, are established.

Dominant readings of *Blue*, taking their cue from the film's narrative focus, devote attention to the loss of Patrice, Julie's husband, a celebrated contemporary composer.[1] His funeral confirms his place in public memory and the collective imaginary. Patrice's music is heard as both diegetic and non-diegetic sound throughout *Blue*. Much of the narrative tension concerns Julie's decision at first to erase his unfinished Concerto, then, as it proves all too indelible and insistent in the public mind and in her psyche, to let it return, be remembered, reworked and finally performed (as we hear in the film's synthetic ending). Music is the medium of public memory and mediated relationality, the means by which Julie negotiates her husband's loss and her own survival. Critics agree on the emotive force, resolution and hope of the end of the film.

But this is only part of the story of loss, memory and survival in *Blue*. The analysis I offer here works to uncover an alternative memory base in the film. This memory base allows me to explore the challenge *Blue* offers to the temporality and teleology of public memory, as well as the reworking it affords of the cinematic medium. This different reading of the film unsettles our apprehension of Julie's recovery and the film's closure, whilst deepening, perhaps, a sense of the emotional complexity of Kieślowski's analysis of love and loss.

At times, in *Blue*, the loss of Anna, Julie's daughter, seems all but forgotten. It is this loss which I want to recall here and which I argue is commemorated, mourned and denied in the chromatic experimentation which accompanies and shadows the play with music in particular and sound more generally within the film.

Anna is the first figure to be seen in *Blue*. As the film follows the car in the moments before the crash, we see her sitting in the back, framed in the glass of the rear windscreen. Her image appears as if through a greenish yellow filter. Behind glass it is always already cinematic, whilst simultaneously pathetic for the viewer in retrospect as the film unfolds. These rare shots of the time before the crash remain isolated in the film. There are no flashbacks; Anna's face, her presence, exists as a receding memory for the viewer, as for Julie. Its image is already tremulous, partial, as the car drives through a tunnel, and the image is lit up, then falls into shadow.

On one level, the opening of the film establishes a brief family intimacy. Yet this is insistently undermined by visual markers which remind the viewer, implicitly, of its imminent loss. The car stops for Anna to pee in the bushes. The image of the child returning to the car is shot from beneath the underside of the car. While the wheel is seen in the foreground, in focus, the image of the child, her dark dress with a white collar, is blurred, is already marked as a mnemonic image, viewed from the perspective of the crash, the car's mechanical failure. We see the brake fluid slowly leaking down the side of the wheel, this ominous detail echoing the child's pee, yet acting too as fatal, unseen forewarning of the crash.

The opening scenes are pregnant with knowledge of the impending disaster. This is conveyed all the more subtly in the filming of the image of Anna in the back of the car. As we first see her, her head is on one side – she seems to be daydreaming. Her eyes are dark in her pale face which becomes an abstract shape. This vision of Anna seems to exist in the film as anamorphic image, as point of fascination and reference which unsettles our reading of the film, and realigns its signification and emotive power.

In evoking anamorphosis, Lacan refers famously to Holbein's painting, *The Ambassadors*. Focusing attention on the blur which hovers in the foreground of the painting, he draws us back from the image to see the form it comes to represent: 'a skull [une tête de mort]' (1994: 88). Lacan suggests that here Holbein makes visible for us 'the subject as annihilated' (*Ibid.*). He explains in his following seminar that this 'magic floating object', this blur in our field of vision, 'reflects our own nothingness, in the figure of the death's head' (1994: 92). Žižek, reading Lacan, explains that anamorphosis, in a picture, forms a 'meaningless stain that "denatures" it, rendering all its constituents "suspicious", and thus opens up the abyss of the search for a meaning – nothing is what it seems to be, everything is to be interpreted, everything is supposed to possess some supplementary meaning' (1991: 91). The anamorphic image of Anna's pale face, a prefigurement of death, allows us to realign a reading of *Blue* and rethink its representation of trauma, mourning and recovery.

In making this link between the image of Anna in *Blue*, and Lacan's discussion of anamorphosis, I draw on potential visual similarities between the image of the child's head, with its dark almost empty eyes, and the image of the skull in Holbein. While the image in *Blue* is seen centre-screen and in focus, rather than at the periphery of our vision, in the chronology of the film and its temporal sequence, the image is positioned liminally. The image as *memento mori* gathers force and pathos, indeed the film only seems to yield this reading of the image, after the death of Anna in the crash. Yet I suggest that the image of the child as death's head, as annihilation of the subject, also has broader resonance and reference within the context of Kieślowski's film-making, and contemporary art cinema in general.

One of the questions which will return throughout this study is that of the challenge faced by the film-maker who attempts to represent the death of a child. How does film offer some intervention in debates on childhood and death in contemporary culture? What diagnosis do contemporary directors offer of the fantasies, the malaise, the fears and horrors of our cultural dominant? How does Kieślowski's film-making intersect with this collective anxiety about innocence and loss?

The death of a child figures previously in Kieślowski's film-making, notably in the first film of his *Dekalog* (1988). Here the death takes place close to the end of the film. But repeat viewing shows that this death is always already known, that it is the film's point of departure and point of reference. A child, Pavel, drowns in a skating accident on a frozen lake. The first shot of the film is ice melting; the edge of the ice dissolving into water stands as the image at the limit of our vision. The film cuts to shots of a woman weeping. Her tears are inspired by television pictures of Pavel running in a crowd of children. Like the children in Italian Neo-realist cinema, like Anna Torent in *The Spirit of the Beehive* (1973) or *Cria Cuervos* (1975), like Anna in *Blue*,

Pavel (Wojciech Klata) is a dark-haired, large-eyed child. His image on the television screen, close to the start of *Dekalog 1*, is in monochrome black and white. The image is in slow motion as he approaches the camera, his face gradually blurring in close-up, then stilled as the image freezes. Before the film unfolds, it is stained, skewed, by this *memento mori*; Pavel's death is always already known. We do not see the accident on the lake; instead it bleeds into the consciousness of Pavel's father. As he is working, he catches sight of a stain of spilt ink slowly seeping beneath his papers (an echo of the premonitory red stain in *Don't Look Now*). The child's death, sensed and unspeakable, figures as a disturbance in the visual field, as amorphous, nauseous image which draws the representation aslant and disrupts its normative, redemptive power.

It is this exploration of the distortion of visual representation in response to savage loss which is pursued in *Blue*. Kieślowski shows how grief may contaminate art (and here the force of seepage, staining and bleeding is felt). Yet he shows too how an art form, cinema, may be moulded, may metamorphose to meet the challenge of an irreparable subject.

Anna, and her image, are lost in long stretches of *Blue*. Nevertheless her name is one of the first words heard in the film, as Julie calls her daughter before the crash. It is heard again as Julie awakens in the hospital. Anna is her first word as she questions the doctor about her daughter's survival. The force of Julie's grief for her daughter, outstripping the loss of her husband, is felt as she views their funeral. Although brief, this becomes one of the key representations of maternal loss and mourning in recent cinema (bearing comparison, for example, with Manuela's grief represented in *All About My Mother*).

Olivier, assistant to Julie's husband, has brought a miniature television into the clinic where Julie recuperates after the crash. This allows her to watch the televised funeral of her husband and daughter; the small screen opens out a space within the enclosure of the clinic, and of Julie's suffering, where we see a public act of commemoration and mourning. She switches on the television and, as its interference subsides, we see the two coffins. At first Julie turns away from the funeral. She lies hidden under her bedclothes. But then we follow her watching the images. In the televised funeral footage, the camera offers an overhead shot of the two coffins, one a smaller copy of the other. From the right hand side of the screen, we see Julie's finger silhouetted as she painstakingly, hesitantly touches the image of her daughter's coffin.[2] This attempt to find contact with the lost daughter, the contact of finger on screen, signals the poignancy of Kieślowski's work in close-up. The distance between the distressed, tender mother and her lost child is at once avowed and denied by the prosthetic televisual images.

The television footage continues to record the funeral oration, where Anna's death is a secondary detail ('We also mourn his five-year-old daughter who died by his side'). These words appear to trigger Julie's tears and expression of grief. As if to suggest the enormity and inexpressibility of her sensation (the partiality of its representation), the camera holds Julie's face in extreme close-up, focusing only on parts of her face, her mouth, her cheek. We cut from this intimate view of Julie back to Anna's coffin where we see her name imprinted and a single white rose. Julie's finger approaches the image once more, and the film cuts back to her face now contorted, her lips drawing in her emotion, tears running down her cheek. As she weeps, the television images blur and disappear in interference. In the last images of the scene, Julie's face entirely fills the screen, in close-up, in shadow, the scar under her eye showing in deeper relief. Her eye now looks straight at the camera in an image which attempts some contact with the viewer, some breakdown of mediation in the sheer presence of Julie's grief before us.

In the blanking of the television screen she watches, Julie's numbed horror erases the public images of grief and commemoration. Julie has tried to touch and animate those images, to make contact with them, as the film itself offers some opening for contact with its viewer. From this point on, however, *Blue*, will shy away from direct representation of Anna's life and death. Now Anna apparently only returns as point of denial, as force of negation: Julie asks an estate agent to find her an apartment in a building where there are no children, she borrows a cat to kill baby mice which infest this apartment. By the end of the film Julie can offer love and generosity to Sandrine, who is carrying Patrice's second child. She can give her house to Sandrine so the child may have his father's name and home. Again Anna seems forgotten.

Yet, could *Blue* be so cold in its eradication of the daughter? Could the mother's grief be so short-lived, so effectively repressed? Anna, the signifier, echoes the Greek preposition and prefix *ana* (as heard in anamorphosis) meaning up, back, throughout. Anna comes back throughout *Blue*. I argue that Kieślowski finds different means to commemorate the daughter, her link with her mother, the trauma of the severance of this bond, and the welling nostalgia this loss inspires. This different memory base, and means of commemoration, commands the film's chromatic experimentation. Indeed the colour blue evoked in the title emerges in the film in the scene following Julie's response to the child's funeral. To explore the meanings and expressivity of the colour blue, in and beyond Kieślowski, I turn to the work of Julia Kristeva.

In 'Giotto's Joy', Kristeva writes: 'Blue is the first colour to strike the visitor as [s]he enters the semidarkness of the Arena chapel' (1980: 224). The chapel here becomes a space of 'choric' fantasy, of somatic memory, coloured blue. As Kristeva puts it: 'such a blue takes hold of the viewer at the extreme limit of visual perception' (*Ibid.*). Her theory of colour privileges the colour blue. She writes, for example: 'all colours, but blue in particular ... have a noncentred or decentring effect' (1980: 225). In dim light, short wavelengths prevail over long ones; before sunrise, blue is the first colour to appear. This primacy given to blue – at the start of the day and at the start of the perception of light – is also linked by Kristeva to biological development where she surmises that centred vision (the identification of objects) comes into play after colour perceptions. This leads to the conclusion that all colours, but *blue in particular* as the first colour perceived by the child's retina, take the adult back to the stage before the identification of objects and individuation. Blue is linked by Kristeva to the semiotic and to the space of symbiosis between mother and child.

For Kandinsky, famously, 'blue is the typical heavenly colour. The ultimate feeling it creates is one of rest. When it sinks almost to black, it echoes a grief that is hardly human. ... In music a light blue is like a flute' (1977: 38). These terms evoke the spectrum of colour, music and emotion in *Three Colours: Blue*. The film's images of Julie against blue and in blue appear to create a contemporary *Mater Dolorosa* who signifies chromatically the divinity, rest and grief of which Kandinsky speaks.

Blue is a liminal colour. Neurophysiologists note that as it grows dark, as the eye begins to adapt, it becomes more sensitive to blue light. For this reason blue flowers look brighter than others at twilight. In the words of Derek Jarman, 'Blue is darkness made visible' (1994: 14).

Kieślowski's *Blue* is, for some, an aesthetic exploration of colour, an experiment with the ways in which manipulating and limiting colour may alter the visual style and emotive effect of a film. This concern is witnessed earlier in his film-making in the use of colour filters in *A Short Film About Killing* (1988) and *The Double Life of Véronique* (1991); the project will be pursued in the latter two films of the trilogy. *Blue* has received both praise and criticism for its chromatic experimentation. For the critic Vincent Amiel, the film stresses 'the mediation of the image, its illusory quality' (1996: 74). For Almodóvar, 'the cinematography ... is very beautiful but it is too self-conscious, there are too many filters, too many personal touches by the director of photography' (1994: 83).

Whilst acknowledging the status of *Blue* as aesthetic construct, I argue that the use of colour forms an integral part of the film's analysis of trauma and mourning for a lost child. Here the intimations of the psychological effect of colour expressed by Kristeva partially underpin my argument. I suggest that the use of blue, in *Blue*, is simultaneously mimetic and expressive, objective and subjective. Coloured light, and colour itself, become means to reflect and designate Julie's mourning for her daughter.

Figure 2 *Three Colours: Blue*

Julie's state of mind, as she is represented as victim of trauma, is revealed in two ways: through music and reflected light. We see this for the first time as she sits outside the clinic, supposedly asleep. Blue light plays over her face and she jolts awake as music interrupts the silence of the scene. Blue light floods the frame as a moving camera closes in on Julie and her reaction. Sound and light vanish as a journalist appears and speaks. Her intrusion triggers the blanking of the screen and the irruption of music once more before image and language return. Clearly this is a scene of involuntary memory: Julie is prey to aural and visual disturbance which disrupts the blank denial of her mind and shocks her into sensation. We cannot know whether Julie herself supposedly experiences these traumatic intrusions as blue light and music, or whether the film finds sensory analogues, the very raw materials of audiovisual representation, to connote her traumatised perceptions.

If Julie's mental disturbance is two-fold, appearing in music and light, this represents her double loss, of husband and child. The colour blue bears association, on several levels, with the lost child. In the first place this association is shown quite literally. The blue lights of Julie's mental disturbance reflect her real blue crystals. This hanging ornament, a glassy fetish and source of some of the most ravishing images of the film, is the only object remaining in the blue room (Anna's room) when Julie, released from hospital, revisits her family house. Julie pulls at its threads of crystals, venting her grief. Yet this is one of the few objects she cannot leave behind. We see it hanging in her new apartment, a reflective, if silent, reminder of the missing child. The crystals here gather links with childhood and memory, where Lucille, who lives below Julie, marvels at the mobile as she enters the room, remembering that she had one just the same as a child. Links between the colour blue and childhood memory – Anna's liminal presence – are further established in images of the blue foil wrapper from a child's lollipop. Before the crash, Anna's small hand is seen holding the wrapper out the car window, letting it blow in the wind. This fine detail is recalled as Julie finds a similar lollipop in her handbag and rapidly, painfully, devours it. This association of colour with private loss, with the unspeakable mourning for a daughter, is actualised with more psychological complexity in the lush swimming scenes which cut through the film.

On a literal level Julie swims; the pool becomes a point of refuge in the film. This search for refuge has been read as a return to the pre-Oedipal phase;[3] such a reading coheres with the sense that the colour blue, so luminously saturating the swimming scenes, works as reminder of Anna and her interior presence. Julie retreats into a watery space which recalls or reflects her symbiosis with her daughter. One may wonder whether the return to these spaces is melancholic or regressive, or whether indeed the blue pools of water return in the film to open a space in which memory of the daughter can surface outside the normative trajectory of Julie's life and the film's tentative narrative of recovery.

The swimming scenes are haunted by images of both drowning and rebirth.[4] Differences between the scenes seem to reflect changes in Julie's psyche. The published screenplay records three swimming scenes.[5] In the first scene, Julie's swimming form is seen in a series of long shots. She is an anonymous shape for the camera; the focus of the scene is rather on the senseless, rhythmical repetition of her swimming strokes. In the second scene (arguably of rebirth), the camera is closer to her face as her strokes cut through the water. She emerges from the pool, lifting herself so we see her skin ghostly pale – almost bruised – in reflected blue light, transfixed by the hallucinatory music of the soundtrack. The third scene apparently breaks her isolation: Lucille comes to the pool and comforts Julie. At the end of the scene, children – a swimming class of little girls – jump into the water, shattering the surface of the pool and the refuge it offers. (Lucille and the swimming children perhaps bear association with the lost daughter.)

The first two pool scenes are distinguished chromatically and temporally: the film explores a closed space of reflecting light and water shot through a blue filter; the pool seems cavernous, enclosing. The screenplay informs us that these are night-time scenes. This literally accounts for their chromatic specificity, yet hints too at their dreamlike quality, at the role they play in figuring the night and blankness of Julie's psyche. The third scene, apparently the culmination of her swimming progress, is a daytime scene. The colours and contrasts are quite different, light and brightness enhancing the water's transparency, placing emphasis on the pool as public rather than private space.

There is, also, a fourth swimming scene which does not appear in the screenplay, but which immediately follows a scene where Julie confronts the pregnant Sandrine in a restaurant restroom. This scene returns to the chromatic intensity of the night-time scenes. Julie is seen diving into the pool. The camera pans from right to left, with an apparently animate, even anxious gaze, searching for Julie's absent swimming form as she disappears for long moments beneath the water. Just before the close of the scene she breaks the surface, sudden sound and image shocking the viewer.

Focus on this hidden fourth scene recognises that the film disrupts as much as instates temporal and curative teleology. Julie may still sink below the surface once more. The scene ends with her body floating, a fetal or inchoate mass in the water, a further blur in our field of vision. In returning to this immersion in the hidden scene, the film re-enacts and repeats Julie's compulsive encounters with death and survival. Psychiatrist Judith Herman reminds us in *Trauma and Recovery* that: 'Resolution of the trauma is never final; recovery is never complete. The impact of a traumatic event continues to reverberate throughout the survivor's lifecycle' (1994: 211). In a more contracted form, this seems also Kieślowski's point in *Blue*. The narrative progress of the film is disrupted in its editing in the return to a night-time pool scene, possibly an alternative take of one of the earlier swimming scenes. The psychological progress of the film's healing protagonist is equally cast in doubt.

Kieślowski maintains a divide between bodily and mental trauma. Changes in the body as it heals are one of the few markers of time passing in the film: the healing of Julie's sutured cuts, her grazed hands, offer visceral signs of temporal change. The healing of the mind is far less certain: Kieślowski leaves Julie's mourning for her daughter unresolved, still insufficiently imagined and represented by the end of the film. The pool scenes, in their cyclical repetition, are the locus and insistent, unresolved reminder of the mourned daughter. These are spaces of somatic intensity, without language and without time. The moving blueness which fills the screen creates an effect analogous to Kristeva's description of entering the Arena chapel where the blue takes hold of us at the extreme limit of visual perception. For the viewer of *Blue*, these swimming scenes afford moments of near abstraction, interludes of nostalgic sensory pleasure and clear, intense blue light. These episodes disturb, yet demarcate, the structure of the film and its internal dynamic of recovery and its denial. They are central to the film, since both chromatically and psychologically they are prime spaces of the semiotic: they are spaces which allow the viewer to question the imbrication of colour, trauma and denial. They are spaces in which the loss of the daughter is denied in symbiosis. They offer a prefiguring of a space which will be re-entered at the close of the film.

In the final shots of *Blue*, the status of the images remains uncertain. We see a collage, a fluid sequence of shots which juxtaposes the separate spaces and psyches with which the film has dealt. Julie and Olivier are seen making love, appearing as if behind glass in a human aquarium: Julie's face is pressed against the glass, the point of contact blurred, distorted. Aquatic foliage, bubbles, points of light and the viscosity of the water impede our view of the scene. The lovers' bodies turn as if in amniotic fluid. Amiel, responding to this scene, lays emphasis on the importance of Julie's relation to Olivier here, saying: 'Julie must then come back to herself, in a known space, and envisage with the other a relation which refocuses her' (Amiel 1994: 24). Yet his reading seems to ignore the very strangeness of the image, its metaphoricity, the uncanny difference and unknowability of its location. Amiel suggests a compulsory move from the semiotic, or imaginary, into the symbolic, and a compulsion to recognise an image of the self and distinguish this from the image of the other. Yet equally the film might be seen to image and envisage the semiotic in a conclusion which will refuse closure. And it is here that Anna will again resurface.

In each wave of images in the closing sequence Kieślowski dwells on confected images of the semiotic. We begin with lovers like twins in the womb. We move to Antoine asleep in the enclave of his room, shot through a blue filter. Above his bed is a double image of women kissing, their heavily glossed lips reflecting one another. The camera moves then to a reflection of Julie's amnesiac mother, appearing ghostly in glass, then in a looking glass and then by herself, her expression absent. Homoerotic sensuality emerges from darkness again as we see the red-lit lesbian floorshow in Lucille's strip joint. Finally, and with the least element of surprise, Sandrine becomes the focus of the shot and the frame is filled with a flickering blue ultrasound image of the unborn baby in her womb.[6]

The decision to leave the wave of images as we see the blue ultrasound picture, offers confirmation of the implicit links between the film's insistent return to the colour blue, its aquatic (and amniotic) imagery and its means of commemorating mother-child symbiosis. Kieślowski appears in keeping with Kristeva, then, in his sense of the psychological depths response to this colour opens and probes.

Throughout this discussion of *Three Colours: Blue* I have argued that memory is double-stranded, mourning is public and private, for a husband

and for a daughter. While mourning for the husband is brought full circle in the completion of the Concerto (which plays over the final collage of shots), mourning for the daughter opens out the meanings of the ending of the film.

Readings of *Blue* tend to privilege a normative trajectory, willing Julie to emerge from the water of her mourning and mnemonic swimming, yet this does not recognise the final immersion in the semiotic of the film's ending. *Blue* envisages new modes of memory and representation which transform the possibilities of the semiotic and of mourning within the search for recovery. The semiotic becomes not merely a point of return but a point of departure. At the end of the film, Julie's identity, her psyche, is projected for us as a product of a mobile series of images borrowed from her external reality. Kieślowski images a fluid series of identifications which are moving and interchangeable (the use of dissolve allowing one image effectively to emerge from another). This seepage, this merger, offers almost unconscious recall of the union with the daughter, a memory of symbiosis which is not death-bearing but death-defying as memory allows the illusory return of the lost object. This merger, whilst melancholic, also allows the othering of the self as she becomes open to alterity. The film makes use of the semiotic to open up a new field of (nostalgic) significations for the self and hesitant possibilities of survival.[7]

Cinema is a mourning art, as Bazin, Barthes and others remind us.[8] The collage coda to *Blue* is self-consciously cinematic, a model in miniature of the film which reminds us of the mediation of viewing. (A comparable scene is found at the end of the feature length version of *A Short Film About Love* (1988).) Cinema has the power to animate lost images; its pleasures are nostalgic, inherently melancholic. In the ascetic sterility, the numbness of *Blue*, Kieślowski refuses any simple comfort for Julie or her viewers; he refuses any direct recall, any retrospective imaging of Anna, the daughter desperately loved and irrevocably lost. The film indicates, I think, that this loss is precisely unspeakable, that it ruptures the symbolic order, that it is silent through the duration of the film. The loss recurs, and is commemorated, however, in colour and in space, two modes which precede language and lie outside its reach.

The loss of Anna appears, as I have said, ostensibly obscured, almost forgotten in the film on first viewings. Yet insistent return to *Blue* allows the film to be aligned differently. In its margins, in the disruption in the visual field Anna's image affords, *Blue* finds different means to commemorate the lost daughter. The film offers no repair or cure for this loss; it merely institutes a mode of endurance and nostalgic survival. Yet the film's prospective optimism lies in its refusal of curative norms, its renewed representation of the traumatised and mourning subject, and its transformation of the uses and affect of the cinematic medium.

The lost child as locus of cinematic reinvention releases fears and fantasies which will return. Kieślowski's lost daughter is effectively a liminal presence in this study as a whole, as we shall see, a haunting image whose insistence offers new alignments in a mapping of contemporary cinema and its investigation of emotion and horror.

CHAPTER TWO

The Female Adjuster: Arsinée Khanjian and the Films of Atom Egoyan

A tom Egoyan's *Exotica* (1994) explores the disturbing subject of a man's search to mourn and deny the loss of his daughter in erotic ritual. The film's investment in creative modes of commemoration bears comparison with Kieślowski's *Three Colours: Blue*, yet the ethical risks *Exotica* takes are entirely other. My aim here is to analyse these risks and their implications for spectatorship. I question whether Egoyan's *Exotica*, in its melancholy eroticism, offers any safe spaces for the viewer.

This chapter is a study of fascination. It has evolved out of my fascination as a female viewer with the actress Arsinée Khanjian, and with the roles she plays in the films of Egoyan. In this way, and more broadly, it is a chapter about 'intra-feminine fascination' (in the words of Jackie Stacey and Teresa de Lauretis).[1] Yet it is also about a film-maker's fascination with his partner, and about the meaning of her presence in his films. Egoyan dedicates the published screenplay of his film *Speaking Parts* (1989) to Arsinée, his sleeping muse. Khanjian appears in all Egoyan's feature films to date. I question here what is special about this presence, and the presence of this relationship both emotionally and cinematically in Egoyan's work. In this partnership Egoyan moves beyond the polarity of film-maker/muse relations embodied, say, in Godard's relation with Karina. The Egoyan/Khanjian relation seems to replicate one of the heterosexual myths of narrative cinema (as it has developed out of the visual arts of the nineteenth century and in Surrealist art and writing), only effectively to undermine its bases and authority.

The questions I raise here about the spectator and her desires owe much to the thought of recent theorists and film-makers on the ways in which film theory and criticism can (or cannot) contend with emotion, in response and in representation. In her article, 'The Little Girl Wants to be Heard', Annette Kuhn asks: 'How can film theory address itself to the emotions films evoke, to the ways in which these emotions enter into people's fictions of the past, their own past?' (1995: 27). This seems an apt question to pose in discussion of a film-maker such as Egoyan who admits: 'To me, the highest aim of any film is to enter so completely into the subconscious of the viewer that there are moments and scenes and gestures which can be generated by the spectator's imagination. That becomes part of the film they're playing in their mind, and I hope the film [*Exotica*] has enough space to allow that type of room, that type of exchange' (1995: 50). Egoyan's ideal of spectatorship seems a more intense version of Wenders' ideas about viewing in *Emotion Pictures* where he states: 'Everybody sees and creates his/her own film, the reviewer too. Like anyone else he is guided by the film on the screen adding (or subtracting) his own emotions, memories, opinions, sense of humour, openness, colours and so on' (1989: viii).

Theorists and film-makers alike stress an interchange between film and viewer, an experience which is both emotional and memorial. Wenders names this simply the addition (or subtraction) of emotion or memory. Egoyan, in more intangible terms, speaks of the scenes which we imagine we have viewed in retrospect but which are absent from the film presented. Film becomes for Egoyan a type of memory text or trace which is etched in the viewer's imagination, a virtual space in which the viewer contends with the phantoms generated by her own emotions and memory. Here the terms Egoyan uses, referring to the 'film' the viewer is 'playing' in her mind, seem amply ambiguous, blurring the boundary between cinema remembered and the specificity of psychic life. (Egoyan comments similarly in the same article, sounding like one of his own characters: 'there's something phenomenal about the fact that every night, every person in this world turns on a little projector in their brain when they go to sleep and creates *movies*' (1995: 54).)

Kuhn herself appears cleverly to blur the same boundary between film and psychic life. Her title, 'The Little Girl Wants to be Heard', refers neatly both to the hearing-impaired child in the film *Mandy* (1952) which is her subject, and to her own response which informs her appeal to theorists to bring emotion back into the cinematic equation. In making this appeal, and re-thinking emotion and memory in film theory, Kuhn reminds us that 'the child's response can only speak through the adult's interpretation' (1995: 38); it is only latterly that the little girl can be heard. Kuhn's desire to move away from intellectual detachment is bound up in the book *Family Secrets* with an exploration of the possibilities of memory work for enriching our understanding of how we use films and other images and representations to construct our identities and histories. For Kuhn, it seems, theorising emotion in spectatorship is interrelated with the therapeutic, healing aims and ends of memory work. In her terms, the emotional and the memorial are linked, as they are for Egoyan (who reveals, nevertheless, a rather different and more troubled investment in therapy). Further, for Kuhn, film viewing is understood in the dynamics of family history; realising this becomes key to unleashing and theorising an emotional response to film. For Egoyan, such family dynamics are an integral part of his film-making.

In an interview with Egoyan in 1995, Geoff Pevere comments: 'A few months ago, in a national weekly newsmagazine, a full-page picture appeared of you and Arsinée and your son Arshile. Since Arsinée has figured so prominently in your films, your relationship has developed a public as well as private dimension. How do you feel about your private life becoming part of the publicity package of your own career?' Egoyan replies: 'I'm uncomfortable about it, but it's a given. There's no turning back. Once *Calendar* [1993] was released and people started asking me if Arsinée and I had actually broken up, I realised in a strange way that our relationship is part of the alchemy of the films themselves. That's dangerous as hell and I understand that' (Egoyan 1995: 65–6). Egoyan's films repeatedly explore the contamination of art (cinematic, televisual, photographic) and life. In *Calendar*, he plays a photographer who travels with his partner, played by Khanjian, through the Armenian countryside, the land of their origins, taking images of churches to form the calendar of the film's title. In *Speaking Parts*, a television screen-writer obsessively attempts to re-enact her love for her brother, who has died donating his lung to her: this drama becomes the subject of her writing, and her writing provides the script for her love affair with the actor who plays her brother. This intersection between art and life has been aptly understood by critics as Egoyan's reflection on the age of electronic representation. As Pevere comments: 'In Egoyan's films, media become environment. Since he sees experience as something circumscribed entirely by mediated message systems, his films are about people whose very existence depends on the media that make experience possible' (in Egoyan 1995: 17).[2] What interests me is the way in which this fascination is itself mediated and rendered metacinematic in the relation between the film-maker, his partner and the films they make between them. Egoyan illustrates the contamination between art and life which is his subject in his own relation to his films, and in the knowing narrative of this relation he constructs in interviews and publicity material. That he should name this personal dynamic between art and life, this alchemy, dangerous is particularly telling.

One of Egoyan's early films is called *Next of Kin* (1984), another *Family Viewing* (1987). As Carole Desbarats reminds us: 'Egoyan is too fascinated by the "family romance" – or the "family film" – to give up telling stories; he just does it his way' (1993: 14). Egoyan deepens our awareness of the network of familial relations, both invented and real, upon which his films depend, by locating them within the dynamics of his own family. Eve Egoyan is the pianist in *Family Viewing, Speaking Parts, The Adjuster* (1991) and *Exotica*; his son Arshile has starred in the short film *A Portrait of Arshile* (1996) with which Egoyan followed *Exotica*. Egoyan appears willing to place his family in what he perceives as a danger zone of representation. This seems all the more ironic given that he frequently takes as his subject the issue of abuse, both sexual and cinematic. This issue surfaces compulsively in his film *Exotica*; it is Khanjian's role in this film which I examine in more detail below.

Throughout her career with Egoyan, Khanjian has played the part of intercessor. In *Calendar* she literally plays a role as translator, mediating between the photographer and their Armenian guide. In *The Adjuster* Khanjian plays the role of Hera, a cultural adjuster, who works at the provincial Censor Board. In constructing these literal roles of translator, or censor, for his partner, Egoyan seeks to reflect the part which Khanjian plays crucially in his film-making. In his film-making to date Egoyan has demonstrated a fascination with sexuality and its imbrication with both vision and trauma: a tricky area, as much of this study seeks to demonstrate. Egoyan relies on Khanjian in this territory: he relies on her embedded role as female viewer, or as female adjuster.[3]

Ron Burnett describes 'a landscape of debauchery' in the film *Speaking Parts*, 'the "raw" material for soft-core pornography, heterosexual and homosexual love' (in Egoyan 1993: 13). This landscape is the very stage for the later film *Exotica* whose location is the strip club of the film's title. We enter this space of eroticism, of abusive sexuality and its re-enactment, as the camera follows a character, Christina, in a series of forwards tracking shots. Christina, the dancer whose story unfolds, leads us from the street into a space of fantasy: a fluid camera moves in this space, echoing the motions of the semi-naked lap-dancer whose dance it frames. The blue lighting, tropical plants, lush atmosphere and intense rhythm of the soundtrack create a space whose tension is tangible. The film seems to be dallying in the spaces of soft-core pornography, in an underworld which represents a present reality in the lap-dancing bars of Toronto, and a recurrent cinematic fantasy of female bodily display and heterosexual male voyeurism.

My interest in *Exotica* lies in a conviction that Egoyan is critiquing the erotic system he constructs in his film whilst refusing to deny its fascination.[4]

Khanjian as partner, as compere, is crucial to the maintenance of this double position. Khanjian plays Zoe, owner and hostess of the club. We see her greet Christina as she arrives: she is heavily pregnant (in reality with Arshile), both sensual and protective. She is the Sibylline presence at our side as we pass through the underworld of Exotica. Zoe says, 'Exotica is a special place. My mother was dedicated to creating a very particular type of atmosphere, and I would like to maintain that' (Egoyan 1995: 135).[5] Zoe is both guide and guardian of the film: her presence is deeply ambiguous.

Zoe's centrality to the film is emphasised spatially in the set and *mise-en-scène* of the Club Exotica. Zoe inhabits an ornate Rococo office which is spatially and conceptually a panoptican. From her desk Zoe can watch Eric the emcee as he introduces the dancers: she is seen to monitor and censor his behaviour from this position. Zoe's surveillance is also facilitated by the one-way mirrors which decorate and fissure the observatory hallway which is the spatial intersection of the office and the club. Through these mirrors an observer can watch the lap dancing unobserved. This hallway becomes a space in which the viewer may reflect on the dynamics of observation and voyeurism within the film. It recalls necessarily the space of a customs office in an airport, where two inspectors watch behind a one way mirror. The double status of the mirrors in *Exotica* is telling: these are mirrors of identification and desire, mirrors to see into and also to see through. Christina comments to Zoe: 'You know, I remember when your mother built this hallway. She built it for this very rich man who used to come here. He used to get off watching us dance for other guys so he actually paid her to construct this very special place that he could watch us from. Your mother never told us that. She said it was to protect us, so she could patrol things. And I believed her' (Egoyan 1995: 104).

For Christina, the mirror represents betrayal: the space of protection is infiltrated. Her intimation of this betrayal is apt within the film. Christina is a character who has been abused within the family context. This we learn implicitly in the draining coda to the film, a flashback to Christina as disturbed teenager returning to a family home which offers her no protection. The dynamics of vision in the hallway offer a spatial reminder of that betrayal. Her reaction to Zoe, matriarch of this unsafe space, is thus transparently negative. As bell hooks argues: '[Zoe] is the daughter of a mother who has betrayed her and other females. It is Christina who names the mother's betrayal, who articulates that masking and deceit was the foundation of the mother/daughter bond both real and symbolic and not love' (1996: 31). hooks offers no further comment on Khanjian's role as owner of the club: her analysis of Zoe's role, whilst important and ethically desirable, works to deny some of the more insidious complexities of the film.

The mother-daughter bond in *Exotica* is founded on masking and deceit, but on desire as well. Zoe wears her mother's mask in running the night-club: she even dresses up in her gowns and wigs. She seems engaged in a melancholic identification with her dead mother, a denial of her absence in her own body.[6] This is only apt in a film which, to a large extent takes mourning and its rituals as its subject. We witness, indeed, a general interest in distorted processes of mourning in Egoyan's cinema. He comments in interview with Jonathan Romney: 'There's a group of analysts in Toronto who have looked at all my films. They've told me that from their point of view, all my films deal with a process called "faulty mourning" – when a patient builds up a ritual of mourning which only accentuates and exaggerates the sense of loss which they think they're dealing with' (in Romney 1995: 8). Faulty mourning may be Egoyan's subject, but what is difficult to determine is how far, for Egoyan or his viewer, this process is at fault. Questioning this may lead us to a different reckoning with Zoe's role in *Exotica*.

Central to the film is the death of a young schoolgirl, the daughter of Francis who comes to the club. The film engages the viewer in a search for the body of this child, punctuated as it is by a series of retrospective images of the search party scouring the fields of the Ontario landscape. The child's body, its abject shape, which will be glimpsed in the closing seqences of the film, is the point of focus of the intersecting narratives of Egoyan's drama (making it comparable with *L'Humanité*). What the viewer comes to realise, by a series of visual echoes, is that we have always already known the form of the child's body in the series of displaced images *Exotica* perpetuates.

The first image of a schoolgirl is seen as Christina dances in the club. She wears a white shirt, short tartan kilt and tie, thick black stockings and lace up shoes. She carries a school satchel. Before we see her, we hear Eric's hushed, lurid introduction: 'What is it that gives a schoolgirl her special innocence? Her sweet fragrance? Fresh flowers? Light spring rain? […] Or is it her firm, young flesh inviting your every caress, enticing you to explore the deepest most private secrets?' (Egoyan 1995: 74). With these words Christina appears and begins slowly dancing to Leonard Cohen's 'Everybody Knows'. Eric's words act as voice-over in the film, eroticising the image and framing it in illicit fantasy. As emcee he creates an intersubjective monologue, choreographing the desires given 'safe' expression in the club, constructing the adult Christina as schoolgirl Lolita.

The image of the schoolgirl does not remain in the confines of the club but is disquietingly seen again as the camera enters Francis's house. This white house of memory holds pictures of Francis's dead daughter Lisa. Though she is still very young in these images, we see the same uniform that Christina wears in the club. The photos act as so many reminders of the dead child, and of the interweaving of memory and denial in Francis' erotic viewing at Exotica. After we have seen these photographs, the film begins to make the links between Francis' desires and his loss more explicit. He asks Christina as she dances for him: 'I was just thinking, what would happen if someone ever hurt you?' (Egoyan 1995: 94). He finds in her the figure of his child at risk; he constructs with her the image of himself as protector, playing out the role in which he has failed for his own daughter.

What the film leaves ambiguous, and what Francis himself seeks to discover in Exotica perhaps, is just how far he too put his daughter at risk. Later in the film, we learn from Christina that Francis was implicated when his daughter was murdered. She continues: 'I don't really know the details. He was cleared and then they caught the guy who did it. But it's obviously had this incredible effect on him. I mean, he's just so fucked up about it' (127–8). The film seems to test whether the wrongful accusation unwittingly revealed to the suspect his potential if not actual guilt. This Francis himself tests in the crippling sexual obsession Exotica and Christina's dancing have become for him.

The film is not openly judgmental about this relationship, and this may be disturbing for viewers. Francis is seen to experience his grief, his memories of his lost daughter, as a home movie continually rewound and replayed in his mind. One scene, for example, shows Tracey (his niece) in Francis's house, looking at photographs of his daughter. The scene cuts to videotaped footage of Francis's wife and daughter playing the piano, the image hesitant, stopping and starting. We hear the sound of the daughter's laughter, almost ghostly, then we cut to the next scene where Francis is seen 'breathing heavily and looking pained' (96) in a washroom stall at Exotica. The film's editing gives us the illusion that we have witnessed his thought process unawares. When we next see Francis with Christina, he asks her: 'How could anyone hurt you? Take you away from me? How could anyone?' (105). The film echoes Resnais' device in *Hiroshima mon amour,* where the French woman addresses her Japanese lover as 'tu', transferring onto him her love of the lost German in a scene of erotic reenactment and mnemonic denial.

In its re-viewing of Francis's cognitive and mnemonic quest, *Exotica* leads me, and perhaps other viewers, to sympathise with the very compulsion surrounding his loss. Where I may be more dubious about his search for recovery, the film again challenges me to distance myself from his desire. On one level it seems necessary for the viewer to perceive that Francis is engaged in a sick ritual, sexualising his dead daughter in retrospect and acting out a 'safe' (abusive) relationship with her, with the lap dancer who by definition he must not touch. But Egoyan takes time to explore the space of this obsession, this ritual of denial. The film encourages us to understand the pleasure of this faulty mourning (whilst showing in the end that this cycle of support must break down).

Eric observes to Christina: 'It used to be wonderful watching you dance for him, seeing how you could soothe him. It soothed me. You soothed me. Do you understand that?' (Egoyan 1995: 138–9). The viewer, too, is brought to question the pleasure she may take in this illusory comfort. Christina herself, victim of abuse in her home life, does not judge Francis. She explains her feelings: 'Francis and I have a very special type of relationship' (Egoyan 1995: 128). She continues: 'We've always had this understanding. I mean, I need him for certain things, and he needs me for certain things, and that's the way it's been' (*Ibid.*). She seems to need the role of protecting angel that Eric and Francis together construct for her. Egoyan constructs our pleasure in this, only to puncture the illusion on which it rests.

Eric, inspired by jealousy of the protective, almost symbiotic, relation established between Francis and Christina, chooses to orchestrate its violation. He appears in this as the dark conscience of the movie, but also its agent of action (despite his own aimlessness and stasis). He incites Francis to touch Christina as she dances; Francis's love must cross the line from protection to abuse and break the club's rules against contact. This breaks the ritual, as Christina regrets the violation of their relation, as Francis himself is ejected from the club. The film in enacting these losses effectively distances itself from the erotic compulsion it sets in circulation, calling into question, in turn, the faults in the process of mourning it has appeared to perpetuate.

Here, recalling my earlier points, Zoe's role as manager of the club is significant. She polices this behaviour, in effect, and reminds Francis how far his search in denial is misplaced. As she interviews him after he has been ejected from the club, Zoe says to Francis, almost like a mother to a child: 'Mr Brown, we're all aware of what you've gone through. You've suffered a lot. But you have to understand that Exotica is here for your amusement. We're here to entertain, not to heal. There are other places for that' (Egoyan 1995: 135). Egoyan raises questions here about film itself as therapy or entertainment. One irony is precisely that these words are spoken by Zoe to Francis, since Zoe herself is engaged in a ritual of mourning, a search for healing, in Club Exotica. But it is perhaps this very point of contact which allows her insight into his ritual. What *Exotica* asks is where the viewer draws his/her boundaries in the face of such pathological ritual. We may be called on to judge, yet the film seeks at every step to implicate us in its very activities and to confuse our response.

The proximity between Francis and Zoe in their mourning, his for his daughter, hers for her mother, is further underlined in their parallel desire for Christina. Just as the film counterpoints the similarity and difference of their mourning, so it draws into question whether his desire, his voyeuristic activity, is more culpable than hers.

Zoe is presented as a female-identified protagonist who knows a continuum between her love and loss of her mother and her future object choice. Her fascination for her mother as object is vocalised as she says to Christina, her object of desire: 'I used to be very shy as a child. I used to watch my mother for hours, just admiring her sense of freedom' (Egoyan 1995: 103). As Zoe finds her own freedom playing her mother's role, the film raises the possibility that Club Exotica is passed on as object of exchange within a female homosocial bond. It is important, however, that Zoe does not merely replicate her mother's choices, but makes her own in her sexual identification. In the closing stages of the film, as its intersecting parts are revealed, Zoe is finally framed as desiring viewer herself watching Christina through the glass of the one-way mirror. This is shown in brief intercut scenes.

In the first of these, we see that Zoe herself has now taken up Eric's role as MC, fully inhabiting her chosen role as choreographer and subject of desire in the club. As Zoe introduces Christina's last dance, the film cuts to an exterior shot of the club as we see Francis who is now waiting to shoot Eric (seeking revenge for the loss of his relation with Christina). We see the interior once more where Thomas, who is used here as Francis's instrument, waits to watch Christina dance. The film cuts quickly from exterior to interior again, from Francis to Christina. Then we see Zoe now viewing Christina as she dances. Zoe watches her through the one-way mirror. The film cuts to an exterior shot once more where Francis now points his gun at Eric, who, untouched, reveals that he was the one who found the little girl. The film cuts to flashback of the discovery of the body of the little girl, cuts back to the club and to Zoe viewing once more, and back to the field and the moment of horror and grief that the film has repressed until this point of culmination.

Khanjian's role here is highly complex. She is shown as voyeur or desiring viewer within the film's diegesis as she is now positioned behind the mirror. Equally her fascinated and reactive position stands to reflect that of the external spectator. The film's editing works to create a panoptical effect once more offering the illusion that Khanjian, akin to ourselves as spectators, is witness to the film's ultimate scene of revelation, the discovery of the child's body in the field by Eric and Christina, the ultimate key to relations between desire and mourning in the film. Khanjian mediates here between the viewing in the film and the viewing of the film. It is in these terms, and through Khanjian's intercession, that *Exotica* enters familiar debates about gender and spectatorship.

Egoyan creates two generations of female spectators in Club Exotica. Under Zoe's mother's regime, as Christina has revealed, a heterosexual binary

Figure 3 *Exotica*

of viewing relations was in place where the male client sought a perverse form of visual pleasure. An analogy with the viewing relations constructed by the classical cinematic apparatus (as theorised by Mulvey (1988)) can be made here. But, more recently, as Linda Williams reminds us, 'the single, unitary spectator of … gaze theory has gradually been challenged by diverse viewing positions' (1994: 3). For Williams, 'the classical model of spectatorship, which too easily assumed fixed ideological and psychic effects on spectators, needs to be viewed, as Judith Mayne puts it … as a more complex set of paradoxes' (1994: 14). One such paradox for Mayne is created by the discord between a view of cinema as a homogeneous institution and the heterogeneity of different spectators (of different races, classes, genders, socialisations and subcultural affinities) who engage with it. Difference itself is necessarily now theorised in spectatorship in a direct critique of homogeneous categorisation. Queer theory has further reminded us that identity categories are themselves always already fissured and fictive, dependent, as Judith Butler reveals, on their very difference to themselves.[7] For Butler this difference allows the possibility of mobilising sexual and social roles. The non-self-identity of identity categories is itself of political import in her view. But how does this re-thinking of identity categories impinge on the ways in which we might think about spectatorship and on the ways in which a film such as *Exotica* already contends with such an issue?

In response, I argue that it is not only queer cinema which reflects the challenge to thinking on gender and sexuality which queer theory has demanded. A film such as *Exotica* troubles the heterosexual matrix by framing the performance and performativity of identity categories, and the instability of such performed identities. Here the nightclub setting, the emphasis on costume and persona for the protagonists on the stage of Exotica seem to show in hyperbolic terms how far identities are part of a masquerade. Yet beyond this theatrical interpretation of performance, Egoyan offers a real insight into the performative nature of identity, showing how his chosen individuals are almost unwittingly playing out, citing and replicating the parts available to them within a distorted family romance and within a specific microcosm of gender relations.

In these terms, in its deconstruction of gender relations, *Exotica* can be considered typical of the sexual hybridity of 1990s Toronto cinema as exemplified in Jeremy Podeswa's *Eclipse* (1994) or Patricia Rozema's *When Night is Falling* (1995). As hooks acknowledges: 'Club Exotica is a diasporic landscape, a place where individuals meet across boundaries of race, sex, class and nationality' (1996: 28).[8] Categories of difference are brought into play which correlate almost exactly to the diverse identity categories which queer theorists and the second generation of theorists of spectatorship explore. Much has been made of the heterosexual assumption behind gaze theory as it was first formulated. In *Exotica* Egoyan challenges such assumption in his construction of Zoe as woman who takes pleasure in watching female heterosexual erotic performance. This form of 'intra-feminine fascination' goes thus far largely unaddressed in film theory, though it finds its analogies in Linda Williams' (1990) analysis of pornography from the 'other place' of a heterosexual feminine desire; or in Teresa de Lauretis' (1994) work on spectatorship and lesbian sexuality. Yet where de Lauretis, exploring fascination, maintains a distinction between identification and desire, (separating the homoerotic from the homosexual), Egoyan appears to follow Butler conversely for whom 'identification and desire can coexist' (1991: 26). Zoe, looking through the one-way mirror, can figuratively see herself and see her object of desire in the figure of Christina. Her melancholic identification with her mother merges seamlessly with her erotic viewing of Christina. The boundaries between homosexual and heterosexual are eroded.

The destruction of boundaries relates itself to the film's disquieting discourse on proximity, on the proximity between protection and abuse, on the proximity between survival and mania. In her interrelation of memory work and film theory, Annette Kuhn reminds us of the ways in which a personal history is also part of a shared history, that memory has cultural as well as personal dimensions. Her response to *Mandy* works to remind her of the ways in which loss and possibility are written into the world her generation inherited. In *Exotica* Egoyan explores a narrative of the loss of childhood, of the loss of the child who wants to be heard. This offers in effect a narrative of a generation and its sexualities, performed, divergent and abusive. As we apprehend the figure of Zoe, Egoyan's partner, we may be led to question the fragile borders between cinema and existence, between cinema as spectacle and identity as performance.

Mayne has argued that 'one of the distinct pleasures of the cinema may well be a safe zone in which homosexual as well as heterosexual desires can be fantasized and acted out' (1994: 176). Egoyan's viewer comes to learn that there are no safe zones in his cinema. The space of protection is also a space of voyeurism; the family romance masks sexual abuse. Art, and cinema as art form, offers no safe space but is always already contaminated by life. Khanjian's presence seems precisely to remind us of this. Egoyan takes the muse, the actress, his partner, and makes her signify differently. He dismantles a heterosexual myth of narrative cinema in order to offer an apparent empowerment of the female spectator as subject of her own desire. Egoyan reveals the strip club as a place of erotic pleasure for women as well as men, for the enactment of homosexual as well as heterosexual fantasy.

Egoyan may challenge the heterosexual assumption which underlies the theorisation of spectatorship, yet I want to say in conclusion that the female viewer who, like Zoe, takes pleasure in the performances in and of his films, must know the risk of perpetuating a system of voyeurism and erotic display in her fascination. In *Exotica*, as in his earlier films, Egoyan offers Khanjian a role of interrogation and intercession, yet here he overtly reveals that role to be highly ambivalent. Zoe may protect her dancers from her position of surveillance, but that is only in order to maintain the 'safety' of the club she creates. In Khanjian's role, Egoyan seeks to represent and implicate the female viewer within his film, in order precisely to forestall and to complicate her response.

The final view of the film which emerges in my reading is then, inevitably, ambivalent. There is intense emotional satisfaction in the breaking of the film's compulsion: this is felt in the late scene where Eric whispers to Francis, 'I found her, man' (Egoyan 1995: 144). Francis reaches out for Eric and embraces him. Touch is no longer illicit in the film; it is the means of crossing the distance between the characters. Eric brings Francis up close to the reality which underlies his obsession with a force none of the other characters have achieved. This contact appears to release the flashback of the coda, offering the viewer a glimpse of the pre-history of Francis's relation to Christina.

hooks suggests: 'It is the image of her pain that stays with us. An image so intense that we find release only by remembering the movie in our minds, so that we can see that Christina moves from the wounds of childhood into an adult world of symbolic repetition of trauma to a space of healing where she can let the past go and be free' (1996: 33). hooks seems to see beyond the end of the movie, generating in her reading a therapeutic narrative, envisaging a space of healing which the film may lead us to imagine but never itself enters. This is the very type of imaginative investment Egoyan claims to summon or seek in his cinema.

Khanjian's role as Zoe allows the film a desirable openness in its internal representation of desiring spectatorship; it also allows Egoyan to explore the risks and pleasures of the emotional, mnemonic response to cinema that he courts. Where hooks' reading brings a sane, restorative framework to the film, the representation of Zoe allows the film to question the ways in which the memories, fantasies and imaginary projections which are mobilized in film-viewing may be less politically correct, more troubled or subjective. This we may appreciate in our gradual acquaintance with Zoe, our apprehension of her sexuality, of her identity in Exotica and her own pleasure in erotic display. It is one of the film's subtleties, then, that the protagonist who plays the role of mediator, of adjuster in the film (the wife whose presence implicitly protects the film-maker from charges of abuse or exploitation) serves ultimately to remind us of the complexities of illicit desire.

Egoyan does not attempt to police the viewer's desire. He seeks instead to implicate the viewer in the network of desires on which his films depend. He does this to create our awareness and responsibility as viewers. The lost child remains the still point of absolute horror in the film (her death far outstripping that of Francis's wife in the film's emotional system). While the search to deny the loss of the child in erotic pleasure and reenactment is seen by the end of the film to be asphyxiating, a trap of traumatic repetition, Exotica asks the viewer whether she can fully indict any activity in which Francis engages as he encounters, and seeks to avoid, the pain of loss, guilt and mourning.

Spectatorship, for Egoyan, is subjective. It brings into play the viewer's pre-history, her memories and desires (as Zoe's own desiring viewing reminds us). In making so emotionally loaded a film as Exotica, Egoyan tests his viewer's responses. He leads us into an underworld where unconscious desires turn and surface like fish in an aquarium. He leaves me with the sense that I have to ask myself what brought me to this point. What have I seen that has channelled me here? Is it something hidden I still have to find?

CHAPTER THREE

New Jersey Childhood: *Happiness*

In an article in *Sight and Sound*, Charles Taylor writes: 'When the history of American independent cinema in the 1990s is written, one of the major influences cited may well be the freak show. Indie film-makers' fondness for presenting their characters as grotesques and fools is perhaps best represented in the work of Todd Solondz (*Happiness*)' (2000: 36–7). Taylor reflects the range of grotesque images of Solondz's film-making where American suburbia is seen in a series of tableaux recalling the unease of Nan Goldin or Diane Arbus photographs. Missing in Solondz's films, however, is the masquerade or performance of the freak show as spectacle. Solondz, instead, makes his images an apparent record of everyday life. This adds to their unease: viewers speak of their experience of troubling proximity with Solondz's characters. The achievement of *Happiness* lies, precisely, in this refusal of distanciation. The film speaks of the horror of equivocal values, of mitigating circumstances, of tightly knit interconnections. The risk it takes is to domesticate the child molester and show him within the range of familiar (and family) experience.

Solondz says of his own approach to paedophilia:

My politics on the issue are simple: you do this kind of thing, you go to jail. I have to say I'm sympathetic to that whole Megan's Law thing. If I have kids I gotta know if there's a paedophile on my block. But I wasn't thinking from a political perspective at all. I read a piece about this Russian serial killer ... who had killed over fifty kids. At the end of the article it said he had a wife and two children, and I thought: what does that mean? (in Hearty 1998: 36)

Happiness takes as its subject the grotesque and pathetic imbrication of paedophilia and family dynamics. The film is an exercise in imagination (as it visualises what a child molester in the family may mean) and in compassion. On another level it works as a vivid and crucial diagnosis of interpersonal relations, trust and betrayal in 1990s America and beyond. Indeed, specific though it is in its representation of New Jersey – we see a billboard in the film saying 'Welcome to New Jersey. The Garden State' – *Happiness* represents a more generic suburbia, a filmic cliché re-presented and a dystopic space of home, childhood and domesticity.

Happiness has proved notorious in US Independent cinema. In July 1998, the film was dropped by its production company October Films 'because of content that October's parent companies, Universal and Seagram Co., deemed too controversial' (Kaufman 1998: 8). The *Happiness* 'drop' raised questions about the autonomous status of 'independent' film distributors and about the future release of films dealing with disturbing or controversial material. Critics writing on *Happiness*, whether positive or negative in their response to the film, tend to offer a litany of its transgressions. Kitty Bowe Hearty, in *Interview*, lists: 'paedophilia, on screen ejaculation, sexual dysfunction' (1998: 34); Trish Deitch Rohrer, in *Première*, elaborates: 'These characters – not portrayed satirically, but with tenderness – vomit; they fantasize mass murder; they ejaculate on the wall (and use it as glue), on the railing of a terrace overlooking a swimming pool in Florida, and in their pants in the day-lit parking lot of a New Jersey mall while children are walking by' (Rohrer 1998: 61). Such cataloguing may leave us surprised the film was released at all (as it was by Good Machine, one of the film's original producers). Further it may make viewers agree with Andrew Lewis Conn, who writes in *Film Comment*: 'Solondz uses shock tactics no different from the stabbings and beheadings of a splatter film … *Happiness* offers cum shots and paedophilia as special effects for intellectuals' (1991: 71). I argue, by contrast, that the film is more than the sum of its parts and that *Happiness* offers an interrogation of its subject matter which demonstrates renewed modes of cinematic representation and response. Kimberley Cooper refers to the film briefly in an article, 'Beyond the Clean and Proper', linking it rightly to films such as *Seul Contre Tous* (1998), *The Idiots* (1998) and *Romance* (1998). She finds her links between these films in both the visceral reaction they have created in their audiences and in the moral polemic they have aroused.[1] A belief in the seriousness of the moral debates engendered by *Happiness*, and the importance of the film as interrogation of representation (rather than sensationalism or pornography) encourages me to include it here.

What is most significant about *Happiness*, for this study, is the way in which it disputes a diagnosis of malcontent about the treatment of children as singular issue. It offers instead a broader representation of contemporary social relations. *Happiness* is Solondz's second major feature film. It builds on the success of his first film, *Welcome to the Dollhouse* (1996), a film also set in New Jersey, about a young girl's painful adolescence. *Welcome to the Dollhouse* already introduces an ambivalent portrayal of child abuse. The main protagonist, Dawn, has a younger sister named Missy. Missy is prettier and more petite than Dawn; in signature shots she is seen dancing on the family lawn and drive in a gauzy pink tutu and ballet slippers. She is an image of the female child as desirable miniature adult (recalling the aesthetic of child beauty pageants). When she is abducted from the family, the (melo)drama is dissipated swiftly as it transpires that Missy was kidnapped by Mr Kasdan, a family neighbour. In video footage the family has watched of an anniversary party, Missy has already been seen riding Mr Kasdan piggyback as he dances. The film steadily downplays and ironises Missy's abduction. Dawn's brother Mark reports that Mr Kasdan kept Missy in a little underground room beneath the shuffleboard court. He says: 'actually, I think she may have liked being there, 'cause she had her own TV and total control over the pusher. And she also got to have as much candy and McDonalds as she wanted'. While Mr Kasdan is taken away by the police, and we learn that his wife is filing for divorce, the film shies away from representing the child molester as monster. Instead the film seems to show how the loving family has itself created the child as spectacle in the video footage. Further, as the film simulates a '60 Minutes'-type news/interview show, it points ironically to the complacency and innocence of the local community ('… Friends and neighbours, however, shocked at his arrest, described Joseph Kasdan as a regular family man who would often dress up as Santa at Christmastime'). Most of all, in placing Missy's ordeal in the context of Dawn's life, *Welcome to the Dollhouse* relativises the ways in which child abuse is represented; implicit seems the notion that the family's relative disinterest in and ridicule of Dawn, her experiences of being bullied at school and her painful attempts to relate to other children, are alternate forms of damage and suffering in childhood which are muted and ignored in contemporary media fascination with sexual attention to children.

While a recognition of the general discomforts and horrors of childhood is inherited in Solondz's later film, *Happiness* raises the stakes in its investigation of child abuse. Bill Maplewood is on one level a neighbour of the earlier film's Mr Kasdan, a family man and pillar of his local community.

Yet in *Happiness*, Solondz appears to follow through with his representation of the child molester, realising him, his horror and his sickness, in their fullest, most dangerous and most ludicrous form.

Where *Welcome to the Dollhouse* is an acid coming-of-age movie, *Happiness* moves outwards, in line with a number of other contemporary movies – *Short Cuts* (1993), *Magnolia* (1999), *Wonderland* (1999) – in order to embrace an ensemble cast and a small community. Solondz questions child abuse within a larger context of domestic trauma, anomie and regret. The film focuses on the Jordan family. There are three sisters: Helen, a poet; Joy, an amateur musician; and Trish, mother of three, married to Bill Maplewood. The film charts a series of connections between the lives of these three women, their neighbours, parents, colleagues and children. From this set of relations, the film draws difficult conclusions about proximity, community and the relay of individual desires and fantasies.

Lauren Berlant, in her essay 'Trauma and Ineloquence', has looked at the ways in which a film such as *Magnolia* manifests the shocking parallelism of the experiences of a set of individuals. She writes: 'That the film repossesses the individual's distinguishing marks – turning the separate stories into truly ensemble acting – devastates' (2001: 55). She continues: 'It seems inhuman to depict persons as essentially the same, once they have been thrown into the isolation chamber of traumatic experience. It is as though the details do not, after all, (have) matter ... the details are at best asterisks or epitaphs to fantasies of will in the privatised world' (*Ibid.*). Berlant's broader argument illustrates the ways in which the form and rhetoric of testimony have been deprivatised and collectivised. The move in contemporary film from the case history, and intense subjective experience, into broader, interwoven composite pieces seems itself to belie a search for an intersubjective, cultural reckoning with trauma as subject and testimony as mode of representation. *Happiness* offers the chance to witness the effect of this collectivisation on the representation of child abuse.

In his study, *Erotic Innocence: The Culture of Child Molesting*, James Kincaid argues strongly for the centrality of child sexuality, as spectacle, and as site of repression and fear, in contemporary Western culture. He writes:

> It would hardly be an overstatement to say that the subject of the child's sexuality and erotic appeal, along with our evasion of what we have done by bestowing these gifts, now structures our culture. It would not be an overstatement to say that the way we are handling the subject is ripping apart our young people. I do not deny that we are also talking sincerely about detection and danger. We worry about the poor, hurt children. But we worry also about maintaining the

particular erotic vision of children that is putting them at risk in the
first place. (1998: 14)

This territory of sexualisation and incendiary responses, mapped by
Kincaid, forms the backdrop to Solondz's film. However, *Happiness* does
not necessarily corroborate the view that child sexuality and sexual abuse
structure contemporary American culture; rather it interrogates the belief that
this is the case, questioning the singularity of this specific fear and its counter-
responses.

The film's strategies in this enterprise are clear and effective.
Importantly *Happiness* minimises the spectacular representation of the child
as erotic subject. The film carries its own self-conscious discourse about
representations of child sexuality and child abuse. One of the Jordan sisters,
Helen, played by Lara Flynn Boyle, is a poet, author of a volume named
Pornographic Childhood. This volume, visible in the film with a dark matte
cover and thick cream pages, contains on consecutive pages poems entitled
'Rape at Eleven', 'Rape at Twelve'. Helen's self-hating voice-over is heard:
'What the hell do I know about rape? I've never been raped. I'm just another
sordid exploitationist. Oh … if only I'd been raped as a child! Then I would
know authenticity.' Inclusion and mockery of Helen's volume of poems seems
set to counterbalance the effect of *Happiness* itself as artistic enterprise,
inviting us to ask questions about the film as possible exploitation. Helen
critiques her own lack of experience as her poetry claims the privilege of
the victim position. *Happiness,* by contrast, while occasionally picking up
the thought patterns of its protagonists, like so much radio interference, is an
objective, unemotional and unassuming representation of its subject matter.

This approach is manifested in the visual aesthetic. In large parts of
the film Solondz observes his characters using a still camera, simple cuts and
shot/reverse-shot editing. This straightforward *mise-en-scène* is criticised by a
reviewer in *Cahiers du cinéma,* for whom the film is reminiscent of American
sitcoms (S.B. 1999: 79). While sitcoms are certainly an ironic point of reference
in the film, as much in its jarring use of jaunty music and suburban spaces as
in its visual style, I suggest too that Solondz, like Aki Kaurismaki, favours
stillness as a deadpan means of paying stark attention to his characters.

Stillness and careful framing also allow the film to allude to the aesthetic
of family photography. *Welcome to the Dollhouse* opens with a close-up family
photograph. In *Happiness* the camera dwells on a blown-up photograph of Bill
Maplewood, his wife and children, just before the frenetic scene where Bill
prepares to drug Johnny Grasso so he can rape him. As both Marianne Hirsch
and Anne Higonnet acknowledge (as does Lauren Berlant, as discussed in
the introduction), the family photograph is a space of renegotiation of family

history and of ideals of the family as structure.[2] Solondz's use and abuse of the structure and image, both literally and in his still *mise-en-scène*, work to signal the ways in which the family is central to his analysis of contemporary interrelations and the ways fractures in the structure of the family will be figured in the form as well as content of his films.

Where Woody Allen, analysing adultery and disaffection in *Husbands and Wives* (1992), uses an interview technique such that his protagonists speak to an absent Other (analyst, reporter, director), Solondz recalls more discretely interventionist documentary techniques where a hidden camera observes the family in its private and public spaces. This sense of reportage is conveyed through the equal attention to family members across three generations, through the careful use of establishing shots (notably the exterior of the Maplewoods' ideal family house) and through the repeated return to particular spaces (the dining table, the family couch) after transitional events. Like *The Truman Show* (1998), *Happiness* imbricates sitcom, photography and documentary, aligning these dominant (visual) modes of representation of the family. *Happiness* is elastic in its attempts to encompass various modes of representation, yet the film is most testing and ethically safe in the moments at which it avoids or elides representation altogether.

The character who most effectively warps and disrupts the film's objectivity and transparent aesthetic is Bill Maplewood. Early in the film we pass seamlessly into the virtual reality of Bill's visualised dream narration; it is only as he starts to shoot indiscriminately in the scene (echoing his child Timmy) that we see that this is not the film's diegetic reality. Although we see flashbacks (real or fantasised) from another character's perspective later in the film, and hear voice-over from various characters, Bill's presence creates the greatest challenge to clear-sighted viewing and interpretation of the film. This warping effect is marked visually in the *mise-en-scène* of the first scene where Bill's paedophilia is revealed. He stops to buy *Kool*, a magazine for pre-teen boys, in the 7-11. In the parking lot outside he is seen approaching his car with the magazine. The car is positioned between the camera and Bill so he is seen at the edge of the frame, no longer as the film's direct central focus. The film seems to adopt surveillance techniques as these shots of Bill are captured. As Bill gets into the back of the car and unzips his fly to masturbate, his image is seen through the reflecting layers of glass of the car windows. As he is seen masturbating, the voices of a wife and children approaching the neighbouring car can be heard. The sounds seem reminiscent of the family reality in which Bill has falsely established his identity. They seem to impinge on his hidden pleasure, tokens of fear or guilt, residue of his psychic reality.

Simpler disruptive techniques are used in a later scene, at a baseball match. Here Bill first sees Johnny Grasso as object of desire. Bill himself is seen framed behind the crosswires of the pitch fencing. The wires separate the child and his observer; they also serve to frame Bill, to show him locked in his perversion and to anticipate his incarceration (understood but not seen at the end of the film). In these various ways, Bill as both subject and object of the gaze is a disturbed, distanced or disrupted presence.

While registering Bill as disturbance, the film is all the more cautious in its representation of Johnny Grasso, Bill's object of desire. The child is first seen at the baseball pitch where he is wearing a baseball helmet with his name printed on the side. The film cuts a few times between Bill watching and Johnny watched, establishing the child as desirable to Bill. The child is clearly appealing: he has soft colouring and delicate features. He is hesitant, slightly tremulous, blinking his eyes a few times as he waits to bat. The film does not underplay his possible appeal, yet it avoids any sexual or flirtatious presentation or behaviour on the child's part. Further, it focuses on the child as a child. The character may be gay: the film seems reminiscent of *Ma Vie en rose* (1997) in its imaging of a pre-adolescent child whose sexuality may be liminally apparent. Whatever his sexuality, his sexualisation is rather the work of his father, Joe, and his friend's father Bill. Joe stands in the film, indeed, as a no-wins alternative to Bill as abusive father. In discussion with Bill at a burger joint, Joe labels Johnny – 'my son's a fag' – and thinks aloud about getting him a professional (hooker). In a hospital scene where Johnny is questioned by police Joe angrily says to his child: 'You've been fucking raped!' *Happiness* shows Johnny as vulnerable, an object upon which adults' fantasies of love and hate attach and settle. The film does not imitate this process, however, largely refusing his idolisation as visual image. He is seen as convincingly child-like: overexcited with Billy, then absorbed in playing a gameboy, then politely picky about food when Bill wants to feed him a sleeping drug.

This latter scene, the film's seduction scene, is both lurid and ludicrous. The film follows the connections in Bill's ideas, cutting from the permission for Johnny to sleep over to an image of Bill melting sleeping draughts into chocolate fudge. As Bill enters his family living room bearing the drugged ice cream desserts, Johnny is seen lying on the floor in the foreground in his pyjamas, propped up on his elbows with the Gameboy. The pose is at once childlike, yet, seen by Bill, inadvertently sexual. The tension, pace and humour of the scene detract from its status as spectacle, however. Attention becomes focused on Johnny's animation. Where Trish, Timmy and Billy all succumb to the sleeping draught, Johnny, uneating, remains awake, almost sphinx-like, until he finally begins to eat a tuna salad sandwich and the scene fades to darkness. Throughout the scene the child remains childlike, unselfconscious, absorbed in the bonus round of his game. The film shows Johnny as Bill's object of desire, yet labours to avoid the actor becoming the viewer's object likewise.

Figure 4 *Happiness*

This caution dictates the total absence of viewed sexual contact between Bill and Johnny, or indeed between Bill and Ronald Farber, his second victim (a child not seen at all in the film). The film cuts from the eating of the sandwich to a static, eerie image of the exterior of the Maplewoods' house, then a tense breakfast scene between Bill and Johnny. In the prelude to the second abuse scenario, Bill, who has learned that Billy's classmate Ronald Farber is home alone, drives in the dark through the neighbourhood, calling Information for the Farbers' address. He turns into their drive and we just have time to see a 'Watch Children' sign illuminated, before the film fades again to blackness and then cuts to Bill coming home to his family house.

These two fades, or elisions, mark the point of the film's refusal to represent. For Cynthia Lucia and Ed Kelleher, writing in *Cinéaste*, this proves a failing. They argue: 'In failing to show more sustained interaction between Bill and Johnny Grasso ... the film also fails to implicate the presumably middle-class art-house audience by allowing refuge into the same recesses of respectability where Bill himself has hidden' (1990: 82). For me, the refusal to represent perpetuates the film's caution over spectacularisation (and concern, perhaps, for its child actors). The film avoids reproducing images which can themselves be mishandled (like the images in the magazine *Kool*). Yet this refusal also demonstrates, I think, the way the sexual damage of children exists as an image outside representation. These moments of darkness fissure the film and point to an encounter with a space that cannot be assimilated into the structure of the film or the surface world of the Maplewoods' family reality. These two scenarios of abuse are missing from the film visually, yet they structure its affect and determine its outrage. Hence their critical power.

Removing the scene of Johnny's rape from view, *Happiness* nevertheless reminds us distressingly of its visceral effects. This system of reminders works through imagery of food, vomit and defecation: such imagery shows the body as interior, impregnable and violable. The rape itself can finally take place because Johnny is cajoled into eating the tuna salad sandwich. We see him bite into the soft fishy paste of the sandwich. The object exchanged between Bill and Johnny seems to cling, stickily associated with the act which will follow. The tuna salad returns too, physically, as Johnny throws up at the breakfast table the next morning. Although his sickness is not exploited visually, this mixing of food, sex and bodily detritus seems reminiscent of Cindy Sherman's still life photographs of the 1980s. In *Happiness* the vomit signals Johnny's bodily expulsion of the drug, of the food, of Bill's advances, as polutants. It makes Johnny, too, insistently only a sickly child.

He asks Bill to drive him home and the film cuts to queasy shots of Bill and Johnny in the car. Shadows of tall trees along the roadside pass over the car as Bill drives, intimating tension. Yet Johnny's response to his trauma is somatic; he seems to have no consciousness of his abuse (we assume he was unconscious as it happened). The car journey home echoes the extraordinary scene at the end of *Exotica* where Francis is in the car with Christina. Johnny, like Christina, is seen to respond to the (in this case) abusive adult figure as carer and comforter. Johnny apologises for being sick and then says: 'Dr Maplewood, you're so cool.' Bill has his arm around Johnny as he drives.

While the child's queasiness seems to signal the abuse of his body, evidence of his rape is found as he sees the next day that there is blood in his faeces. The film shows Johnny briefly, again in pyjamas, in the bathroom at home. While his bodily exterior is little pictured by the film, his bodily interior becomes the thoroughfare through which the film drives its meanings about abuse. Indeed a sickly link can be traced between Johnny's experience of rape and vomit and another of the film's voiced sexual fantasies. Close to the start of the film, an adult character Allen is speaking to Bill Maplewood, who is his psychiatrist. In the 'safe' space of Bill's office Allen says: 'I want to undress her, I want to tie her up and pump her pump pump pump 'til she screams bloody murder. And then I want to flip her ass over and pump her even more and so hard that my dick shoots right through her and that my cum shoots out of her mouth.' Although the scene is not connected to Johnny's rape in the film, on repeat viewings Johnny's sickness and vomiting start to echo Allen's sadistic fantasy. As this interconnection becomes clearer, the film appears to achieve an intersubjective representation where the fantasies and experiences of the characters impinge on and overshadow one another. This is particularly sensitive, and disturbing, in the film's representation of child abuse. While Bill himself is a circumspect, contained character, the fantasies and (auto)erotic activities of his client, Allen, appear to speak something of the excess and mess of his sexuality. It is in this mess of adult sexuality that Johnny is mixed up; this seems indicated in the returning bodily images.

Whilst seeing nothing of Johnny's rape – being unconscious like the child himself – we imagine its horror and degradation as we attach other visceral and emotional memories to it. Solondz's cinema seems to depend on the viewer's own bodily recall as she or he consumes the different sensory images represented. Laura Marks has observed: 'Sense memories are most fragile to transport, yet most evocative when they can be recovered. ... What is left out of expression registers somatically, in pain, nausea, memories of smells and caresses. What does not register in the orders of the seeable and the sayable may resonate in the order of the sensible' (2000: 111). Marks is concerned with intercultural cinema and with the recovery or recall of sense memory in innovative haptic cinema. The memories she studies, often nostalgic and born of exile, have barely found their way into the public record. Her remarks have resonance in the different context of the cinema of trauma and abuse where, in different circumstances, the unseeable and unsayable may yet register somatically (as we find in Johnny's bodily experience, his delayed response and regurgitation). I suggest that, for the viewer too, the representation of abuse is found in the diffuse sense impressions conjured by imagery of food, ingestion and vomit. The film's meaning is gradually constituted in the mnemonic associations of the viewer as she or he perceives structural and fantasmatic repetitions.

As ensemble film-making, *Happiness* is a film where the protagonists act as so many distorting mirrors to one another's actions. Like Johnny, Allen himself is sick while Christina is there; Johnny's car-ride home is followed by a scene where Joy is beaten up by Vlad's girlfriend, her bodily vulnerability like a delayed reaction to Johnny's rape. This repetition, or contamination, works in such a way that a fractured, disseminated image is finally recognised as a piercing reality. This is the case, further and more generally, in the film's engagement with the representation of childhood.

While Johnny Grasso and the unseen Ronald Farber are the film's most obvious children at risk and victims of abuse, the film offers a more widespread engagement with discourses, practices and representations of child/adult contact and of disturbed borders between childhood and adulthood. Solondz is extremely good on the literal contemporary detail of childhood: the Gameboy, the Tamogotchi, the Robocop costume, the grape Hi C. In representing Trish as mother and Timmy as child (who cries 'Die, Aunt Joy!

Die'), Solondz parodies contemporary family anxieties about childhood, its invasion and erosion. Trish says to Joy: 'I blame it on cartoons. They are so full of violence.' Later, when she has learnt that one of Billy's school teachers is a junkie, she says: 'I'm sorry, but when it comes to drug abuse ... and children, my children ... Uch, they should all just be locked up and throw away the key.' In the words of the Christian Right, Trish continues: 'Now I know, Bill, I may sound harsh, but we're talking about our kids. Not to be too grandiose, but this is the future, the future of our country we're talking about, after all.' Ironically for Trish it is her husband who is, in the words of the graffiti on their family house, a serial rapist and pervert.

Happiness works both to ironise the unthinking repetition of clichés about children and their safety (it is 'National Children's Month' at the hospital where Johnny Grasso is examined), yet simultaneously to acknowledge the gravity of the fears, suspicions and abuses surrounding children. As we have seen, James Kincaid has argued that fears for child safety and, for him, hysterical attempts to ensure that safety, have gone hand in hand with the (erotic) idealisation of children which puts them at risk in the first place. Solondz works to divorce this paranoia and converse gloating attention.

Kincaid links the idealisation of the Romantic child to 'deep escapist nostalgia' and in particular to the notion of the inner child. He writes: 'The idealisation of the prepubescent child and its location within the sad adult is not simply fuel for therapists and best-selling self-helpers; one sees it all over our culture' (1998: 70). In an image peculiarly apt to the imbrication of food and abuse in *Happiness*, Kincaid says of the healing child within: 'This child rechurns our cultural curds, innocence and purity, into a modern snack food we can ingest and use to nourish, excuse, and explain ourselves' (*Ibid.*). Solondz refuses childhood as sugar sweet snack food; food itself in his films is viscous and mushy – mashed potato, wilting lettuce and flaccid burgers. Further, in debunking the child-centred culture of which Kincaid speaks, Solondz shows up the pathos and real horrors of and for adults in touch with their inner child. A panning shot round thirty-year-old Joy's bedroom in her parents' house pauses on her crocheted toy animals, her spider plants and sprigged curtains. Another character, Kristina, is like an overdressed little girl with her pastel dresses, ribbons and her appetite for 'a half-gallon of strawberry ice cream, two boxes of fudge, and a key lime pie'. Even Kristina's comfort food is disturbing as she eats a sundae while describing how she cut up her doorman's body after he tried to rape her. Joy and Kristina, childlike women, are both sad and partly grotesque (though Joy is also one of the most sympathetic characters of the film).

The idealisation of childhood is undone further still in a series of peculiar exchanges between Bill and his son Billy. There are three key scenes of dialogue between Bill and Billy. All begin with Billy saying, 'Dad?', and Bill replying, 'Yes, Billy?' They have a dead-pan rhythm, reminiscent of the family voices and dialogues in Egoyan's films. The content of each exchange between Bill and Billy is uneasily sexual. In the first Billy asks Bill what 'cum' is and Bill explains in patient, liberal, pedagogical terms. In the second scene, Billy asks Bill about penis size and length. In the third, Billy asks Bill about his abuse of Johnny Grasso and Ronald Farber. On one level the scenes further demystify childhood. Another side of adult/child sexual negotiations is the parent's responsibility to offer some reasonable sexual education to the child. The scenes reflect the part-practical, part-deeply embarrassing tone of such discussions. Billy is a plain child, solemn, sympathetic, slightly fat. The film avoids any sexualisation of the visual presentation of the scenes. Nevertheless in the first two scenes, Bill's responses, as a responsible father, are surprising. In the first scene he offers to show Billy how to masturbate. In the second he offers to measure his own penis to quell Billy's anxieties about penis size. Despite the film's black humour manifested in the matter of fact tone of Bill's patient questions and answers with Billy, the exchanges still belie his excess sexuality.

The third scene is the most traumatic and offers the greatest shift in power balance. Billy now appears as Bill's confessor, drawing words from him. This underlines the way these scenes function in the film as a whole. They work as a type of catechism where Bill and Billy repeat and gradually subvert the terms and meanings of father/son identification and bonding. Billy's questions also serve to voice the viewer's questions and concerns. This becomes most apparent in the third scene where he tries to get Bill to find words for what he has done and finally asks crucially: 'Would you ever fuck me?'

The scenes actualise Solondz's concern to question how the child molester and serial rapist functions in the family. What sort of father is he? How does he relate to his son? For Solondz, Bill's fatherhood opens questions about his identity and redemption. He says: 'if there is redemption for this man it lies in [his] honesty and the love he has for his son, before whom he cannot but tell the truth' (in Hearty 1998: 36). The statement is disturbing as a result of the set of interconnections the film sets up between Bill's paternity and his paedophilia. Solondz explains further, saying of Billy: 'He can't really understand the full ramifications of what his father has done and what it really means but he knows enough that his father is a terrible man and that his father has done wrong and that his father loves him' (*Ibid.*). It is to this set of irreconcilable truths that the film offers no resolution.

In the same interview with Solondz, the interviewer says of the film-maker that he is 'looking for human connections beneath domestic chaos' (Hearty 1998: 34). More than this, *Happiness* demonstrates the horror of inextricable connections between individuals in inter-relation, between love and abuse, between survival and denial. The structural interconnections and repetitions on which the film depends as art, are seen to bring absurdity, pain, frustration and irresolution in human inter-relations. This absurd inextricability is represented at its most grotesque in the film's own bonus round, a scene six months later where Billy finally comes. His cum is licked up by the family dog who in turn goes to be petted and kissed by Trish. Again the transfer of bodily fluids seems sick and excessive. The film ends with this mess of interconnection.

Happiness offers a complex engagement with its subject. On the one hand the film pushes us to the limits of what we want or can bear to see. Yet it also works to suggest that its subject – child abuse – encompasses so much more which resists the viewer and remains outside representation. What we see in this devastating film is the 'happy', sanitised version, the starkly humorous, picaresque narrative. Offering a self-consciously edited view allows Solondz to hint that society and cinema are as yet far from grasping the pain and mess of child abuse. This failure to grasp seems due to the difficulty of experiencing and testifying to abuse (Johnny Grasso, for example, is far from being able to assume the subject or victim position). It derives, further, from the difficulty in cinema's spectacular and erotic regime of denouncing and critiquing sexual acts and sexual objects placed on show. Further still, the incendiary social context of contemporary art and its reception (as witnessed, rightly or wrongly, in responses to works by Robert Mapplethorpe, Larry Clark, Sally Mann, A. M. Homes and others) makes any intervention in this field highly charged, risky and liable to legal and moral censorship.

A solution, for Solondz, is to represent through interconnections. Indeed it is in its summoning of unwelcome similarities and inescapable connections that the film marks its visceral impact in the viewer. This means of representation itself reflects the film's ensemble cast and outreach to a whole (smalltown New Jersey) community. The whole cast of characters work in one way or another to reflect questions about child abuse and child sexuality. Yet, further, the charting of the many protagonists' own diverging griefs and horrors simultaneously sets child abuse in the relative context of other contemporary losses, agonies and anxieties (divorce, suicide, theft, betrayal, rivalry, self-disgust, rape). Solondz accepts blurred boundaries: perhaps Bill is in some difficult way a caring father. Child abuse and parenthood queasily merge. *Happiness* respects the excessive horror of its subject, yet also indicates its frightening banality and familiarity. It avoids idealising children or making them objects of desire for the viewer; it is within these parameters that Solondz finds an interrogative and critical approach to his subject. Crucial, perhaps, is his observation: 'I don't think anyone is getting off on this movie' (in Hearty 1998: 36). I think he's right.

CHAPTER FOUR

Uncanny Families: *Olivier, Olivier*

More elegiac than *Happiness, Olivier, Olivier* (1992) revisits the classic spaces and emotions of loss in childhood: the enclosed security of the mother/child relation, the ambivalent space of the open fields and the fearful structure of fairy tales and their initiatory dynamics. In this chapter, pursuing thoughts of adult/child relations rather differently, I look at the way the missing child film offers the means of rethinking the loss of childhood itself as drama (and trauma) for adults and children. The exceptional event, the *fait divers* occurrence, acquires resonance, even horrific familiarity, in the ways in which it magnifies and literalises a set of psychic losses which are encountered as a child grows up. Hence its fascination, and terror. In *Olivier, Olivier* in particular, the missing child film is used to open up and interrogate the family. While the film offers emotive images of maternal love and nostalgia both for the safety of home and the green paradise of childhood innocence, it is most radical in its imagining of a transformed and renewed post-traumatic family.

Agnieszka Holland herself has not avoided the association of *Olivier, Olivier* with aspects of her own experience of maternity and loss. When martial law was declared in Poland on 12 December 1981, Holland was in Sweden, promoting her film *A Woman Alone* (see Holland 1996). She was warned not to return to Poland, so went to Paris. She had no information about her husband and her nine-year-old daughter, who had remained in Warsaw. She kept vigils at the airport in Paris. Eight months later her daughter was allowed to leave Poland. Leon Steinmetz writes:

Olivier, Olivier was a very personal film for Holland. … She thought she would never see her daughter again. She knew that, as someone noted, 'for her daughter, she had disappeared, vanished as abruptly as had Holland's own father [who died in KGB custody when Holland was thirteen]'. 'When my daughter finally arrived in France, she could not speak to me,' Holland recalls, adding 'later, she told me she had been sure that I was dead'. (in Holland 1996: xii–xiii)

While I claim no direct relation between Holland's experience and her choice of subject in *Olivier, Olivier*, I want here to signal some awareness of the ways in which her involuntary exile and her circumstances as a Polish director, filming in France, may transform and inflect her treatment of a missing child drama.

Olivier, Olivier was based on a true story, like Holland's earlier *Europa, Europa* (1991). In 1984, Holland had come across a piece in *Le Matin de Paris* about the disappearance of a nine-year-old boy, and his return as a teenager six years later. Holland recalls: 'the basic story interested me, but I wanted to fill it with my own experience, with things close to me. I wanted to be able to see myself in the character of the mother. I wanted my characters to be more lucid than the protagonists of the real event.'[1] The achievement of *Olivier, Olivier* is its ability to work as a mirror not merely to the real *fait divers* by which it is inspired, nor simply to the drama of Holland's own experience, influential and formative though both must have been, but to broader issues about severance between mother and child, about rupture and loss. The particular situation reproduces and renegotiates archetypal concerns. Holland presents a contemporary fairytale in whose confines open out questions of home and safety, maternal love, loss and adolescence. In Holland's film, public and private, personal and historical fears and complexes effectively coalesce. *Olivier, Olivier* is thus in another sense inspired by a 'true story' of psychic investment in questions of childhood.

While Holland has treated a wide variety of subjects in her films, the management of loss in childhood returns as preoccupation in *The Secret Garden* (1993). The point at which *The Secret Garden* comes closest to *Olivier, Olivier*, seeming to provide a moment of psychic intensity missing from the earlier film, is in a singular dream sequence. The child Mary dreams of herself as a toddler in a wild garden where she is dwarfed by broad-leafed plants. Her mother appears before her as a memory image, her arms outstretched to the child. Then she disappears. In a high-angle shot, we look down on the tiny child, now alone, calling out 'Mummy' and, almost inaudibly in her tears, 'I want to go home'. For a brief interval the film shows the fear and disorientation of the missing child, almost unbearable to view.

The image of the child lost in greenery resonates with the pastoral imagery with which *Olivier, Olivier* begins. The first shots of the film show the expanse of the French countryside. In a tracking shot Holland marks out the territory and space of her film; the pastoral Eden in which the child is at risk has become a key point of reference. In *Exotica*, as we have seen, search parties comb the fields for the child's body, eventually found in grasses by Eric and Christina. More explicitly, in *L'Humanité*, the child's body is displayed in the stark, barren landscape of Northern France. Disturbingly these pastoral images return in media reporting of the cases of missing children. (In England, in summer 2000, meadows in the Sussex countryside were a recurring image accompanying reports of the abduction and murder of the child Sarah Payne.) Such imagery appears to work doubly, recalling a lost paradise of childhood (where the pastoral here is linked with nostalgia), yet also highlighting this mythic, emotive space as the very locus of rupture and loss.

Olivier, Olivier keeps in play this set of double meanings, yet works further, too, to historicise and contextualise this space of childhood loss. The colours of the landscape are luminous in the film: Olivier cycles through a field of poppies. The image is reminiscent of the field of poppies where Dorothy sleeps in *The Wizard of Oz* (1939), a space of beauty and childish pleasure, yet also of danger, where Dorothy's animate fragility is tested by the Wicked Witch of the West. The film alludes to children's literature (and liberally to 'Little Red Riding Hood'). Yet the poppy field and yearning pastoral landscape have a further historical point of reference. The colour of the red poppies seems to anticipate Olivier's trauma and tie it loosely to the losses which have scarred the French landscape (the children are playing in the grass and bushes of a trench that dates from the First World War). Holland makes the national context of the film subliminally significant.

Critics have read *Olivier, Olivier* in its French filmic context. Jonathan Romney considers *Olivier, Olivier* in the French tradition of 'bucolic family drama', typified by films such as *Le Grand chemin* (1987). He suggests that Holland, in *Olivier, Olivier*, allows 'gaps to remain in a way that French family stories rarely do' (1992: 54). Such gaps arguably work in *Olivier, Olivier* to leave the viewer space to question the stability of the family and its status as social structure, and indeed the ideology which structures the family story as such. In this questioning *Olivier, Olivier* comes closer to some earlier French films of childhood, in particular *Les Jeux interdits* (1952), recalled where Olivier and Nadine are seen playing in a small cemetery with wrought iron crosses. *Les Jeux interdits* similarly maps a historically grounded narrative of childhood and loss in a French pastoral landscape. In such references, in its setting, language and in the (French) nationality of its cast and crew, *Olivier, Olivier* claims identity and reference as a French film. Yet it also recalls certain Polish filmic images of a pastoral landscape of childhood, as found, for example, in Andrzej Wajda's *The Birchwood* (1970) or, more recently, in the films of Dorota Kedzierzawska. Holland's own exile from Poland (she describes herself as an orphan of Poland) arguably adds its own mnemonic intensities to her filming of a lost world (home as well as childhood).

Indeed central to this film, I argue, is a conflict between home and abroad, between familiarity and difference, between the *Heimlich* and the *Unheimlich*, between nostalgia and futurity. This, as we will see, is crystallised in the film in its competing concerns on the one hand with pressing nostalgia for the mother/child relation, for similarity and symbiosis, and on the other with a set of motifs of estrangement, of difference, of flight into the future. These contradictory emotions are mobilised in the drama of love and losses leaving childhood necessitates. Further, as Freud has familiarly demonstrated, the very signifier for the safe and homely (which I associate here with nostalgia), the *Heimlich*, always already bears a double meaning: 'on the one hand it means what is familiar and agreeable, and on the other, what is concealed and kept out of sight' (1985b: 354). For Holland, the sunlit fields of this missing childhood seem at once the familiar place of the homesick dreamer, and a space of historical and emotional rupture. Further, home in *Olivier, Olivier* harbours these double, hidden emotions: associated at once with the nostalgic and familiar and with rupture and difference. The familiar and agreeable will be drawn into question as an uncannily familiar child returns home to the family. In the return of the missing child, the cravings of nostalgia and preemptive mourning are arguably satisfied. Yet as the child is further inserted into the family unit his difference and transformation of the family become steadily more apparent. Holland seems to open up the family to change and futurity rather than leave it locked in nostalgic repetition. Estrangement and the defamiliarisation of the family are themselves the insistent subjects of *Olivier, Olivier*. Stringent, and morally complex, the film asks us to reconsider maternity as loss, and disavowal as a possible prop in kindred living. Such disavowal becomes one mode of survival of traumatic loss, a means of renegotiating memory and moving into the future.

At the start of the film, we hear the voices of the children, Olivier and Nadine, before we see them. Holland takes us directly into the acoustic net which surrounds the children and knits their relations to one another. We are eavesdropping on an intense imaginary game, led by Nadine. Despite the pastoral archetypes on which it draws, the film lands firmly in the present: Olivier and Nadine are fighting aliens. Questions of the alien(s) and of estrangement enter the film from its start and run through as recurring motif. Nadine frightens Olivier with tales of aliens when they are in bed at night; she later leads the small child Paul to believe that aliens have taken Olivier away.

The children's game proves premonitory as the family's neighbour, Marcel, comes cycling into the landscape. This is the first of a series of shots of Marcel, then the little Olivier and the older Olivier on a cycle or moped. On this first encounter, Nadine pretends to aim and fire at Marcel. As if struck by her imaginary shot, he loses his balance and falls off his bicycle. Marcel's identity as Olivier's murderer goes undiscovered for large parts of the film, and for six years of diegetic time, yet he is always the obvious suspect. The film might be criticised for its stereotyping of Marcel as child molester. Yet this underestimates its guardedly non-judgemental treatment of him. An elegy of sorts seems to be offered, after his arrest, as the camera dwells on cuttings and photographs, small ephemeral details, he has pinned to his wall. Further, one of the most successful ways in which the film creates unease and distress is in its testing of whether, finally, guilt rests with Marcel alone. This lends complexity to its treatment of the missing child theme, and underscores the way in which such films may also usefully question the nexus of emotions which make up familial relations.

Rather than merely identify Marcel as perpetrator of the crime, *Olivier, Olivier* leads us all the more painfully to interrogate the feelings of guilt of its other characters and their respective investment in Olivier's loss, his remaining in childhood and his future return and rediscovery. In this way the film differs crucially from the classic detective story. As Colin Davis points out: 'Žižek describes how the resolution of the mystery [in a detective story] relieves us of our own unconscious guilt' (2000: 62). Žižek writes, indeed: 'the detective's act consists in annihilating the libidinal possibility, the "inner" truth that each one in the group might have been the murderer' (1991: 59). Žižek suggests that the act of singling out the murderer guarantees our innocence. Davis looks at texts with unresolved mysteries and open endings which 'offer no such restoration of normality and relief from guilt' (2000: 62); he argues that, 'Instead, they suggest that guilt has not been, and cannot be, removed by the expulsion from the community of the convenient scapegoat' (*Ibid.*). Despite the seeming resolution of its mystery, a similar conclusion may be drawn about *Olivier, Olivier* which works not to cast blame but to interrogate love and guilt. The drama of the missing child is used as a point of departure from which the other characters are constrained to trace their own desires and fears.

Central to this examination of guilt in the missing child film is an analysis of the mother/child dyad, sibling rivalry and the complexities of such familial love relations. *Olivier, Olivier* is strategically ambivalent about the mother/child bond, its intensity and asphyxiation. Olivier has reached the age of eight or nine by the time the film starts, although the child actor (Emmanuel

Morozof) looks younger. The first scene in which we see mother and son together is staged as a bedtime drama. They are held together within the frame in relatively long takes. The lighting of the scene is soft and intimate: Elisabeth drapes a scarf over Olivier's bedside lamp. The textures of the scene are equally soft and tactile, in particular the satin of Elisabeth's dressing gown. She appears visually to encircle her child and sings him a lullaby. The scene of intimacy identifies Holland's work with the domestic strands of the work of French women film-makers who have represented the making and breaking of the mother/child relation (Diane Kurys, Sandrine Veysset). Holland appears to seek a visual form of the pre-Oedipal unity of mother and child. Tender though such a scene is, this bedtime drama, like a later bathroom scene between mother and child, in retrospect seems stark evidence of the mother's over-weaning attention to her child (which she fears has driven him away). This mother/child relation is the lost love the film takes as its subject, detailing Elisabeth's profound regret that her child will leave her (even before Olivier has disappeared).

The symbiotic, very physical, relation between Elisabeth and Olivier, seen in the bedtime drama, is disrupted by Nadine, the jealous elder child who watches from the doorway. Nadine upsets the singularity of the shots and the exclusivity of the mother/son dyad. Her jealousy of Olivier, her teasing him with alien games, and the accident that it is Olivier, not Nadine, who takes the lunch to their grandmother's house and so goes missing, also combine to make her too feel guilty when her brother goes missing. It is as if she has broken the mother/son bond from which she has been painfully excluded; as a result she is punished by the wish-fulfilling loss of Olivier.

Looking at mother/child relations in *The Acoustic Mirror*, Kaja Silverman remarks that, 'it has become something of a theoretical commonplace to characterise the maternal voice as a blanket of sound, extending on all sides of the newborn infant' (1988: 72). She explores what she describes as this fantasy turning upon 'the image of infantile containment – upon the image of a child held within the environment or sphere of the mother's voice' (*Ibid.*). Silverman comments that where she herself has tried to describe this image as neutrally as possible, 'in fact its "appearances" are always charged with either intensely positive or intensely negative affect' (*Ibid.*) (she cites the work of Guy Rosolato as an example of the former and the work of Michel Chion as an example of the latter). For Silverman, the contradictory views point to the profoundly ambivalent nature of the fantasy, an ambivalence which finds filmic form in *Olivier, Olivier*.

In contrast to the film examples critiqued by Silverman, however, the primary concern of *Olivier, Olivier* is not the child's perspective, but the mother's response to and reception of the binding unity of the mother/child relation. Holland's film in this sense is innovative in its attention to the signs and meanings of the mother's subjectivity and her investment in her relation to her child. Rather than perpetuate the containment and devaluation of the maternal – (defensive gestures of self-supporting male subjectivity) – the film works instead to tackle the possibility of a maternal (over)investment and pleasure in the fantasy of imaginary fusion and plenitude. Elisabeth is seen to wish to perpetuate an illusion of her relation to Olivier in such a way that their severance is denied. She props up her illusion through a repetition of the retroactive fantasies of the maternal voice: she reads and sings to her child, she takes refuge in the softly-lit and mirrored interior of the family house, listening to music and often sleeping in the day. Holland shows very poignantly the density of investment in this fantasy for Elisabeth, and leads us to suspend judgment on its sanity.

Here the role of Nadine, Olivier's sister, is again crucial. Nadine has been seen as onlooker to the scene of her mother's umbilical love for Olivier. Interestingly (in keeping with Silverman's account of the negative Oedipus complex explored elsewhere in *The Acoustic Mirror*) Nadine is a rival to Olivier for her mother's love. What the film confronts is the mother's greater love for her son than for her daughter. This is tested in a demanding scene where Elisabeth says she wishes it had been Nadine, not Olivier, who had gone missing. When they are reconciled, Elisabeth holds Nadine, rocking her like a baby, like a replacement Olivier. Despite her mother's ambivalence, Nadine is seen still to choose her mother's affection over that of her father. After Serge (the father) departs for Chad, Nadine acts as mother to Elisabeth as they stay on in the family house (with Marcel playing surrogate father). There is a gentleness and easy physicality between mother and daughter which replicates the unity between Elisabeth and Olivier. The strength of the mother/daughter relation is privileged, yet this is the daughter's choice, not the mother's.

Olivier, Olivier shows how the trauma of a missing child can disrupt the family unit and allow its love relations to be realigned. Here I think it is crucial that the film is open and non-judgmental. The household Elisabeth and Nadine create between them is in some senses a mausoleum to Olivier, yet mother and daughter are shown to find a different interrelation and a love which both recalls and displaces the unity between Elisabeth and Olivier. This (homoerotic) relation depends on both nostalgia *and* futurity. It allows Holland to double the mother/son relation, with a different mother/daughter relation. This love, and the stability and familiarity of the family unit is put to the test still further in the seeming return of Olivier.

Part of the challenge of *Olivier, Olivier* lies in its creation of two missing children: the child Olivier and his adolescent counterpart. The film poses the question of whether these two individuals can be equivalent, whether they can be one and the same. Over and above the real, and extraordinary, issues of identity or difference tested in the real *fait divers*, the film questions the seeming non-identity between a child and his later adolescent self. This is an issue addressed in *Empire of the Sun* (1987) or the documentary on the Kindertransport, *Into the Arms of Strangers* (2000), where adolescents find their families again after the trauma of World War Two and are barely recognisable to them. In *Olivier, Olivier*, this drama of loss and change is literalised still further in the real doubts which surround the adolescent Olivier's identity. The returning child, nostalgically remembered, does not fill out or fit with the remembered child who was lost. While the returning Olivier is really not the Duval's missing child, the film also asks the question of whether any missing child who returns could be entirely and easily recognised as familiar.

In *Olivier, Olivier*, the adolescent Olivier is found by the policeman, Druot, who headed the enquiry into the child's disappearance. The adolescent is a son in search of a mother. The boy offers several narratives of his identity, finishing up with another fiction of a missing child: 'My name is Sebastian Blanch. My stepfather took me by force the first time in our bathroom at home, while my mother was out' (Holland 1996: 34). Druot rejects this narrative, and it remains an uncharted line. He seeks instead to insert the missing boy into a different family drama. He carries files of children who have disappeared – an eerie staple, like the images of missing children seen on American milk cartons. Holland alludes to the larger network of losses into which her film is inserted; in this it acquires pathos and resonance. In the face of these innumerable and irredeemable cases, Druot attempts to return one child to a family, believing the adolescent to be Olivier and setting himself the task of restoring him to Elisabeth.

The new Olivier, back in the family, is used as a figure of both truth and disavowal: again the film privileges ambivalence. He is the support for Elisabeth's fantasy of her son's survival and return. When they take the train back home, she talks to Olivier without noticing that he doesn't hear her. She touches him while he is asleep and speaks to him: 'You're going to forgive me, aren't you? From now on everything will be normal … I'll do my best … a normal home. A real home … a real life …' (Holland 1996: 39). This, in keeping with my reference to Žižek above, seems to indicate Elisabeth's sense of guilt over her missing child, her notion that her family and her love have been abnormal or excessive, and have failed to keep him and keep him safe. The return of the missing child allows the illusory possibility of recreating the family unit and now shoring it up through knowing denial.

The family becomes an artificial, wish-fulfilling double of itself. Its harmony is dependent on the illusory knowledge of the perfect resemblance between the new Olivier and the lost son. Ironically Olivier is nostalgically desired within the family because he supposedly resembles the lost child, yet he seduces the family members through his uncanny difference. Grégoire Colin, playing Olivier, seems to play a different part for each member of the family, winning them over by his ability to anticipate their needs. He remains silent and enigmatic about his past in Paris, though hints of his work as a prostitute, in its difference, again draw the fascination of the family (in particular Nadine). The new Olivier as false, seductive family member plays a role akin to that of Terence Stamp in *Theorem* (1968) or Elias Koteas in *The Adjuster* (1991). A new mobility of gender roles is initiated where the (Freudian) distinction between identification and desire is broken down.

As *Olivier, Olivier* explores a negative Oedipus complex in Nadine's relation to her mother, thus transforming the family unit, so the film also moves to open out homoerotic bonds between father and son. Marking Olivier's return, indeed, Serge himself has returned from Chad (leading to their resemblance as returned family members). Serge brings a pet monkey with him for Nadine: the introduction of the animal into the family and the animal's sensitivity to family dynamics again seems to mirror Olivier's alien, exotic presence within the familiar home space. Serge forges a new relation with Olivier, drinking with him and buying him a moped, realising the identification with his son which was prevented previously by the exclusive mother/child relation.

While both Serge and Elisabeth wonder at their new-found son and his transformation of the family, Nadine is responsible most completely for putting Olivier's identity to the test, as it was she who previously interrupted the relation between mother and son. The film seems to imply, indeed, an uncanny similarity between the denial and wish-fulfilment of the scenes after Olivier's return and the amniotic unreality of the mother/child relation. Nadine goes as far as sleeping with Olivier in order to test his familiarity or difference. Her mother too has sought to test somatic evidence of Olivier's identity: like a nurse in myth or fairytale she has been overjoyed to discover an appendix scar on Olivier's side, seeming bodily proof of his self-identity. Nadine, sleeping with Olivier, usurps the love between mother and son by which she herself has been previously displaced. In the morning she sees Olivier playing a peeing game with the child Paul in the yard, a game she has seen her brother play with Marcel in the past. This uncanny repetition (like the scar) seduces Nadine again into a belief that her brother has returned.

In addition to his new role in the family, Olivier also, however, uncovers the identity of Marcel as the real Olivier's murderer. In a ghastly repetition of events, the new Olivier finds Marcel sexually abusing another small child, Paul, brother of Nadine's friend Babette. If the new Olivier himself has been abused as a child, as his narrative in the police station has suggested, it is apt, and cathartic, that he should rescue Marcel's next victim, putting a stop to the proliferating series of events: tying and binding Marcel. With the discovery of the child Olivier's body in Marcel's basement after his arrest, we learn that any line we have drawn between child and adolescent Olivier is illusory. Further, any fiction of the child's escape or future is foreclosed. The film does not remain content with this brute reality, however, and works further to question the possibility of disavowal.

Holland points to the series of disavowals on which the other characters have depended. Firstly Druot's; he reveals to Olivier wistfully: 'You were supposed to be my big success' (Holland 1996: 74). Then Marcel's; he confesses: 'I swear to you … I only wanted to touch him … and … he was afraid … he wanted to run away … I didn't know what to do … I wanted to forget … It wasn't my fault! … I loved the kid a lot! And she … Elisabeth … I…' (1996: 75). Marcel's words reveal his will to 'forget' or disavow his crime and Olivier's disappearance. His words indicate too his peculiar identification with Elisabeth who, as grieving mother, also faces the truth of her own disavowal. Despite the discovery and burial of the first child's small body, Olivier will still return to the Duval family. He tells Druot that he is going 'home' (he too is a missing child, in search of a mother and family). Olivier returns to continue his imitation of their missing son. In a return to the image of the aliens, the film ends with Olivier saying: 'Come back to earth, Mom, I'm here' and Elisabeth replying: 'You're here, Olivier. You've come back after all' (1996: 78). Through the window we see Olivier's empty swing in the garden. It is swinging back and forth, against the darkness and rain.

Critics of the film have stressed the ways in which the last image of the empty swing points to the destruction of the family. Frédéric Richard argues that there is no illusion of refound stability (1992: 41). For Inga Karetnikova: 'The last shot is beyond the story. Here Holland reminds us that the little boy is gone, his place is empty' (in Holland 1996: 86). Romney argues, however, that 'in mourning, Elisabeth still sees the new Olivier as her son' (1992: 54). It is this illusion, and substitution, on which I think more can be said. Here, the very motion of the swing, in its movement back and forwards, seems to hold meaning. The swing imitates the double movement of disavowal, swinging between acknowledgement and denial. The swing is empty, yet its motion, its animation, recall and conjure the illusory presence of the lost child. It is in this illusion, and recall, that the film closes. In this image, too, Holland seems to provide a self-reflexive comment on the privileged status of cinema as medium of disavowal. Cinema can offer the illusion of presence of animation, a photographic trace of lost objects and lost loved ones. Hence its poignancy, I think, as medium in which the missing child drama is explored. This poignancy, this play between nostalgic illusion and painful recognition, is exploited in *Olivier, Olivier*. Before we see the empty swing at the end, we have glimpsed a shot of Paul swinging back and forth. Seen briefly, the shot raises doubts for the viewer as to whether this is a memory image, or even a flashback to Olivier himself, now and always a phantom presence in the family house. Film allows the viewer to visualise the constant presence of the missing child in the space his family inhabit. Yet Holland prefers to show how a family might not merely find comfort in fleeting representations, psychic or photographic, of their missing child, but seek further to identify another son as theirs and deny his difference.

Holland makes her familiar drama rich and strange. She shows not merely how the family unit is defamiliarised, but shows further how the representation of the family, its dynamics and emotions, can be re-oriented, made to differ from itself. This is achieved by approaching a familiar complex in cinema (as demonstrated by Silverman), namely the enclosure and castigation of the over-weaning mother. Holland re-enters this fantasy, taking us into the enclosure of the mother's extraordinary love and derangement, interrogating its bases, neither to idealise or exonerate maternal love, but to explain its intensities, the horror of its losses and myths of self-abnegation.

In this exploration of the mother/child relation, and its seriousness, Holland presents, nevertheless, not merely regret or nostalgia for sameness, for similarity and the intensity of the mirroring bond. I have stressed that the film suspends judgment and privileges ambivalence. If it offers any final resolution of its complexes, it seems to be in the embracing of both alterity and disavowal. The new Olivier, although other and alien, can uncannily recall the lost child. In the double movement of disavowal, where his real identity is both known and denied, he offers if anything at least distraction from the lost child. For him likewise, perhaps, the Duval family is an uncanny double of the family he has lost; Olivier too can disavow his own alienation.

Holland's film makes of the missing child drama a meditation on family, loss and fantasy. It enacts a mobility of roles, opening up the family unit and showing it as surprising and surprised at itself. A case is made for the denaturalisation and renewal of the family (as social and psychoanalytic unit), for its opening both to other members and other desires. I want to stress that this is lived, still, as a form of commemoration of the loved child, not as recovery. Yet, rethinking the family and redirecting its libidinal investments affords at least a force of renewal.

In mourning a lost child, an experience realised in much of its pain in Brigitte Rouän's performance as Elisabeth, any search for comfort seems to make sense (as I imply throughout this volume). In the force of its representation, and the compassion it engenders, *Olivier, Olivier* is finally most radical and unsettling in its call to think through disavowal as a mode of survival.

CHAPTER FIVE

Mater Dolorosa: *All About My Mother*

Pedro Almodóvar's 1987 film, *The Law of Desire*, closes on an image of a lavish *pietà*. Before a burning shrine, bedecked with flowers, a man weeps as he cradles the inanimate body of his younger lover. In discussion of the earlier *Dark Habits* (1983), Paul Julian Smith speaks of 'the redirection of Catholic iconography' in Almodóvar's films (1996: 30). Almodóvar himself, in conversation with Frédéric Strauss, explains the motivation behind his recourse to, if redirection of, Catholic images: 'Kitsch exists in all my films and it's inseparable from religion' (in Strauss 1996: 36–7). He continues to say that he uses religion to comment on purely human feelings: 'What interests me, fascinates me and moves me most in religion is both its ability to create communication between people, even between two lovers, and its theatricality' (1996: 37). The visual style of Catholic imagery may be flamboyantly present in Almodóvar's earlier films – memorably in the opening images of Mary and Jesus in ravishing red and blue in *Tie Me Up! Tie Me Down!* (1989) – yet in his later films, and the loose trilogy formed by *The Flower of My Secret* (1995), *Live Flesh* (1997) and *All About My Mother* (1999) in particular, the emotions and drama detectable in religious imagery, feelings which have moved Almodóvar, intensify erotic and family relations.

In the discussion of *All About My Mother* which follows, I am indebted to the readings of Almodóvar as postmodern and constructionist film-maker as offered by Smith. My interest is in the ways in which issues of emotion, trauma and passion intersect and interact with the sophistication, self-consciousness and radical sexual politics of Almodóvar's cinematic practice.

Redrawing notions of charity and devotion, Almodóvar challenges the uses and meanings of religious images. He admits: 'Pain moves me. It's like a religion to me, a religion that everyone can understand because everyone knows what pain is' (in Strauss 2000: 140). *All About My Mother*, more than any of Almodóvar's films, reaches out beyond its specific context. Almodóvar comments: 'I have the impression that important elements in my work can by understand by anyone, anywhere. The final proof has been *All About My Mother*, which inspires the same emotions whatever the country or language' (Strauss 2000: 186). Such a statement seems to allow the type of decontextualisation necessitated by my own reading of the film in a study like this. Grief, Almodóvar suggests, stretches out beyond its own context. Film as medium offers a means of imagining such grief, of reflecting on ways it might be managed or denied. Urgently, Almodóvar's film-making seeks to represent not redemption, but some transitory forms of comfort or relief.

All About My Mother represents the fullest flowering of Almodóvar's constant interest in the passion of love and loss between a mother and child. As Paul Julian Smith points out, 'Manuela is Mary in a new Holy Family (hence the appearance of the Sagrada Familia), the grieving mother of a son of doubtful paternity' (1999: 30). Manuela is shown as a *Mater Dolorosa*, a weeping mother. In his choice of Cecilia Roth to play Manuela, Almodóvar effects an inversion of the signs of his earlier cinema. Roth appeared in *Labyrinth of Passion* (1982) where she played a nymphomaniac, Sexilia. (A memory of Sexilia hovers in the later film as Agrado conjures images of Manuela's past – 'Oh, Manolita! The *Barceloneta*! Those were the days!') *All About My Mother*, wistful in its evocation of memories, is lachrymose from its start as drops of liquid fall like tears (the opening shots show the drugs fed intravenously to Manuela's hospital patient).

The image of the Madonna circulates in various conceits in the film: Lola has stolen a statue of the virgin treasured by Agrado; Rosa's mother is seen copying Chagall's *Madonna of the Village* (1938–42). Central, however, to this proliferation of images is the framing of Manuela as Madonna. Derek Jarman, in another film about mourning, also enmeshed with questions of the losses wrought by AIDS, *The Garden* (1990), offers self-consciously pictorial images of Mary as Virgin Mother. Almodóvar creates a more restrained and secular series of 'devotional' images. We first see Manuela in the hospital where she is working, before her son's death. The camera travels up her body to pause over her face as icon. Her hair is tied back, her face is contemplative, in repose, her mouth slightly open. The image is still, conjuring the forms of portraiture or photography. Manuela's face is calm and contoured, but barely readable: it figures as veil concealing and containing her emotions. The colours of the image are muted, dominated by the sea-green of her hospital scrubs (a colour recalled later in the shots of the sea seen through the glass front of the Hospital del mar in Barcelona). The composition of the image and its colour scheme are repeated in the images of Manuela in the training seminar (dressed in blue), in her kitchen with Mamen (the blue-green cupboards unifying the colours) and on the train to Barcelona (with blue-green upholstery behind her head). The background colour appears again, half within the frame, as Manuela later speaks of her son's death to Huma.

In addition to the melancholy of these images, the film offers other images of Manuela as mourning mother with more urgent emotion. In the accident and ensuing hospital scenes, Manuela's face is far more expressive. As she learns the news that her son is brain-dead, her head tips back violently and flops forward, her hair flying, her whole body (within the frame) now a contorted sign of her grief and horror. In this scene, later as she weeps in the theatre, and later still in a scene with Rosa's mother, Manuela puts her hands to her face, in an image of mourning. Her tears align her with both Rosa (the 'virgin' who dies in childbirth) and with Rosa's mother, in whose relations the fusion of maternity and mourning are played out once more in the film. Almodóvar has acknowledged: 'I recognise that there is no spectacle which fascinates me, as a director, as much as that of a woman crying' (Strauss 2000: 140).

Marina Warner has explored the imagery and meanings of the *Mater Dolorosa*. She argues: 'She made the sacrifice on Golgotha seem real, for she focussed human feeling in a comprehensible and accessible way' (1978: 211); she continues to suggest that the *Mater Dolorosa* brings consolation because her tears 'belong to a universal language of cleansing and rebirth' (1978: 223). Julia Kristeva, offering a psychoanalytic investigation of work on the Virgin Mary, suggests that in evoking human grief, the *Mater Dolorosa* represents a return of the repressed (of emotion, of the mother/child bond) in Western culture, recalling the non-verbal and the pre-history of the subject (1983: 295). Both Warner and Kristeva seek to understand the image of the *Mater Dolorosa* beyond its specific Christian context, and in more universal terms. *All About My Mother* works more lavishly to secularise religious imagery, yet draws on comparable universal resonances in the image of the grieving mother.

As an exploration of grief and the process of mourning (for a child), *All About My Mother* examines in particular an investment in an ideal, sacred image of maternity. This, I will suggest, is shown to be Manuela's means of keeping her relation to her son alive, of disavowing the loss which undoes her identity. Extending the interest in disavowal in *Olivier, Olivier, All About My Mother* leads us to observe and attend to the disavowal upon which Manuela's trials of mourning depend. We witness how a woman becomes an actress in her son's choreographed drama of her afterlife, her survival in grief.

Manuela's son, Esteban, is a writer. His notebook is his prop while he is alive and his remainder after his death. In this first scene where we see Esteban and his mother, they sit down to watch *All About Eve* on television, eating a meal Manuela has prepared. As Esteban watches the titles of the film, and criticises the Spanish translation, *Eva al desnuda* (*Eve Unveiled*), he suddenly takes up his notebook again and writes: *Todo sobre mi madre* (*All About My Mother*). We see his hand in a close-up as he writes. The film then cuts to a shot of the pencil lead writing directly on the glass of the lens, as if our point of view and the notebook on which Esteban writes are one. The film cuts back to a shot of Esteban and Manuela, both in the frame, on the sofa. In the space between them we see the same title repeated, superimposed over the image, confirmed as the title of the film. The film is marked as the creation and product of the consciousness of the adolescent who will be its victim. Esteban seems to be author of the film, explaining the possessive pronoun in the title. (Jean-Pierre Jeancolas questions in *Positif*: '*All About My Mother*. About whose mother? About which mother? ... Who is speaking? The child who dies at the start? The one who is born later in the film?' (1999: 12).

The first scenes establish the ways in which Esteban's love for Manuela is bound up with his vocation as an author. She reads to him from Truman Capote's *Music for Chameleons*, which she has given him as a birthday present. The passage she reads from the preface, where Capote outlines his own childhood vocation as a writer, serves to mirror Esteban's role in the film. This desire to hear his mother read aloud is a conscious recollection, and re-enactment of his childhood. (He says: 'Read me something. Like when I was little.') Yet the shot/reverse shot editing, and bedroom setting, hint at romantic associations. Manuela is shown to be aware of Esteban as her (desiring) observer. He has asked her, just before: 'Would you prostitute yourself for me?' The early scenes between Esteban and Manuela might be interpreted as a representation of the transition between the symbiotic unity of the mother/child dyad and more openly erotic relations. For Esteban, writing all about his mother becomes a way of playing out his desire for her at one remove.

'If you were an actress', he says, 'I'd write parts for you.' His interest in choreographing her, introduces a further strand in the film, linked directly with the mother and son's family romance. Manuela shows Esteban an image of herself in an amateur theatrical production, with her partner amputated – cut out of the image. This photograph, and Manuela's role as actress, form part of the postmemory Esteban inherits. Marianne Hirsch specifies that 'postmemory is distinguished from memory by generational distance and from history by deep personal connection' (1997: 22). Hirsch uses the notion in relation to the memory heritage of the children of Holocaust survivors and victims. I use the term more loosely to refer to a missing parental history, or family romance, which has bearings on the child's identity, which is absent to him, but fantasised by him. The tale of Lola, Esteban's transvestite father (cut out of Manuela's photograph) is the missing history in *All About My Mother*, a history which will be rediscovered, in compensatory terms, after the traumatic loss of the son himself. The theatre provides a drama of Esteban's prehistory, and postmemory, which is in some senses the film's constant subject, especially after his death.

The imbrication of Esteban's love of Manuela and his vocation as a writer are reflected in his two birthday wishes: to attend one of the training seminars in which Manuela partakes (for he is writing a story of her life) and to go to the theatre to see the actress Huma Rojo. Both scenes serve to sow doubts about the nature of the images viewed, as event or fantasy. They develop the film's concern with Esteban as spectator, as viewer of his mother. Both are central to the trauma, the death of Esteban, that the film takes as its repeated subject.

Manuela is a nurse in the transplant service of a hospital. Her character has been transplanted from *The Flower of My Secret*, where a nurse of the same name, though played by a different actress, takes part in training videos. In *All About My Mother*, Almodóvar actualises the drama which has remained virtual in the previous film. He confirms: 'The first note that I wrote which then led to this script [came] from that scene in *The Flower of My Secret*. And in the beginning it was much more present than at the end of the script. I was very interested in the capacity of people who are not actors professionally to act, or to represent' (in Pincus 1999: 47). Almodóvar attended actual training sessions about breaking news to bereaved relatives and was particularly touched by the ease with which the hospital nurses played their roles as mourning wives and mothers (see Loiseau 1999).

In a circle of repetitions, in *All About My Mother*, we encounter three scenes which play on the theme of organ donation. First a literal scene of Manuela at work, finding a recipient for a donor's organs; second, the (seminar) scene where she plays the role of a bereft wife who is persuaded to donate her husband's organs (this scene itself is videotaped and played back in the film, as well as being watched by Esteban); and, third, and most viciously, a scene which realises this simulation, where Manuela herself must determine the fate of the organs of her brain-dead son. The mechanism of the film seems caught in a compulsion to repeat (Vincent Remy speaks of 'this obsessive idea of repetition, of eternal return' (1999: 29)).

In the filming of the training session, the role of Esteban as spectator is particularly significant. The scene opens with Manuela facing two doctors; she plays her part as bereft relative. The camera sweeps sideways to show us Esteban as observer, then the other seminar participants. The film cuts back

Figure 5 *All About My Mother*

to a close-up of Esteban responding to the simulated scenario, again making notes in his notebook. We cut back from Esteban to a grainy video image of Manuela. Literally we see the filmed training video. Yet figuratively we also view a subjective image, Esteban's fantasy of a film of his mother. The tape is rewound after Manuela has acted her false, poignant hope that her 'dead relative' can be given someone else's organs rather than be a donor himself. This becomes a sticking point in the viewing of the training video, the point of disavowal of death, the point at which Almodóvar's film itself rewinds, having nevertheless left its viewer a prescient image of the horror to follow.

On their trip to the theatre Esteban is again Manuela's audience, her observer. This is revealed spatially in the scene which is the source of one of the major marketing images of the film: Manuela in her red coat waiting for her son in front of a vast blown up poster image of Huma Rojo. (Almodóvar comments: 'that billboard outside the theatre theatricalises the exterior of the theatre – it's a set, and in a way it's more theatrical than what's inside on the stage' (in Pincus 1999: 48)). Esteban has been seen in the previous scene through the window of a bar opposite the theatre, again with his notebook. The glass and window bars which divide son and mother, her imperviousness to his presence and his almost voyeuristic observation of her, seem to imply that the Manuela we see is as much a product of her son's story as she is a 'live flesh' character. We see another close-up of his hands as he writes in the notebook. In a possible gesture to late Kieślowski, whose melancholy style Almodóvar

70

appears momentarily to have absorbed, Esteban's writing hand is itself seen beautifully reflected in the surface of the table. This play with reflections only imitates visually the doubts about virtual and actual, fantasy and reality which begin to inhabit the film.

As with the training scene, outside the theatre the film offers a rehearsal of its central trauma. As Esteban crosses the road to meet his mother, he is almost knocked over. The scenario is repeated at the exit from the theatre. In the second scene, Esteban is run over in the darkness and the rain as he tries to secure Huma Rojo's autograph. The scene, consciously reminiscent of Cassavetes' *Opening Night* (1978), is shot from several disconcerting perspectives. In a backwards tracking shot, the camera pulls away from an image of Manuela in the rain shouting after her son. We cut to an anonymous point of view within a moving car, behind the glass of the windscreen. Esteban falls onto the window, appearing suddenly in the driver's field of vision. The pace of the editing quickens as the film cuts to Manuela screaming and back to the radiating shattered glass of the windscreen. Disconcertingly, the film then cuts to Esteban's point of view as we suddenly view the scene tip sideways, upset from its axis. From the traumatised boy's perspective we see Manuela's legs as she runs towards him, her hands and her wet hair as she reaches out to him. The scene closes with her screams.

Almodóvar suggests that when he was writing the screenplay he imagined the scene rather differently:

> Jerkily, from shot to shot, the car moves forwards, close-up on the wheel, the impact, Manuela's umbrella which rolls away, the son lying in the torrential rain, a stream of water, the trickle of blood seeping outwards, reaching Esteban's notebook, the mother who runs towards the body and who takes her son in her arms, a *pietà*. It could have been amazing. (in Loiseau 1999: 34)

The water and staining blood are reminiscent of *Don't Look Now* (and Kieślowski's tribute to it). Yet Almodóvar finally chooses instead a warping and unbalancing of the visual field to figure the trauma at the centre of the film, decentring it indeed. The missing *pietà*, which is figured emotionally, if not visually, throughout the film, is also restored on the soundtrack. The desperate words of Manuela as she repeats 'hijo mio' ('my son') offer a rhythm, an angst, to the scene which moves beyond sentiment to pain and distress. Sound replaces image here in the representation of mother/child love and rupture (reminding us of Kristeva on the *Mater Dolorosa*). Manuela tries helplessly to restore, and recall her relation to her lost child (her sounds will be echoed as she plays Stella weeping in labour). By the

71

roadside her brute noise figures only the violence and unrepresentability of the sudden trauma. A lack of synchronisation in sound and image seems to convey the rupture and disorientation of the scene: Manuela's sounds appear disembodied and distanced, an intrusion of her desperate mental reality in the numbed, rainy scene.

For moments after the accident, the film pauses between life and death. Manuela waits outside the Intensive Care Unit. The film offers deceptive signs of his survival (as in the cut to Esteban's point of view immediately after the accident). As Manuela waits, holding her son's notebook, voice-over narration from Esteban is heard, edging us towards belief in his survival. The consolatory voice-over speaks the words of his notebook as he makes himself up as a character: 'Tomorrow I turn seventeen, but I look older. Boys who live alone with their mothers have a special face, more serious than normal, like an intellectual or a writer.' He seems to live on as his voice is heard. Even after Manuela has signed the paper agreeing to the donation of her own son's organs, the camera still seems to contradict the knowledge that Esteban is brain-dead. As he is wheeled down a corridor to the operating theatre where his heart will be removed, we see a point of view shot of the ceiling. The camera then pans down to the form of Esteban on the trolley. His autonomous role in his film is almost complete. From here onwards, although his heart will continue to beat in the chest of the organ recipient (briefly followed by Manuela), his image and words will exist only in photographs, his notebook and evanescent flashbacks. From this point on Esteban is an unseen presence, the imagined creator and witness of the film (as he has been insistently seen as writer and observer) for whom Manuela acts.

If the narrative and action of the film, including its protagonist's death, are the wish-fulfilling construct of Esteban as young author, it is now that he consciously exits from the scene to allow Manuela to appear centre stage. Where we are left in doubt as to Esteban's presence or absence, what we may also wonder, all the more painfully, is whether the presence and observation of Esteban are a fantasy conjured by Manuela to palliate her loss.

Diana Fuss cites Freud, writing: 'If one has lost a love-object … the most obvious reaction is to identify oneself with it, to replace it from within, as it were, by identification' (1995: 1). Manuela, however, does not attempt specifically to identify with the lost love object and absorb his qualities. Rather, she is seen to identify with the image of herself – perfect mother, radiant actress – that Esteban has constructed in imagination and writing. Manuela constructs herself in relation to a literally absent, yet omniscient son, an Other in Lacanian terms, by whose imagined dictates she now lives out her life. In exploring such complex matter, *All About My Mother* offers a variation on the means of managing loss theorised by Freud. The film is by no means theoretical or

Figure 6 *All About My Mother*

prescriptive in itself. Instead it allows the viewer to witness, close up, the rituals of mourning in which Manuela engages. We see the obscure comfort obtained in performance, in theatre for Manuela and in cinema for the viewer. Cinema itself can offer the illusion of presence in the face of absence and loss. Stanley Cavell reminds us of 'photography's metaphysically hallucinatory character, its causing us to see things that are absent: it makes things present to us to which we are not present' (1996: 69). As the film moves further into its post-Esteban sequences, we are made increasingly aware of the illusions and pleasures of cinema's reparative devices. These are used by Almodóvar to intimate the illusion and fantasy which keep Manuela alive.

Returning from her trip to follow Esteban's heart and see the organ recipient, Manuela enters Esteban's room. His words are again heard in voice-over: 'Last night, Mama showed me a photo of when she was young. Half of it was missing. I didn't want to tell her, but my life is missing that same half.' While this resurgence of the voice of Esteban is a reparative privilege of cinema, here his words appear to be summoned from Manuela's consciousness, the voice-over coinciding with her memory, and present fantasy of the presence of Esteban. Almodóvar notes: 'In the catalogue of human suffering which is, unfortunately, so exhaustive, as experiences are weighed up, everyone says that nothing is comparable to the loss of a son' (in Altares 1999: 23). He envisages the possibility that there is no recovery from this loss: 'either the mother commits suicide or she finds an excuse to move on' (*Ibid.*). Manuela's excuse comes in her bid to play the part Esteban has scripted for her. This will be a part played out on the private stage of her traumatised psyche. The compassion and generosity of Almodóvar's cinema are sufficient to give us access to this space of desire and denial (in contradistinction, say, to the blankness which we face in Kieślowski's *Three Colours: Blue*). The viewer gains luminous access to the space of Manuela's refusal to relinquish her son. This space is too brutally at odds with her son's empty room in the Madrid apartment; to escape loss, through fantasy and theatre, Manuela embarks on a (temporal and) physical journey back to Barcelona.

On this journey Manuela is inhabited by thoughts of her dead son. We hear Manuela speak in voice-over, alluding to a still prior trip: 'Seventeen years ago, I made this same journey, but in the other direction, from Barcelona to Madrid. I was running away then too, but I wasn't alone. I was carrying Esteban inside me.' The symmetry of the film hints at the difference between the state of pregnancy in which Manuela holds her child within her, and the later state of mourning where she can only summon his image in memory and fantasy.

The film creates an elegy to the lost, symbiotic relations between mother and son. The journey is seen as regression and escape; yet the film seems to champion Manuela's tactics. The train enters a long tunnel, a birth canal and spatialisation of Manuela's state of mind, only to pull out into one of the most ravishing sequences of the movie, an aerial view of twilight Barcelona, with lights shining over the city and the song, 'Tajabone', playing over the shots. A new rhythm and mood is offered to the viewer, as we too find comfort, beauty and relief. Movement is the major motif here, as the view of Barcelona is filmed from a moving helicopter, as we cut to a scene of the Sagrada Familia shot from a taxi, and then to the circling near dance of the prostitutes on the wasteland outside the city. The golden colours of the night time lights, the illuminated stone of the Gaudi façade and the encircling darkness of the field, together with the hypnotic music, create an effect both sexual and amniotic. As Manuela in memory recalls her pregnancy with Esteban, the film in its return to the space of Barcelona appears to echo something of the cradling, pre-linguistic pleasure of mother and infant. Music takes the place of language. Manuela seems almost numbly moved onwards and backwards into the space where she can refashion an identity for herself, reconstructing her relation to Agrado, the character who will create the soothing mood of the scenes in Barcelona.

For twenty scenes or more Esteban seems to be forgotten, his loss too painful to be remembered. Manuela deliberately delays saying anything about her recent past. This resurfaces only when Manuela, sitting like her son previously by a café window, notices an advertisement for Huma Rojo's play, now transferred to the Tivoli theatre in Barcelona. This chance triggers the gradual resurgence of her grief in our view and its emergence in language. In a following scene, Manuela speaks of Esteban, only very briefly, to Rosa, identifying his photograph, saying he died in an accident, and telling her not to touch his notebook. Manuela's grief is still essentially private, dependent on an imaginary game she seems to play, in spite of herself, which will, in illusory forms, allow her son's resuscitation. In the next scene she goes to the theatre to re-view Huma Rojo in *A Streetcar Named Desire*. She seems to look for Esteban on the pavement opposite. The film offers a palliative hallucination: we too see a brief glimpse of Esteban (and a confirmation of cinema's capacity to conjure phantoms). The film's stance is double. It shows us Manuela's illusion and her real state. In the theatre we are reminded of Esteban's anterior presence and present absence in the empty seat beside Manuela (we assume she has bought a ticket for her dead son). Acknowledging his absence, she nevertheless has his photograph in her handbag (a displaced signal of her desire to hold on to him and contain him). Almodóvar notes in the screenplay: 'She isn't following any plan. She only thinks about her son. It is Esteban who directs her, from the Beyond. Or wherever he is. She lets herself be carried along' (Almodóvar 1999: 89). This confirms Manuela's state as automaton, as actress playing the part her son has directed for her.

It seems a form of filial wish-fulfilment that the mother should keep the son's place so painfully absent in her life. He remains her sole object of desire as she returns to the space of his prehistory and conception. If we conjure the illusion of Esteban still alive as writer, or more strangely of Esteban watching from the afterlife, we see parallels between *All About My Mother* and a particular science fiction genre which, as Constance Penley points out, dramatises infantile curiosity about the mother.[1] Penley writes: 'The desire represented in the time travel story, of both witnessing one's own conception and being one's own father or mother, is similar to the primal scene fantasy' (1989: 128). In *All About My Mother*, the return to the past is strictly in memory and geography, not time itself. Nevertheless Manuela's journey after Esteban's death is a journey to find his origins and to fulfil his desire to view the primal scene which has been absent for him in the absence of his father from his life.

In this search for a prehistory, *A Streetcar Named Desire* is significant in several ways. Manuela herself says: 'A *Streetcar Named Desire* has marked my life.' (The screenplay tells us that she says this as if she means literally that she has been knocked down by a streetcar.) This is the play she viewed with Esteban on the night of his death; it is also acting in *A Streetcar Named Desire* that Manuela met Esteban's father, who played Kowalski while she played Stella. Where Esteban's birthday is also his death day, the play he watches on the day of his death is also, aptly, the drama of his primal scene. It is this primal scene, re-enacted, that Manuela will compulsively re-view as she returns to the theatre in Barcelona, fulfilling her son's, or her own, reparative fantasy. The play's overdetermination in her life appears to trigger her imbrication in the drama and life of Huma Rojo, Esteban's idol, allowing a further facet of the film's tight structure to come fully into view.

As suggested above, theatre offers some release or relief in Manuela's mourning. While she is involved in a drama of disavowal, replaying the last night of her son's life (and its opening), her *fort/da* game focuses on a locus precisely of performance and repetition (one of the key differences, of course, between theatre and cinema being the compulsory repetition of the staged play). She begins to live out her loss in her relation to Huma Rojo, again finding the means to fulfil the wishes of her son, fan and admirer of the actress. It is to Huma that Manuela reveals, 'my son said I was a very good actress' and it is to Huma and her girlfriend Nina that Manuela will first narrate the story of the crash in which Esteban dies, triggering Huma's own flashback to the taxi, the rain and the night of Esteban's death. Yet, as soon as Manuela has revealed her motivation for inserting herself into the lives of Huma and Nina and taking Nina's role in *A Streetcar Named Desire*, she withdraws from the confessional mode: 'I don't want to talk about my son. I can't.' The film is attentive to Manuela's access to her trauma, then withdrawal from its conscious recall. We follow the rhythms of her grief, controlled and uncontrolled. Huma seems in accord with Manuela's feeling, witnessed in the letter she writes to Esteban and delivers to Manuela: 'Dear Esteban, this is the autograph I never gave you and not because you didn't try.' Huma follows Manuela's desire to maintain an illusion of Esteban alive. In addressing a letter to the dead son, Huma again raises the spectre of Esteban's absence, yet omniscience, his continued ability to exist as addressee.

Paul Julian Smith comments that in *All About My Mother*, 'letters, photographs and children circulate among the cast, eventually reaching their destination. Esteban never sees a photograph of his father, but his father will see a picture of the son s/he never knew before s/he too dies. Huma will write the autograph for Esteban she refused him on the fatal night. And a third Esteban (Rosa's son) will come to take the place of his lost father and brother in Manuela's care' (1999: 30). This formal control and structure offers order to the morass of emotions with which the film contends. It confirms the notion of the film as artifice, and also as possible wish-fulfilment on Esteban's part. Indeed, if this is the son's fantasy, his film of his mother's emotive response to his own demise, then of course all the pieces will fit together. This order and sense of symmetry and predestination works well, on a different level, as consolation for the viewer. The film takes care of us, in the way Manuela takes care of those around her. That such a devastating event should, filmed, become heart-felt drama, is testament to the justice and judgment behind Almodóvar's artistic choices.

Manuela survives through fantasy and in maternity, in a fantasy of herself as mother. José Arroyo points out that 'Almodóvar's detractors will … find ammunition here. The two good mothers have no active sex lives and work in traditionally feminine and caring occupations (Manuela is a nurse, Rosa a nun)' (1999: 40). The idealisation of nurturing femininity in the film, meaningful or touching, arguably, for women as well as men, seems more motivated if Esteban is reckoned absent author of the drama. Of course his mother, in his afterlife, will devote herself to his memory and then to his namesake, Rosa's child. (As Kristeva comments, the *Mater Dolorosa* is faithful to the body of her dead son.) Manuela's sexuality, necessarily numbed in mourning, is sublimated in the exquisite attention she pays to others. This is not a limit of the film, or a sign of its sexism, but rather is an indication of its self-conscious focus on a fantasy of femininity.

In Manuela's devotion to her son's ideal, the film appears to reveal the pleasure achieved in playing out the roles desired by others. This is not reciprocity: Esteban remains absent; but it is an intimation of the way an other can, and does, in fantasy or actuality, direct the actions of the self. Further, in keeping her relation to Esteban alive, Manuela also works selflessly (sometimes even in spite of herself) to help others: she helps Agrado, Huma Rojo, Rosa who she nurses with tenderness, Rosa's mother and, in the end, Rosa's small child. This marks a difference between *All About My Mother* and *Opening Night* where a traumatic death outside a theatre triggers merely the crisis of the actress herself. For Manuela, survival comes in a relation to the other which is at first a fantasy, but which almost imperceptibly, and by extension, becomes literal, practical and humane.

Indeed, relations to the other, and the embrace of alterity are key to *All About My Mother*. In this respect the film seems to follow Hélène Cixous' view of maternity and femininity: 'For potentially or really mothers, all women have even so an experience of the interior, an experience of the capacity to hold the other, an experience of non-negative transformation by the other, of good receptivity' (1989: 142). *All About My Mother* makes of the capacity to hold the other an ethical imperative in a general validation of alterity. Hence the aptness of the film's juxtaposition of mothers, nuns, drag queens, lesbians and others, all of whom, through maternity, charity, gender or sexuality have been open to the other and have taken it into their body and/or displayed it on its surface. That this openness to the other is a construction, not a natural property, seems underlined in Agrado's confessional monologue delineating the artistic (surgical and silicone) moulding of an identifiable female body. Rather than offer any essentialist view of maternity or femininity, Almodóvar seems to open a Cixousian economy of the gift where even body parts (Esteban's heart) are transplanted, where maternity is the product of (desiring) identification and flamboyant performance.

In placing Manuela as *Mater Dolorosa*, Almodóvar fleshes out the image of the *pietà* which has haunted his film-making, and indeed a vein of Spanish art. As Smith reminds us: 'All *About My Mother* ends ... with a very Spanish reference as Huma rehearses the role of the mourning matriarch in Lorca's *Blood Wedding*' (1999: 39). *All About My Mother* is most successful, perhaps, in bringing to full term a theme nascent in many of Almodóvar's own previous films. Smith shows the ways, '*¡Atame!* will hint at a matrilinear and parthenogenetic lineage of women' (Smith 1994); Marsha Kinder (1992) speaks of the vindication of 'the powerful sexual mother' in *High Heels. All About My Mother*, whilst it displays close ties to *The Flower of My Secret* and *Live Flesh* (where Penelope Cruz plays a mourned young mother), should not be considered solely a part of this latter trilogy, but be realigned too with the body of Almodóvar's earlier film-making. Indeed there is an elaborate continuity in the exploration of themes of memory, mourning and maternity in Almodóvar's cinema, despite its stylistic evolution. *All About My Mother* achieves a fine coincidence between the stylized repetitions of postmodern camp and the compulsion to repeat witnessed in response to and recall of traumatic loss. As the theatre becomes a stage of mourning and commemoration, the film contends with permeable divisions between acting and reenactment, disavowal and the suspension of disbelief. The implications of this for Almodóvar's own cinema – existing as witness to pain and as space in which to imagine forms of reparation and psychic repair – are far-reaching. These implications lead me to argue that Almodóvar's cinema is engaged in debating issues of loss and survival crucial to cinema of the last decade, which insist in, yet also extend beyond, its specific Hispanic context.

This context nevertheless partially colours one of the abiding concerns identified in this film and of much of Almodóvar's previous work. Maternal relations need by no means be natural or biological, but the patient care and unconditional love maternity, as image, summons, embody an emotional and even erotic ideal in Almodóvar's films. That the ultimate representation of this ideal, in Catholic iconography, should be the image of the *pietà*, offers a sense, perhaps, of the pathos and universal appeal of this (artistic) image of suffering maternity. As *All About My Mother* reveals, the representation of a missing child always exists in some sense, in symbiotic relation, with the drama of the mourning mother. Such issues will be pursued in the following chapter on *The Portrait of a Lady*.

CHAPTER SIX

Isabel's Child:
The Portrait of a Lady

S oon after Jane Campion won the Palme d'Or at Cannes for her film *The Piano* (1993), her baby son, Jasper, died. Critical material produced after the Palme d'Or and before the release of Campion's next film, *The Portrait of a Lady* (1996), made her bereavement public and set it in the context of her film-making career. Commentators remarked on the ways in which this loss coloured the success of *The Piano*. Further they stressed the links the loss afforded between Campion herself and her next film heroine, Isabel Archer; as Lizzie Francke put it succinctly: 'Like Isabel Archer, Campion lost a baby' (1999: 207). (Campion suggests, with different emphasis, that she felt like Isabel Archer when she was younger, coming from New Zealand to Europe.)[1] In a study of women's poetry about pregnancy, birth, still birth and abortion, Barbara Johnson has noted that in male poetic conventions, 'it is as though male writing were by nature procreative, while female writing is somehow by nature infanticidal' (1987: 198). I suggest in what follows that Campion makes of loss and commemoration such a fertile, feeling subject in her film-making that she works to reconfigure this conflict between child-bearing and female creativity. Child-bearing is shown in her films as source of both pleasure and loss, sensuality and tragedy; its extremes are imbricated with Campion's film-making art.

Campion herself now has a daughter, Alice, and continues to make films (in the face of increasingly ambivalent reception). *The Portrait of a Lady*, which will be my point of focus in the following discussion, has received a number of negative reviews. My aim here is to rethink this critical commentary and to argue that the film works as an important, self-conscious re-vision of the concerns of the nineteenth-century novel. Influenced or not by her son's death (conjecture here seems difficult), Campion reimagines Isabel's losses, offering a new cinematic engagement with mourning and sensuality. Like *Jude*, discussed in the subsequent chapter, *The Portrait of a Lady* redraws the period drama, disrupting its perspective and visual control. The vanishing point in this realigned portrait is the loss of Isabel's child.

In James's novel we learn of the death of the child in a conversation between Madame Merle and Ned Rosier, suitor to Gilbert Osmond's daughter, Pansy:

> 'Mrs Osmond,' Madame Merle went on, 'will probably prefer to keep her money for her own children.'
> 'Her own children? Surely she has none."
> 'She may have yet. She had a poor little boy, who died two years ago, six months after his birth. Others, therefore, may come.'

The death of Isabel's child takes place in the early years of her marriage, elided in the novel, as James moves from Gilbert Osmond's courtship of Isabel to Ned Rosier's courtship of Pansy, some three years later. This ellipsis and editing of trauma looks forward to modernist prose. For Campion, looking back on James, a test seems to come in the decision of how much, similarly, to leave out. In the film, indeed, we encounter the information in much the same way. That Madame Merle reveals the information is not insignificant. She is the hidden mother of Pansy in the novel; in a different manner from Isabel, she too has lost her (illegitimate) child. Laura Jones's screenplay for Campion's film retains the dialogue almost word for word; in addition, however, the film imagines a tableau of Isabel's mourning.

The novel is silent on Isabel's mourning; this history is not consciously evoked even in the extraordinary and famous chapter (described by Tony Tanner as 'one of the high points to which psychological fiction reached' (1985: 41)) in which Isabel sits up, by her dying fire. There are, though, reflections in that chapter which insist in the mind of the reader curious about Isabel's loss. James evokes Isabel's responses in suffering – 'Suffering, with Isabel, was an active condition; it was not a chill, a stupor, a despair; it was a passion of thought, of speculation, of response to every pressure' (1985: 629) – and he images her trapped in a dark, labyrinthine space (almost a sepulchre). There is no equivalent scene in the final film, though one where Isabel is seen to walk down a corridor in near darkness is projected in the screenplay. Campion and Jones also avoid the use of voice-over or of any verbal transcription of the novel's extraordinary evocation of Isabel's states of mind. Instead, in evoking

Figure 7 *The Portrait of a Lady*

introspection, the film more generally exploits spatial imagery, echoing Isabel's intimations of her entrapment in the film's *mise-en-scène*. Space, light and gesture (material signifiers) transpose something of the novel's insights into Isabel's states of mind.

Such a transposition is found in the inserted scene of Isabel mourning which follows Madame Merle's conversation with Ned Rosier. The scene is missing even in the screenplay. It works arguably as Campion's alternative to James's fireside scene of introspection, realigning the emotional centre of the film. The film cuts from Madame Merle's face to a close-up of Isabel's hands (a shot reminiscent of a Stieglitz photograph). Isabel holds a small porcelain effigy of an infant's hand. Her left hand and wrist fill the lower part of the frame. Her right hand touches the infant palm. She cradles it, almost dandles it with her fingers, her hands moving very slowly, with utmost tenderness. Light reflects on the surface of the porcelain; Isabel's hands seem themselves very pale. There is pathos in the contact between the animate hands, arms outreached, and the partial effigy of the missing child. It seems apt in this film of fine art objects and possessions, that the sentient baby should be represented and replaced by a perfect porcelain ornament. Isabel, in her mourning, her 'passion of thought', appears to have the power to invest this small object with feeling and love.

The scene is wordless, but music, its volume slowly increasing, plays against the shots. After lingering on the image of Isabel's hands, the camera moves slowly upwards. Isabel is turned away from us as we watch her in the privacy and seclusion of her loss and sorrow. The bend of her left arm and fold of her elbow create a frame within the frame, as her body hides her from us. The camera moves closer still, however, showing her forehead propped against her right hand, her arm resting on her dressing table. The angle of her face is oblique and speaks of her despair. Her face is all but in shadow, light only reflecting on her diamond droplet earrings and her temple. Her pose is reminiscent of the introspective, despairing women of late Impressionism. She is seated at her looking glass, in whose mercurial surface her hand and the side of her face can be seen reflected. Beyond its pathos, the scene is consciously pictorial in its reflexive reference to the mirror, and in its blanched and shadowy tones. Isabelle's naked arms have the unblemished paleness of photographic models, of the women intimately photographed by Degas or Bonnard.

The scene is gone in moments, yet this, I think, is Campion's personal portrait of Isabel Archer. Embodied, intimate, self-consciously photographic, this portrait makes Isabel's lost motherhood her occluded tragedy. This, in addition to her more liberal focus on sensuality, sexual fantasy and physical travel, marks Campion's reading of James. I argue that she is a passionate reader of the novel (as Lizzie Francke comments: 'Campion's movie is like an intense, intimate reading that explores the darker elements of James's text' (1999: 208)), a reader whose adaptation claims its own right to difference and liberty. Above all the film is a feeling response to the novel, a response embodied in close attention to bodily contact, surface and space, and to the lived experience of femaleness as rapture, adventure and tragedy.

Critics have been quick to find aberrations in Campion's *Portrait of a Lady*. The film has been most readily attacked for its liberal and provocative opening sequences. For me, the film's opening is in line with Campion's interpretation of Isabel Archer and her artistic achievement in adapting the novel. The range of reservations expressed are instructive, nevertheless.

The frankest critic is Robin Wood, who in an otherwise judicious reckoning with the film describes the opening shots as an 'absurd and irrelevant credit sequence in which various young women in modern dress disport themselves amid trees, as if auditioning for modelling jobs somewhere between GAP and Ralph Lauren' (1999: 14). For Ken Gelder, equally sceptical, the opening chimes in with the theme of autonomy and independence he argues is predominant in the film: for him, the film 'begins by announcing its own independence from James's novel through an apparently unrelated prologue which presents a number of young Australian women talking about "the kiss"' (2000: 168). Cynthia Ozick, more reflective, uses the film in an argument which implicitly champions the subtlety of literary texts over cinema. For Ozick:

The film's opening moments startle with the faces and voices of a group of contemporary young women who comment on the act of kissing – and though such a prologue may seem extraneous to what follows, it is plainly offered as a key to the director's sensibility. Self-oriented eroticism (or call it, more generally a circumscribed interest in one's body), a current theme of a certain order of feminism, here replaces James's searching idea of a large and susceptible imagination roiling with world hunger. (2000: 152)

Despite her squeamishness about contemporary feminism, Ozick's comments come closest to my concerns. Certainly Campion uses the prologue to reflect her sensibility, her filter on the film. Questioned about the opening scene by Michel Ciment, she states: 'I thought it was necessary to suggest to the audience what the romantic hopes of young girls could be. The decision was taken very early on to have that introduction, which serves as a link to our era, and which is like a poem before the journey of a young woman' (1999: 180). Several French journalists, in reviews on the release of the film, exploit this notion of 'a link to our era', stressing that the modern preface underlines the modernity, and continuing relevance of the film's themes. Another critic, Susan Saccoccia, approaches this modernity rather differently, usefully linking the opening with another Campion film: 'The scene echoes the final moments of *A Girl's Own Story* (1983), Campion's 27-minute film about a girl's passage from innocence to experience. In the surreal closing scene, a chorus of girls dressed in white are chanting, "I feel the cold."' Campion corroborates the reading, saying of the earlier film, 'It's a mini *Portrait of a Lady*' (in Wright Wexman 1999: 202). Campion's 'frock dramas' (her term) draw resonance and impact from their place within a broader corpus of work. Where they recreate an era, they are also fully self-conscious about their own existence in and influence from the period of their conception (and place in a contemporary *auteur* corpus). Jonathan Romney has pointed to the self-consciousness of Campion's period drama in suggesting that *The Piano* (1993) bears comparison with *The French Lieutenant's Woman* (1981) in its depiction of 'Victorian mores from the standpoint of twentieth-century irony' (2000: 160). I argue, indeed, that the prologue to *The Portrait of a Lady* works not only as key to the director's sensibility, but also as reminder that in period drama we always necessarily look back upon the past from an embodied and sociocultural context: our present and that drama's future.

In another sense, too, beyond reference to *A Girl's Own Story*, a key cinematic intertext is summoned (unmentioned, as far as I can find, by other critics). Campion's prologue to *The Portrait of a Lady* consciously echoes a scene from Peter Weir's *Picnic at Hanging Rock* (1975). The scene echoed is one of the signature scenes of the young girls at the picnic. It occurs not only in its proper narrative place in *Picnic at Hanging Rock*, but also in slow motion as its coda or as an elegy to the lost summer afternoon on which the girls disappear. By the end of the film, it has become a self-consciously cinematic flashback to a time, a period, a paradise whose loss, and passing, *Picnic at Hanging Rock* dramatises and laments.

Weir's film has been mentioned in discussion of *The Piano*.[2] Yet the relevance of *Picnic at Hanging Rock* to *The Portrait of a Lady* seems all the more overdetermined and dependent both, strangely, on Campion's faithfulness to James's novel and on her bid to mark out *The Portrait of a Lady* as self-conscious cinema, as deliberately luminous, spatial, photographic art.

James's novel begins with glorious languor, in 'the perfect middle of a splendid summer afternoon' (1985: 193). The description continues:

Part of the afternoon had waned, but much of it was left, and what was left was of the finest and rarest quality. Real dusk would not arrive for many hours; but the flood of summer light had begun to ebb, the air had grown mellow, the shadows were long upon the smooth, dense turf. They lengthened slowly, however, and the scene expressed that sense of leisure still to come which is perhaps the chief source of one's enjoyment of such a scene at such an hour. From five o'clock to eight is on certain occasions a little eternity; but on such an occasion as this the interval could be only an eternity of pleasure.

For me, there is no lovelier cinematic evocation of a summer afternoon than Weir's. The start of Campion's *Portrait of a Lady* sets up a possible dialogue between James's novel and *Picnic at Hanging Rock*. Yet, more than extend, in glancing light and shadow, James's description of a summer afternoon, reference to Weir's film brings other, more inherently cinematic and mnemonic meanings. Before drawing these out it will be helpful to look more closely at Campion's prologue.

After a pale manuscript page, on which the name of the production company appears in inked handwriting, the film opens in darkness. Against this darkness a young girl is heard speaking in cherishing tones: 'The best part of a kiss is when you see that head coming towards you and you know that you are going to get kissed. That moment before is so exquisite…' Another, older, voice fades in: '…and I'd never ever felt the touch of another person my age and the sensation just flew through me…' Still another: 'I love it. I love kissing.' Campion explains that she 'had the idea of gathering all the lively, intelligent young women that [she] had met in Australia during the preparation of the film and asking them to speak off the cuff of their aspirations and sentimental experiences'. She adds: 'There were absolutely fascinating conversations of which you only hear fragments and which would make an astonishing radio program, were it only with all the stories of kisses that they tell!' (in Wright Wexman 1999: 180). As it is, we have only a brief collage of voices all of which work in some ways as clues to Isabel's sensuality and intimations of her fate. At the film's liminal moment, Campion places a choice anecdote about the anticipation of pleasure. She encourages us to look forward to the point in the film which, apparently, Campion sees as the key to Isabel's marriage: Osmond's kiss at Caprarola. The polyphony of voices at the start speak the feelings Isabel is later seen to encounter.

The words conjure absent female bodies and emotions: there is something addictive, hypnotic about this start in a space of secrets voiced with sincerity, with pleasure and without embarrassment. This is one of the first liberations of Campion's cinema and one of its liberal enthusiasms. As music begins to be audible, the darkness opens to a black and white overhead shot of girls in the grass. Foliage surrounds the frame, again the sense of privacy is crucial (as the foliage at Gardencourt will be the hiding space where Isabel attempts to withdraw from her suitors). The shot of the girls from above is reminiscent of several of the group of sisters in *An Angel at My Table* (1990). Campion seems fascinated by the patterns that can be made by choreographing groups of figures: her study of girlhood, here and in the earlier films, is shown to be generic, as well as individual. The girls here all mysteriously lie down, echoing their counterparts in *Picnic at Hanging Rock* (sounds of the earlier film are echoed as birds are heard against wistful music). The images of the girls create a living, sleeping frame for the central credit: 'a film by Jane Campion'.

The film cuts to a lone girl in a white dress who gently sways to music, against an ethereal, sunlit background. Her walkman is visible, making her, too, a younger sister of Ruth in *Holy Smoke* (1999). Then the film closes in on the girls in the grasses, one wakes in the foreground, another lies, dreamy, outstretched. Girls are seen in the branches of a fallen tree, one plays with another's hair. Their poses are languorous and directly borrowed from Weir. We see a girl, against dark foliage, staring intently at the camera, resembling an early photographic portrait. Another girl joins her in the frame, peering again into the viewfinder. Their doubled pale faces, and dark hair, are reminiscent of the signature shots of Ada with Flora in *The Piano*. The image changes to colour – the pastel shades of the early parts of *An Angel at My Table* – as we now see girls dancing. Then we move back to black and white for more living portraits. The camera is moving always, in tune in part with the hypnotic soundtrack. The girls shown have self-possession and composure. One smiles into the frame. Others are arm in arm as Campion repeats and anchors the homoeroticism of Weir's film. The sequence is brought to a close as the image

Figure 8 *The Portrait of a Lady*

fades into a shot of a long pale wrist and hand, along whose palm and middle finger is written, in ink, the film's title: *The Portrait of a Lady*.

In presenting *The Portrait of a Lady* through the filter and frame of *Picnic at Hanging Rock* (as well as her own film-making) Campion appears to extend its resonance as film about loss and nostalgic evocation. This resonance is felt on several levels. While I have stressed the impact of *The Portrait of a Lady* as a missing child drama through reference to the loss of Isabel's baby (and more subliminally to Campion's too), in its opening the film seems to highlight its importance as lament for the loss of Isabel's youth, vitality and idealism (all the qualities perfectly embodied by the young Australian women). The narrative of *The Portrait of a Lady*, both novel and film, famously traces Isabel's freezing and mortification in her (chosen) marriage to Gilbert Osmond. In the film in particular this is visualised in the loss of her youthful impetuosity and childishness. Before marriage, Campion's Isabel is deeply sensual, almost polymorphously perverse in her pleasure in taste, smell and touch. Her marriage to Osmond contains and controls her, separating her from her pleasure, from the lost paradise of Gardencourt and her girlhood freedom. A lost childhood is the film's subject, too, as much as the missing child whose absence seems to confirm the hollowness of her marriage.

Picnic at Hanging Rock as a film of missing young girls and lost paradise reflects on the very status of the period drama. A parallel may be drawn between the nostalgic spectatorial pleasures of period drama – where a lost era is evoked and its absence denied – and the very self-conscious subject of the film, the loss of childhood, innocence and pleasure. In Visconti's *Death in Venice* (1971) in a still more concentrated form, memories of a lost wife and child, recalled in flashback, form the drama screened by, yet determining, Aschenbach's love of the youthful Tadzio. These two impossible, nostalgic, regretful loves determine further the films' luxurious, yet knowing, romance with the past re-evoked. Lost childhood, a lost era, bears a self-reflexive force in such films.

However, in *The Portrait of a Lady* Jane Campion is not a straightforward inheritor of the heritage of period drama. As her prologue shows, she is keen to keep in play the links between past and present (a similar imperative seems to dictate the futuristic ending of Sally Potter's *Orlando* (1992)). For Campion, this concern relates not merely to her own work as renovator of period drama, but also to her intimations of Isabel's fate in the diegesis of *The Portrait of a Lady*. Indeed, while the film dramatises two losses – the loss of Isabel's child and of her childhood – Campion seems adamant to avoid lapsing into elegy or regret. She does not redeem Isabel's tragedy or render a solution. (Such was imagined as Campion contemplated an alternative ending to the film, offering Isabel a refound solidarity with Pansy, Osmond's daughter. But unlike Potter, Campion does not offer such a feminist resolution.) What she does offer, however, is a means of keeping Isabel alive both to her grief and, more hopefully, to pleasure. Contrary to the strong voyeuristic aesthetic of both Weir and Visconti – the imaging of Miranda as Botticelli angel, the glimpses of the girls in the outback and through clefts of rock in *Picnic at Hanging Rock*, Aschenbach's trailing of Tadzio and surveillance of his image on the beach in *Death in Venice* – Campion favours a haptic visuality, in which touch dominates vision and cinema aspires to become a plastic art. This haptic visuality, this emphasis on touch and pleasure, is privileged already in the mourning scene as Isabel holds her baby's porcelain hand. In more extensive discussion of touch and contact in *The Portrait of a Lady* we will see how Campion's film in fact strains against the pictorial aesthetic seemingly named in its borrowed title. This privileging of touch is the film's aesthetic innovation in its representation of a mourning mother and her remembered connection to her missing child, and her own missing childhood. Where, as in *Three Colours: Blue*, the theme of the missing child may seem forgotten for stretches of the film, and from discussion below, I hope to imply that attention to the haptic is for Campion here bound up with questions of commemoration and elegy, suffering and reparative pleasure.

As noted above, an image of a hand points the way into the film and directs us to its heroine, Isabel Archer. The very writing of the title on skin seems to indicate the direct contact between words and flesh Campion can present: her literary adaptation here will be words in flesh. The image recalls the tattooing and body art represented in *The Piano*, as it seems to recall more subliminally, too, a schoolgirl aesthetic where words are sometimes inked on skin. Hands often serve as signs in Campion's movies: in *An Angel at My Table* an image of a hand points to the psychiatric ward where Janet Frame will be locked up; in *The Piano* Ada literally speaks with her hands, as she signs to her daughter. In *The Portrait of a Lady*, even more than in *An Angel at My Table* or *The Piano*, the hand will point to the film's own interest in the tactile and in touch.

In *The Skin of the Film*, Laura Marks looks at the way 'vision itself can be tactile, as though one were touching a film with one's eyes' (2000: xi). This experience of the tactile in film she defines as haptic visuality, drawing on thinking developed in phenomenology, art history and latterly in the thinking of Deleuze. For Marks, haptic visuality entails and depends on a bodily relation between the viewer and the image. Film is seen to be manipulated in order to work beyond the distance, voyeurism and control of the conventional viewing relations of narrative cinema. Haptic visuality draws the viewer into contact with the image; the image in turn recalls or mourns somatic memories, the experience of the senses often neglected in dominant scopic regimes. Marks is concerned in particular with the texturing of the visual image, with its graininess, with distortions in size and proportion, disruptions of figuration and recognition all of which disturb our visual and cognitive control of the image.

As mentioned in chapter three, Marks studies intercultural cinema and argues for the specificity of such works which 'evoke memories both individual and cultural, through an appeal to nonvisual knowledge, embodied knowledge, and the experiences of the senses, such as touch, smell and taste' (2000: 2). She stresses that her volume should not be read as a more general thesis on the senses and cinema. Yet, given the compelling nature of her conclusions about embodied spectatorship, and her acknowledgement that dominant cinema has itself borrowed and repeated the mechanisms of the cultural forms she studies, I am persuaded of the usefulness of her work in the study of Campion. Indeed Marks herself refers, briefly, to *The Piano*, making the point: 'Haptic images may also encourage a more embodied and multisensory relationship to the image in films that use haptic imagery in combination with sound, camera movement, and montage to achieve sensuous effects, such as *The Piano*' (2000: 172).

Having referred to *The Piano*, Marks also addresses the issue of how her study might relate to 'the recent rash of dramas based on novels by Jane Austen, Henry James and Edith Wharton' (2000: 223). She recognises that these films are 'effectively, ethnographic reconstructions of cultures that no longer exist' (*Ibid.*), but suggests that they differ from commemorative works of intercultural cinema in that the customs detailed in such heritage cinema are themselves 'differentially available in recorded history' (*Ibid.*). The point seems important, yet I would move further to argue that Campion, at least, in

The Portrait of a Lady, works to supplement 'recorded history'. She re-forms her film to testify to the hidden, feeling underside of Isabel's history, the emotion, sensuality and grief wonderfully intimated by Henry James and all too frequently absent in literary adaptations in cinema.

Marks writes emotively about her material, stressing the ways in which the forms of intercultural cinema have been used frequently to interrogate the historical archive and to recreate personal and family memories. Here the story is often 'the product of a process of mourning, a search for loved ones who have vanished' (2000: 5). She continues: 'These lost loved ones may be people, places, or even ways of inhabiting the world.' She describes the film-making she studies as a memorial and mourning process: 'It is the holding on to artifacts of culture, including photographic and filmic images, in order to coax the memories from them' (*Ibid.*). This image of a film-making practice seems peculiarly apt for thinking about haptic visuality (and its relation to mourning) in *The Portrait of a Lady*. It should be noted, though, that in Campion's work, more than in those films studied by Marks, haptic visuality, and the sense of touch, are conveyed in particular through attention to hands, surfaces and physical contact.

Doubtless the key scene in which touch is invoked, and made central to Campion's aesthetic, is that where Isabel mourns her lost baby. This is precisely, literally, a scene where she holds on to an artefact, the child's porcelain hand. Yet, all the more powerfully, and more in keeping with Marks's thoughts, the scene is one where Isabel makes contact with her past ideals and aspirations, with a feeling, sentient, tactile reality and mode of expression which has characterised her engagement with the world before her marriage to Osmond. In this sense, touch itself, as sense, is overdetermined in its relation to childhood and mourning. Marks indicates the ways in which, through Irigaray, touch can be associated with an originary space of pleasure and non-division. She writes: 'More than any other sensory deprivation, the loss of the sense of touch creates a feeling of being an orphan in the world. Irigaray's question, "How to preserve the memory of the caress?", rests on a fundamental sense of loss: of a world of tactility experienced by the foetus and the infant, before language and vision organise its sensorium' (2000: 149). Isabel, an orphan whose mother has died, also loses this tactile relation to her infant son; she is deprived of both being and having both mother and child. The tactile – embodied in the memorial effigy – is her fetishistic way of restoring or commemorating her relation to her missing child, her missing childhood. Isabel's experiences are worlds apart from those of the intercultural cinema Marks studies, yet reading Marks in tandem with Campion offers ways of thinking of *The Portrait of a Lady* as a film about a woman's mourning for her child, her exile from her life (her own childhood), vitality and destiny.

Privileged Isabel may be, yet she is still shown to suffer losses which are commemorated, poignantly, in an appeal to the senses.

Radiating from the mourning scene is a further series of images of tactile contact which draw a variety of meanings. In the first place, in keeping with the tenets of the mourning scene, touch, embraces and hand to hand contact are used to signify parent/child relations in the film. This serves to make Isabel's tactile relation to the inanimate effigy all the more poignant.

In the first scene in which we see Madame Merle with her daughter Pansy, there is a close-up of Madame Merle's hand touching Pansy's waist, her other hand entwined in Pansy's grasp. She then moves to clasp both her daughter's hands, again seen in close-up, filling the frame. Madame Merle's hands are in fine black gloves, while Pansy's are bare. This seems a visual clue to the unequal status of their relations: Pansy is unaware that she is Madame Merle's daughter. Madame Merle offers to make Pansy a gift of a dozen gloves, her projected present at once expressing her bounty to the child and also drawing narrative attention to the hands which have been a visual point of focus in the scene. Madame Merle's hands, wistfully touching Pansy, seem to speak her desire for contact with her child; her position is gently paralleled with Isabel's. (Isabel herself will reach up to touch Pansy's face when she visits her in Florence, after Osmond's declaration of love.)

The play of hands is framed too when Osmond is seen with his daughter. He sits Pansy on his knee as he talks to Isabel. Osmond's hands are clasped around her waist, as the girl's own hands are clasped. Again the image is seen in close-up, the two sets of hands mirroring one another. Pansy seems bound in Osmond's grasp, bound both by his proprietorial encircling of her and by her physical imitation of his gestures. Touch, the clasp and intertwining of hands, seems to indicate inter-relation, connection, kinship and parentage within the film. This is a relation both tender and binding, affectively inescapable. This primary set of meanings is associated with several others, however.

Contact and touch are linked too, and more troublingly, with violence and eroticism, in particular with Osmond's approaches to both Isabel and Madame Merle. This dimension of his inter-relations with women, and motif in the film, is first seen as Osmond assaults Madame Merle. He comes to sit very close to her, with his face beside hers. His hand reaches to touch her garment and her face. His fingers prod her chin, moving her as if she were a puppet or automated doll. He jerks her head backwards, putting pressure on her to fall back on the settee where they are seated. Their conversation, about Isabel, continues as Osmond's hand explores Madame Merle's body. Sensuality is steadily evacuated from the scene in the shadowy colour of the filtered lighting, in the ominous music which plays, and Madame Merle's tense intake of breath. Osmond suddenly breaks their tactile proximity as

Merle says: 'Isabel Archer is better than I.' For a moment we see their faces in extreme close-up, almost fused. Then Osmond withdraws to the other side of the room; Madame Merle puts her gloved hand up to her face. The tactile has been established in the scene through the literal filming of hands in contact and movement, of skin touching skin. Yet the haptic visuality is also created through use of extreme close-up on physical details, where the viewer herself is denied distance from the image framed. Campion offers the viewer the illusion of feeling the senses which the film evokes on every side. This adds a depth and resonance to her film-making, yet also contributes to its manipulation of, even sensory assault on, the viewer. (Notably, for Marks, proximity to the image, and somatic memory conjured, are in general restorative and recuperative; she pays less attention to ways in which haptic visuality may also lead to a more impressionable, vulnerable or risky viewing relation.)

Such tactile tactics are repeated in scenes between Osmond and Isabel. The first physical contact between them comes in the extraordinary scene in the underground chamber of the Palazzo Farnese at Caprarola. Here lighting and shadow add immeasurably to our perception of surface and physical contact. Campion's cinematographer, Stuart Dryburgh, has said of the chamber at Caprarola: 'In the middle of the day, the sunlight comes down through ... gratings and creates these wonderful, very intense shafts of vertical light, which then reflect around the interior' (in Gentry 1997: 56). He works to recreate and intensify this natural phenomenon in the lighting of the film. The effect is one of bedazzlement, of intense light and shade, accompanied by spectral after-images. This works to derealise the scene and gild it. Isabel, in a bright white embroidered dress, catching the light, wanders in the chamber, at first a visual, moving echo of the statues around the wall. The raised texture of her dress is akin to the rough plaster of the walls of the chamber. She seems a tactile work of art in these surroundings. More hallucinatory still is Osmond who appears unexpectedly – she did not know he had left Florence – spinning Isabel's striped parasol, as if to mesmerise her and her viewer. Osmond will cross the distance between himself and Isabel, reaching his face suddenly very close to hers as he whispers beneath her parasol and kisses her. He announces his love for Isabel: she is seen reeling from this, at some distance, by a giddily moving camera. Osmond clasps her hand almost swinging her round; this is the first scene where his physical contact with her speaks of possession as much as sensory pleasure.

This scene is the point of focus for Isabel's obsessive imaginings on her travels with Madame Merle, narrated in the film in *faux* home movie footage. In shadowy, filtered shots, which echo the lighting effects of the chamber at Caprarola, Osmond's hand is seen advancing around Isabel's waist, before a cut to a shot of their faces. It is this scene of predatory contact and sexual difference (the bare male hand closing in on the clothed female body) which appears as one of the signature images of the film in advertising shots and on the cover of the published screenplay. To signify *The Portrait of a Lady*, an image of the body is used: the face is absent. This seems a reminder of the tactile, plastic aesthetic of Campion's film. In the home movie footage, as well as seeing Isabel's body encircled by Osmond, we see a close-up of his lips, very fleshy, speaking the words, 'I'm absolutely in love with you.' Osmond's sensuality seems to draw Isabel to him, yet is increasingly marked as sinister, revealing an underside of Isabel's sexuality.

This is glimpsed in the first scene where the couple disagree about Pansy's suitors. We see Isabel's hand against her face, then Osmond's against his. There is a close-up of Osmond's hands restlessly moving a cigarette over and over. He begins pacing around Isabel and finally, to make his point, prods at her face with his fingers. The gesture is ambiguous, at once correcting and controlling her, as he did Madame Merle before, yet also in part comforting her, seeming to dry her tears. These gestures indicate how far she is in his thrall. A second such scene of disagreement, and physical contact, is preceded by Isabel's words: 'If you really wish hands to be laid on Lord Warburton, you must lay them yourself.' We see an image of Isabel's white hands, then Osmond clasps her round the upper arm, leading her by force. He lifts her onto a raised seat of cushions he has prepared, making a woman again his doll or puppet. As she tries to escape, he lifts her back. As they argue, we see Osmond's hand in close-up taking Isabel's, then he suddenly withdraws it to slap her; the action and slap are repeated, as Osmond seems to lash at her like a master with a dog. As Isabel tries to leave the room, Osmond steps on the train of her dress leaving her to trip forwards, the soundtrack recording her contact with the marble floor. Osmond clasps her arm again, then moves to press his nose into her cheek in a jeering parody of his former sensual contact with her. Isabel nevertheless moves to kiss him, but Osmond, as with Madame Merle, moves away.

In her essay, 'Muteness Envy', Barbara Johnson discusses Jane Campion's earlier film, *The Piano*, devoting some time in particular to the very contrary, and emotive, reviews the film received. She concludes: 'I think these reactions are highly significant. The genius of the movie lies in the fact that it can provoke ... diametrically opposed readings. Like the aesthetic tradition on which it implicitly comments, *The Piano* would seem to be about telling, or not telling, the difference between women's violation and women's pleasure' (1998: 147). The aesthetic tradition to which Johnson alludes is that of canonical poetry written by men, exemplified in her discussion by Keats' 'Ode on a Grecian Urn'. Johnson works to question why female muteness is a repository of aesthetic value for male poets, and uses *The Piano*, and the drama of Ada's muteness, to do so. For Johnson, muteness has aesthetic value for male poets since they contrarily envy the disempowered or victim position. The victim position, paradoxically, carries the greatest (moral) authority.

Johnson's reading is brilliant in its versatile and incisive rapprochement of works from different media and traditions (contemporary film and Romantic poetry). In her important attention to concepts and politics, Johnson spends less time on *The Piano* as visual work of art. Visual analysis of *The Portrait of a Lady* within Johnson's frame, however, may work to extend the set of connections between the aesthetic tradition of canonical poetry to which Johnson alludes and Campion's film-making. As Johnson points out, making her point about the aesthetic value of muteness, 'numerous are the Parnassian poems addressed to silent female statues, marble Venuses and granite Sphinxes whose unresponsiveness stands as the mark of their aesthetic value, and whose whiteness underscores the normative whiteness of canonical representations of women' (1998: 132). Further, Johnson reminds us that a female statue has acquired a privileged position in psychoanalytic thinking about female pleasure; she writes: 'In his efforts to collect reliable testimony from women about their pleasure, Lacan finally turns, astonishingly, to a statue, thus writing his own Parnassian poem: "You have only to go and look at Bernini's statue [of Saint Teresa] in Rome to understand immediately that she's coming, there is no doubt about it"' (1998: 134).

Campion makes fairly extensive use of images of statues in *The Portrait of a Lady*. Marmoreal figures haunt Osmond's study, as he himself seems to embody the figure of the sterile, self-pitying male creator. Unlike Pygmalion seeking to make Galatea flesh, however, Osmond seeks to freeze and mummify his living wife, to still her and stay her as a beautiful artefact, as another object in his collection. Such gestures of control have been seen in the evocations of Osmond's violent tactile attention to Isabel.

Campion herself appears to counter Osmond's aesthetic, however. Her allusions to statuary and marble work, in effect, to deny their immobility and fixity. She works instead to privilege tactility and plasticity. When Isabel and her friend Henrietta go to the Victoria and Albert Museum in an early scene in the film, they repeatedly forget the museum's interdiction on touch, laying hands on the funerary statues they visit. Isabel still possesses this inclination to make contact far later in the film, in Rome, where she and Madame Merle walk past the extraordinary statues of the Capitoline. The mammoth foot and hand by which Isabel pauses are out of all proportion to the characters in the scene. Campion herself has commented that she finds these outsize relics particularly moving. In their incongruity and fragmentary beauty they seem to embody, in plastic form, the disorienting properties of the close-up, of the blown-up haptic image as discussed by Marks. In alluding to statues, Campion moves beyond the proportions of the conventional, marmoreal effigy. Her film breaks laws of representation and observation, proliferating a series of three-dimensional images.

Over and above this irreverence towards the Parnassian aesthetic, Campion works to make the statue and statuesque signify differently. Her *Portrait of a Lady*, unlike *The Piano*, contains very few still portraits of its heroine. Instead, Isabel is seen on all sides, from troubling, off-centre and unprecedented angles. More than a portrait, the film aspires to offer a plastic impression of the dimensions and vitality of its subject. Ric Gentry comments, 'the camera is in a state of constant motion throughout the film, as virtually every shot was executed on a dolly. Ironically, there is no sense of "portrait photography" in the illustrative sense' (1997: 52). Stuart Dryburgh specifies that the camera movement was used to contemporise the film, and break with the traditions of period drama. He suggests too, that the movement works to create emotional restlessness and uncertainty about what is happening, what can be seen. Added to these meanings is a search to make cinema palpably in three dimensions, to seek the aesthetic privilege of plastic art forms.

This plasticity, linked to haptic visuality and the privileging of the tactile in *The Portrait of a Lady*, becomes Campion's means of interrogating a tradition in which the female statue is a staple. In *The Piano*, as Johnson has emphasised, Campion brilliantly shocks her viewer into indecision over the differences between female pleasure and violation. In *The Portrait of a Lady*, Campion works to make cinema tactile, to make it felt, yet the feelings summoned range between traumatic loss and ecstatic pleasure. Sensory cinema, haptic visuality, becomes Campion's mode of countering Osmond's aesthetic and his numbing of feeling. Campion keeps Isabel alive to contact; this ensures that her mourning for her child is unending, as is her pain in her marriage with Osmond, yet it also opens her to the feelings and sensations of mourning and eroticism now merged. In this search for contact, Campion transforms period drama as voyeuristic, static regime. Her cinema may indulge in part in the commemoration of lost children and lost childhood, psychological and even erotic staples of period drama, yet the past is never reified or fixed in her films. Campion places past and present in contact, in both the juxtaposition of prologue and film, and in the restless, moving attention to her present subject. Unlike Lacan observing Saint Teresa, Campion records real women speaking of their pleasure; equally she makes real pains of maternity and mourning palpable in her film. *The Portrait of a Lady* searches within and far beyond personal experience to find mobile, sensate means of testifying to extremes of sensation, to loss and desire, both excruciating and radiant.

CHAPTER SEVEN

Jude: Mortuary Photography and Heritage Cinema

In his study, *Angels and Absences: Child Deaths in the Nineteenth Century*, Laurence Lerner looks at child deaths in late Thomas Hardy. Making a comparison with the death of Tess's baby, Sorrow, in *Tess of the D'Urbervilles*, he observes: 'Hardy's most famous child death, the suicide of little Father Time in *Jude the Obscure*, is more sardonic still, a clear anticipation of modern black comedy' (1997: 144). Lerner indicates the pivotal nature of the child deaths in *Jude the Obscure*. He continues: 'the laboured, grotesque, yet somehow shocking death of Jude's children seems to announce the end of the pathetic child-death, undermined by a weird irony inherent in the scheme of things' (1997: 145). In his film, *Jude* (1995), Michael Winterbottom returns to a text which itself has been seen to mark the end of a sentimental tradition in nineteenth-century England. In this chapter I will be concerned with the implications of such a return, arguing that Winterbottom, like Hardy a century earlier, rethinks the nostalgia and sentiment of the nineteenth-century heritage. For Winterbottom, it is the restoration of such nostalgia and sentiment, in British heritage cinema, which comes under attack. The child deathbed scene becomes the focus of Winterbottom's searching analysis of loss and decay, not preservation, in period drama.

Jude was conceived as a film which would challenge the conventions of the literary adaptation and of British heritage cinema in particular. In interview in *Positif*, Winterbottom argues that such a radical treatment as he offers of *Jude the Obscure* was itself a way of remaining faithful to the ethos and mood of the novel (see Ciment & Tobin 1996: 28). Rather than bedecking the film with ornaments and lavish costume (in the manner associated with the films of Merchant and Ivory), Winterbottom adopts a more life-like aesthetic; as he explains, he wanted the characters to speak like real people. In a preface to the published screenplay, the screenwriter Hossein Amini comments on first viewing the completed film: 'There was a naturalism in the performances that I'd never seen before in period films' (1996: viii). He adds: 'We had jokingly anticipated the hostility of the critics to the "modern" approach we were going to take' (1996: x). In an otherwise lukewarm review, Derek Malcolm nevertheless describes the film as a 'period movie untrammelled by the usual heritage clichés' (1997: 13).

In her study of the heritage genre in the 1990s, Pamela Church Gibson singles *Jude* out as one of the films which has most deliberately challenged and disrupted the heritage tradition. Citing Winterbottom from the press release which accompanied the film, she writes: 'He announced that he intended not to "fetishise the past" but to "highlight its relevance"' (2000: 118–19). She continues: 'His screenwriter, Hossein Amini, went further, stating that his intention was to "destroy the heritage film from within"' (2000: 119). Church Gibson explores the ways in which the subject matter of the novel itself (Jude's failure to gain a place at Christminster; his failed marriage to Arabella and doomed love of Sue; the tragedy which befalls his children) differentiates it from the more glamorous conventions of the genre. She adds to this list of distinguishing features, the darkness of the film (in mood and in literal colour) and its metacinematic self-consciousness and *auteur* status, commenting: 'Winterbottom's cinematic style accentuates these anti-heritage elements. Homage is paid to Bergman, Truffaut, Renoir, Bill Douglas and Carol Reed' (*Ibid.*). Her comments depend on a certain understanding of what heritage cinema means. In several works, Andrew Higson has attempted to define the key formal, thematic, iconographic and industrial chararacteristics of the heritage films of the 1980s and 1990s (see especially Higson 1993). He locates heritage films between the art house and the mainstream, and sees their main pleasure lying in 'the artful and spectacular projection of an elite, conservative vision of the national past' (1996: 233). He suggests that the narratives of these films are typically slow-moving and episodic, that their camerawork is generally 'artful and pictorialist, editing slow and undramatic' (1996: 234). In later work he seeks to pluralise the definition of the specificity of the genre, simultaneously problematising the notion of generic specificity per se.

Higson introduces thoughts on the hybridity and ambivalence of the genre, discouraging pejorative reckonings with heritage cinema as fixed, reactionary cultural artefact. Recognising its hybridity allows critics to mobilise readings of heritage cinema as genre always already interrogating issues of identity, memory, nationhood, marginality, sexuality and so forth.

The genre is gradually understood to hold far greater political, emotional and aesthetic interest (as critics of Higson's early piece had contended). A similar revisionist approach to heritage cinema is found in Pam Cook's deconstruction of national identity and its role in informing the ideology of costume drama in *Fashioning the Nation: Costume and Identity in British Cinema*. Looking beyond her specific objects of study, Cook goes so far as to imply that 'our national cinema [consists] of a heterogeneous amalgam of visual styles and formal strategies appropriated from other cultures' (1996: 8). These terms are apt for thinking about Winterbottom as one of the directors currently shaping British National Cinema.

The common emphasis, found in Higson and Cook, on ambivalence, diversity and hybridity informs this reading of *Jude*. Central to my argument is the notion that *Jude* does not stand against the heritage genre as such, or destroy it; rather *Jude* may be said to interrogate the bases of the genre and offer a re-evaluation of the capacity of (heritage) cinema as art form in which the past and its values can be mourned as well as commemorated. Crucial in *Jude* is what I call a mortuary aesthetic, of which many heritage films fight shy, and within which questions of loss, longing and nostalgia, central to the genre, are placed on display. This mortuary aesthetic is Winterbottom's answer to the 'museum aesthetic' (see Dyer 1994) dominant in heritage films. He is concerned with questions of spectacle, with the film as showcase (as evidenced in the recurring motifs of photography and framing in his films), yet the images he sets on display remind us of the pathos and monstrosity of Victorian entertainment. In *Jude*, this mortuary aesthetic finds its blueprint in the images of the bodies of Jude's dead children.

Writing about his first meeting with Winterbottom and producer Andrew Eaton, Amini recalls: 'They kept talking about "the scene with the children"' (1996: iii). This scene, key to Lerner's evaluation of *Jude the Obscure* and its engagement in nineteenth-century discourses about death, is central, too, in Winterbottom's film-making. The scene is a challenge to a film-maker intent on avoiding either the mawkish or the macabre. The extraordinary achievement of the scene merits mention from *Jude*'s critics. Brian McFarlane speaks of the scene as 'the film's worst horror, involving Jude's son' (1996: 53). For Angie Errigo, the 'catastrophe that ultimately overtakes [Jude and Sue] cannot fail to move' (1996: 15). Church Gibson speaks of 'terrible tragedy' (2000: 119).

Michael Atkinson is the only critic who links the sacrifice of the children in *Jude* to Winterbottom's other films. He comments, with reference to *Welcome to Sarajevo* (1997), the film with which Winterbottom followed *Jude*: 'Children are *Sarajevo*'s relentless focus; couple it with *Jude* (and even the nerve-wracking scene in *Butterfly Kiss* [1995] when it seems that Eu might kill an eight-year-old) and you can read a strong current of parental anxiety invading Winterbottom's conscious filmscape' (1998: 47). Extending this argument, in line with the concerns of the other films discussed in this study, I suggest that Winterbottom's interest in the loss and recovery of children derives more broadly from a generational concern with the limits of representation on the one hand, and, more humanely, with large scale issues of innocence, loss and inheritance.

In his discussion of the heritage film, Higson argues: 'This question "who shall inherit England?" is central to the heritage film. *Chariots of Fire*, *Another Country*, *A Handful of Dust*, *Orlando* – they all deal with this question of inheritance' (1996: 47). Inheritance is the staple of the genre to which, in strongly contestatory manner, *Jude* still partly belongs. Indeed it seems apt that in its attempt to dispossess itself of its filial links with the genre, *Jude* (as an extension of Hardy's novel) should rely so strongly on a scene about the loss of children, heirs and birthright.

Yet, as Atkinson's comment implies, it is not merely in *Jude* that Winterbottom concerns himself with children in crisis. A thread can be traced in his film-making, from *Butterfly Kiss* through to *Welcome to Sarajevo* and *Wonderland* (1999) (released after Atkinson's article). Winterbottom's films are thematically and stylistically diverse: this has been one of the remarkable aspects of his career. Yet through his work, Winterbottom engages in a type of *fort/da* game whereby a child's loss is envisaged, then denied, where the child is lost, and then recovered. This is played out literally in *Wonderland* where the child Jack goes missing.

Wonderland shows Jack's loss from several perspectives. We follow his father's discovery that the child has gone and his search for the boy, with his sister-in-law. We follow the boy himself in scenes shot in a fairground at night. At first the camera traces the child in a series of forwards tracking shots: with a knapsack on his back, like a child in a fairytale, he makes his way down the fairground aisles. While the sounds of the fairground are insistent on the soundtrack, the child is seen wearing a personal stereo: he is placed at one remove from his context and from the spectator, the stereo seeming to underline his self-enclosure. Throughout the film the child appears self-absorbed and self-sufficient: we have seen him in his bedroom, lit by a globe night light; we see him several times through windows and frames, like a small Kieślowski child. His vulnerability is established as he is mugged at the fairground. The scene is fast and jarring, shot from the child's unsuspecting angle of vision, in darkness intermittently broken by the glare of fireworks (the violence of the diegetic noise now exactly reflects the child's sensory experience). Suspense is broken as the film moves to show Jack, now officially a missing child, calling his mother from a police station. *Wonderland* pulls back from the tragedy of *Jude*; here Jack is reunited with his mother. Particularly moving are the shots of his mother cradling him on the backseat of a car. Though this image resembles a *pietà*, it brings the pathos of recovery, not grief, and a different variation on the fear of losing a child. As such, *Jude* is all the more uncompromising.

As suggested above, *Jude* is a film which challenges and changes the aesthetic of the heritage film. One of the first striking ways in which it does this is through the use of a stylised prelude. This prelude works to open up debates about cinema and photography, about fate, fatefulness and the reading of signs. Asked why he chose to shoot the beginning of *Jude* in black and white, Winterbottom replies: 'What Eduardo, the cinematographer, and I wanted to do was to create a circular feel to the look of the film. Start in black and white, and by the end of the film we're back to a kind of monochrome' (in *Films in Review* 1997: 73). He continues: 'In a sense the opening of the film became a miniature of the rest of the film. What happens to the boy Jude is an introduction to what will happen to the man Jude' (*Ibid.*).

Nearly all the film's critics remark on this opening. Church Gibson notes: 'It is not surprising that the film shocked an audience used to more lyrical adaptations; their expectations were confounded from the start' (2000: 119). Geoffrey Macnab echoes Winterbottom's sense of the indicativeness of the early scene: 'As the farmer catches and whips [Jude], there's a cut-away to a crow hanging dead, an intimation of the tragic events ahead' (1996b: 45). Atkinson, more emotively, writes: 'From the very first scene (of Jude as a child chasing crows from a massive plowed field, struck dumb by a cross of lynched crow bodies hanging in the wind), the movie places Jude either at the roiling heart of chaos or at the empty fringes' (1998: 47).

In its opening *Jude* is faithful to Hardy's text. In chapter two of the novel Hardy offers the signature image of the film's opening: 'The fresh harrow-lines seemed to stretch like the channellings in a piece of new corduroy' (1998: 14). Yet there is no anticipatory image of hanging birds: Hardy's intimations of Jude's destiny, its pathos, and the future loss of his off-spring, are more diffuse. Hardy traces links between the living birds and Jude's destiny: 'his heart grew sympathetic with the birds' thwarted desires. They seemed, like himself, to be living in a world which did not want them' (1998: 15). The child Jude harbours feelings which link him to his suicidal son: 'If he could only prevent himself growing up! He did not want to be a man' (1998: 18). In the film, more economically, we see the clear image of the birds on the gibbet signalling circularity in fate as well as visual style. *Jude* is highly imaginative in its discovery of visual means of expression, and in its self-consciousness about the filmic medium and its adequacy for representation and recall of the past.

Jude opens with an image of near abstraction. From the white on black of the minimal titles, the film cuts to a monochrome image of a field, entirely dark, with a mere strip of pale sky visible. The cross formed by the gibbet where the crows hang is distantly silhouetted against this background, as is the far-off figure of Jude himself, moving into the field of the film's attention. The opening is reminiscent of Bergman (on whom Winterbottom has previously made two documentaries). Setting *Jude* in the idiom of *The Seventh Seal*, Winterbottom signals the issues of fate and mortality with which the film will contend. More volubly, *Jude* demonstrates from the start that heritage cinema takes its influences and constructs a hybrid identity within a European art cinema tradition. The unimpeachable 'Englishness' of the genre is challenged. The film questions which heritage it recalls and restores.

As the child becomes the focus of the camera's attention, visual references proliferate and interfere. Critics allude to Bill Douglas (see Church Gibson 2000: 119): such references seem to anticipate how far *Jude* will continue threads in British film-making. Though monochrome, Winterbottom's images of the small Jude also recall Ken Loach's *Kes* (1969) and look forward to Lynne Ramsay's stark images of children in *Ratcatcher* (1999). Visible too, are references to Truffaut's filming of the young Antoine Doinel (as in the fairground scene in *Wonderland*): in the black and white cinematography, the imaging of the young Jude as victim, and the virtuoso crane shot of the flock of sheep, reminiscent of Truffaut's shot of school children.

While such cinematic references mark out patterns of filiation, of artistic heritage, the prelude to *Jude* also reminds us of its own status as visual and mnemonic artefact. Winterbottom has imported one critical scene, absent in Hardy (and in the shooting script of the film): the taking of a school photograph. The film cuts from Jude being scolded by his Aunt Drusilla to a shot of a camera, from behind which emerges Phillotson, the school teacher who inspires Jude's dream of Christminster and who later marries Sue. The film cuts to the image Phillotson is viewing and recording: a village school photograph, with children of various ages, little girls in pinafores and boys in short trousers. The camera is visible in the lower left-hand corner of the screen, constructing this image as representation of the director's work.

Importantly, this school photograph is instantly recognisable: its style conforms to that of many late nineteenth-century images in its composition, in its period detail, in its stillness and monochrome. The image is carefully constructed in the narrative of the film, as well as its *mise-en-scène*: we see Phillotson and the photographer check the image through the viewfinder. We see the image through the eyes of the child Jude too, slightly aslant, before he runs to take his place in the shot. We see how the stillness and organisation of the image is artificially composed. Most jarringly, we see the composition after the image has been taken by the camera. The posing figures break into applause, an unfamiliar after-image.

100

Jude returns not to the cinematography and *mise-en-scène* of previous Hardy adaptations (Schlesinger's *Far from the Madding Crowd* (1967) or Polanski's *Tess* (1979) to which *Jude* has been unfavourably compared), nor to the imaging of late-Victorian England found in other period drama; rather Winterbottom returns to the style and form of the very photographic evidence of the period. This is not merely in search of verisimilitude, but works as a means of questioning the Victorian era as an era in which photography itself was developed, and in which photography functions as a forerunner of film for the preservation of past moments in visual representation.

Although the school photograph scene is missing in *Jude the Obscure*, the novel does already provide its own small trail of photographic images. In the novel, Jude first sees his cousin Sue as a photographic image: 'One day while in lodgings at Alfredston he had gone to Marygreen to see his old aunt, and had observed between the brass candlesticks on her mantelpiece the photograph of a pretty girlish face, in a broad hat, with radiating folds under the brim like the rays of a halo' (Hardy 1998: 77–8). In the film an image of Kate Winslet as Sue sits on Aunt Drusilla's mantelpiece in the film and recurs as insistent reminder of the object of Jude's desire. Removed to Jude's bedroom at Christminster, the portrait sits beside a statue of an angel, whose wings convey the purity and ethereality of Hardy's image. The photograph in both novel and film serves to hold and focus the female character who in many ways marks the tale by her restlessness, her uncertainty and her wandering. Both novel and film seem to display awareness of the ways photographic reproductions fix, arrange and even idealise the subject represented, as much as offering a true likeness.

This ambivalence over the veracity of the photographic medium seems to filter the school photograph scene, too. Here the relation between movement and stillness is telling (and again Winterbottom seems to recall Truffaut in encouraging the viewer to think about the relation between the still and moving image). In representing the movement around the still school photograph and its general arrangement, Winterbottom seems to show up the superior representational capacity of moving pictures over still photographic images. Yet as we witness the falsity, the artificial construction and production of the photographic image, we are reminded of the inherent falsity of representations which always hold a selective view and arrangement of the world.

Jude simultaneously acknowledges the fixative power of photographic imaging yet challenges it and avoids it as well. The heritage genre in particular has been associated with stasis, slowness, with pictorial influences in the construction of the shot, with a museum aesthetic. Whilst *Jude*, like the recent Jane Austen adaptations, makes frequent use of images within frames, seen through glass, through windows and in doorways (see Pidduck 1998), the general pace and direction of the film inversely avoids this photographic stasis. *Jude* is a film of extraordinary energy and movement. Its restlessness is inherited in some degree from the novel: the film follows Jude's moves between Marygreen, Christminster, Melchester, Shaston, Aldbrickham and elsewhere, and Christminster again. On a smaller scale, and in contrast to much heritage cinema, much of *Jude* is shot outside on the streets, with the camera tracking the characters as they go about their business. This is evident in the distinctive first Christminster scenes between Jude and Sue. In addition to faithfulness to the novel, and faithlessness to the heritage genre in cinema, this restlessness derives from an aesthetic concern with the tracing and fixing of evidence. *Jude* constructs its visual subject as forever moving and elusive: this adds a sense of progress, vitality and modernity to the film, as well as rendering its ultimate circularity all the more invidious.

The scene which fixes *Jude*'s concern with the photographic and with the recording of evidence is the notorious scene with the children. As the film leads towards this scene, its circularity becomes more evident. Little Jude (Little Father Time in the novel) visually recalls the child Jude of the opening of the film. His arrival in Jude's honeymoon days with Sue, sets the film on a downward spiral towards its close.

In the novel we are reminded on various occasions that Little Father Time is older than his years; portentously: 'He was Age masquerading as Juvenility, and doing it so badly that his real self showed through the crevices' (Hardy 1998: 276). In this respect Little Father Time is reminiscent of Paul Dombey and sundry other infants of Victorian literature old before their time. (As Laurence Lerner reminds us this was a familiar trope in the representation of sickly and dying children.)

The film *Jude*, avoiding such doom-laden and sentimental aesthetics, opts again for a visual intimation of fate. In the scene which immediately follows Little Jude's arrival in England, Jude and Sue take the quiet child to a magic lantern show. The scene is, like the school photograph, an invention of the film and not present in the novel. In the shooting script, Jude and Sue take the child to a fair and they visit a Haunted House with 'black castles and mists and ghostly apparitions' (Amini 1996: 91). In his preface, Amini tells us: 'It was expensive to build a fairground House of Horror, so the Tunnel of Doom turned into a magic lantern show' (1996: vii). The necessary substitution seems to accord all the more smoothly with the concerns of the original novel, and with the film's cinematic self-consciousness. Early in the novel, Hardy makes use of a magic lantern image; Jude thinks of Christminster: 'In his deep concentration on these transactions of the future, Jude's walk had slackened, and he was now standing quite still, looking at the ground as though the future were thrown thereon by a magic lantern' (1998: 38). In the film, illusory images of the future, conjured by the play of light, are cast over the face of little Jude. The macabre images of Amini's Haunted House are transposed onto the magic lantern show, by whose illusion a moving phantom is conjured, amidst other horrors. The film offers a glancing image of a death's head which functions as visual *memento mori*, framing the mortality of the child Jude. That this reminder of death should occur in a scene which represents a proto-cinematic apparatus, and a scene which is itself reflective of the status of Winterbottom's film as spectacle, begins to raise questions about the intimate relation of photography, mortality and death-denying commemoration. Such questions are debated more visibly, and with all the more pathos, in the scene of the death of Jude's children.

The fateful scene occurs at Christminster again. Jude and Sue return to their lodgings after Jude has just acquired a new position. Although their mood is light, the space they enter is cramped and oppressive, the walls papered in a mouldy green. Sue pauses first before entering the room were the children should be sleeping: she is reading Little Jude's scrawled note pinned to the door. She stops still and Jude passes her: we see their sidelong images echoing one another as they both stare through the door frame. The film cuts quickly to the image they behold: little Jude hanging in the centre of the room.

The image has the quality of early colour photographs. The child's face and pale nightgown are picked out against a receding dark background. A cord is visible round his neck. His face, like his father's, is in profile. We are reminded of the point of view from which the image derives as the handheld camera moves quickly down from the spectacle of the hanging child to a further small child lying on a bed. The urgency of the gaze is echoed as we now see the adult Jude frantic in the frame: the effect of the scene comes, in addition to the sheer horror of its subject, from the play between stasis and movement. The scene is silent apart from the sound of Jude's quickly drawn breaths. He shows desperate energy as he moves from child to child, first releasing his hanging son, then with painful tenderness carrying each of the dead children from the scene of their death into the adjacent room. Jude's movements seem a terrible, animal attempt to animate the children, literally to make them move. The scene seems to have no order or control, as if its horror has disrupted its balance and the camera's stable point of view. The colour scheme, *mise-en-scène* and silence seem reminiscent of Kieślowski's *A Short Film About Killing*. The images of the children's bodies themselves echo a further set of proto-cinematic precedents.

Particularly powerful, in addition to the image of the hanging child, are two shots of Sue's daughter lying out on her bed. First she is seen as if from the corner of Jude's eye, on his entry into the room. She is simply a still, funereal image. The camera returns to her again as Jude tries to release his son and

Figure 9 *Jude*

we see her image in more detail. Her eyes are closed, her body is swaddled in a blanket, as if already prepared for her coffin. The skin of her face seems waxy, sickly grey and her strands of blonde hair trail outwards on her pillow. In this image of the child, *Jude* recalls the nineteenth-century tradition of post mortem photographs which were taken of the loved one soon after death. In such images there is the same combination of fragility and composure, the blankness of expression, closed eyes and stillness, reminiscent of sleep, but starkly distinct.

Jay Ruby has studied such photographs in his 1995 volume, *Secure the Shadow: Death and Photography in America*. He looks at the evolution of a photographic tradition in the nineteenth century which worked to replace the earlier posthumous commemorative or mortuary portrait. Ruby explores the social practices which informed the taking and keeping of such photographs (and indeed his study is primarily anthropological). He argues: 'The motivation for the image contains a fundamentally contradictory desire – to retain the dead, to capture some sense of the essence of a being now gone, to deny death' (1995: 29). This combination of acknowledgement of death, yet disavowal, seems apt to the contradictory dynamics of Winterbottom's heritage cinema which seems to acknowledge the loss of the past, the impossibility of its cinematic reanimation. Yet he approaches an illusion of the recreation of the past, its emotion and aesthetic, most successfully precisely in evoking nineteenth-century images of loss and commemoration.

Throughout his study, Ruby places emphasis on the possibility that post mortem photography is a part of a process of mourning, of the acceptance of loss and of eventual healing. He argues, of post mortem images: 'Their function was not to keep the dead alive but to enable mourners to acknowledge their loss' (1995: 43). His study extends into the late twentieth century which he sees influenced by the resurgence (in the 1980s) of the notion that 'the process of mourning involves thinking and feeling about the dead person' (1995: 181).[1] He looks at the 'reinvention' of post mortem photography by health care officials, and particularly its use for still-born children and neo-natal fatalities: often polaroid images of the child are taken on the ward and used later in counselling with parents. The importance of such imaging in the personal context is doubtless invaluable. Bearing in mind the social basis of his work, and the empathy which informs it, Ruby emphasises, on several occasions, the possibility that photographs can help to resolve grief rather than prolong it. He sums up his work with the words: 'We cannot prevent the loss of those we love but we do sometimes mitigate the loss with a photograph' (1995: 189).

In the context of an artistic representation, here narrative cinema, such a healing imperative is less necessary to uphold. I would argue indeed that the post mortem photograph conjured visually in *Jude* works as an icon of horror and loss whose aim is to unsettle the viewer and mark out the mortuary aesthetic from which the film will not fight shy. Other examples of this aim to strip heritage cinema of its protective gloss come in the early pig-killing scene (which Winterbottom had already filmed for his student exercise at film school) or in the bloody childbirth scene. In the filming of the death of the children, the personal idiom – the post mortem photograph – is transposed into the public medium of narrative cinema. In this transposition, the post mortem photograph, until recently rarely seen as aesthetic artefact, works to renew heritage cinema as art form. The horror of past losses, witnessed in the nineteenth-century experience of death, is made both palpable and visible.

Jude as film works to remind us of a nineteenth-century means of contending with death. As moving picture, in whose narrative the viewer necessarily becomes involved, the film reanimates a drama of loss and mourning, allowing us no complacent acceptance of the deaths on view. We are reminded of the irresolvable horror of the loss of a child (still the same in an age of higher rates of child mortality). Winterbottom, like Barthes in *La Chambre Claire*, returns to the dead evidence of nineteenth-century photographic representations and quickens our reckoning with the pain of the losses (once and future) such images represent. In this respect, *Jude* effects an act of disinterment in emotional terms, opening former graves, and replacing commemoration with stark grief. (Aptly Sue cannot bear the burial of her children and asks for their bodies to be disinterred so she can see them once more.)

Jude offers no process of healing or comfort. Its first representation of grief is visceral. Both Sue's and Jude's bodies are shown to be contorted, literally knocked sideways by grief. Sue is seen crouched in the corner of the room, then heaped on the floor as she lets out unearthly howls. Jude is curled on his bed, foetal and weeping. Grief is represented as a form of bodily regression. Uncannily Jude and Sue appear themselves like mourning children. The film indulges in a set of repetitions, as if motored by a compulsion to repeat. Jude's and Sue's images double one another, in their first sight of the tragedy, in their grieving response, in their later insomniac nights. The novel itself, of course, insists more generally on the couple's similarity to each other. But in the insistence on this visual doubling at his film's climax, Winterbottom seems to allude and return to the circularity he has sought and foreseen from the start of the film. There is no progress here, despite the brief contact between the separated parents in the winter churchyard at the end of the film. *Jude* ends in the churchyard where Jude's children lie buried, again underlining its own mortuary aesthetic.

As I have argued, this mortuary aesthetic is key to Winterbottom's reinvention of heritage cinema. *Jude* is a film which self-consciously questions the psychological investment in the preservation of the past and the denial of time passing. The film offers its own cinematic reanimation of late nineteenth-century England. Integral to this disinternment of the past is a refusal to disavow the poverty, degradation and mortality, indeed the living horror of the period reconstructed. If heritage cinema is seen as cinematic reanimation, then issues of mortality, the very life/death divide, acquire a privileged place and even metacinematic relevance within its confines. *Jude* exploits this in its representation of child deaths. The death of Jude's children represents the loss of his inheritance and heritage, the denial of futurity. The reanimation of the past on which the genre depends, is circumscribed by its own failure in the resolution of the film in death and ungrievable loss.

The question remains why Winterbottom should return to a nineteenth-century sentimental tradition and its re-evaluation precisely at the end of the twentieth century. The heritage genre itself has found new strengths and popularity in the late 1980s and 1990s. It has been noticeable that a number of directors have tried their hand at a heritage film or literary adaptation amidst more contemporary output. For Winterbottom, the pathos of the child deaths in *Jude the Obscure* would seem to mark the novel as privileged subject of adaptation in the context precisely of his interest in children, missing, imperiled and saved in his broader work. *Jude* as heritage film already exceeds its own confines, finding new meanings in reflections and reverberations through Winterbottom's other films. The links between Winterbottom's films, past and present, remind the viewer of the constancy of the fears and horror surrounding child death and missing children per se. *Jude* refuses any wish to angelise the past or set it at a distance from present perception. Nevertheless *Jude* exists as exemplary, self-conscious heritage cinema, facing the viewer with images of the past not as inherently different but merely as irrevocably missing, as a series of losses which can be denied only too ephemerally in photographs, magic lantern images and moving pictures themselves.

CHAPTER EIGHT

Still Time: *Ratcatcher*

Ratcatcher (1999) opens with a close-up image of a child wound up in a net curtain. The child spins in slow motion, so the image seems numbed, poetic and jarring. The white daisy pattern of the curtain is highlighted by the bright light from the window. The child's face is only just perceptible beneath the netted material. The screenplay draws out some of the associations of the image, describing how the child has pulled the curtain over his head 'like a shroud' (Ramsay 1999: 3) and how the child spins round and round 'cocooning himself' (*Ibid.*). The child's features, submerged, recall images of asphyxiation and drowning, as they echo, too, sonogram pictures of the foetus in the womb. The film seems to recall some of the image patterns found in a film like *Three Colours: Blue* and in this opening, slowed image, it creates a moving tableau of the concerns and aesthetics of the narrative which unfolds.

Ratcatcher is Scottish director Lynne Ramsay's first feature film. It opened the Edinburgh Film Festival in 1999 and went on to win the BFI Sutherland Award at the London Film Festival. Two of Ramsay's short films, *Small Deaths* (1996) and *Gasman* (1997) previously won awards at Cannes. Set on a council estate in Govan, in Glasgow, *Ratcatcher* centres around images of drowning and traumatic loss in childhood. Ramsay has expressed her particular interest in childhood, saying: 'For me childhood is an interesting time because your opinions are not yet set' (1999: viii). She continues: 'Childhood is like a blank canvas, in terms of the direction you can take for good or bad' (*Ibid.*). The comment anticipates the way Ramsay will work to convey childhood visually. She links childhood to particular ways of seeing, as she says, 'as a director, I try to look at things from a child's point of view' (*Ibid.*).

The majority of the films discussed here have explored the subject of missing and lost children from an adult perspective. By this rationale, this book has been far more a study of parental anxiety and adult nostalgia than an engagement with the specific experience and sensation of childhood (exceptions come in the attention to Nadine and Olivier in *Olivier, Olivier* and in the vignette of the missing child at the fairground in *Wonderland*). *Ratcatcher* looks at how one child, James Gillespie, responds to (and is responsible for) the death of his friend, Ryan Quinn. Where films about late adolescence and early adulthood – such as *La Haine* (1995) and *La Vie rêvée des anges* (1998) – have looked at the identificatory bonds between live and dying counterparts, few films have addressed so squarely the experience of mourning a lost other, friend or double, in childhood. In this respect, *Ratcatcher* opens a new facet in this study, as it equally echoes the concerns of many of the other films discussed here.

Critics have commented in particular on links between Ramsay's film and Bill Douglas' autobiographical trilogy.[1] *Ratcatcher* is set during the dustmen's strike in the 1970s. Ramsay grew up in Glasgow and would have been a small child in the 1970s. However, she stresses: 'Although the story is set in the 70s, I talked with the designer about giving the film a timeless feel – I don't think it looks period. I didn't want flares or anything that specific; I wanted a mixture of 50s, 60s and 70s influence' (in Spencer 1999: 18). She makes no claims for the film as autobiographical or as influenced by her own life history. Indeed *Ratcatcher* seems distinctive as a film which is *not* attempting to recapture or recall an adult's lost childhood as memory piece. Ramsay seems alive to the very present, and persisting, concerns of her protagonist James. Childhood is seen as largely painful and fractious, although the film is sensitive, too, to the complexity and peculiarity of childish imaginary worlds.

Instead of recalling a lost past, the period setting seems influenced by the visual opportunities offered by the strike setting. In this it bears comparison with another National Lottery-funded film, *Billy Eliot* (2000), far more redemptive than *Ratcatcher*, which calibrates its hero's successes to the miners' strike of the 1980s. This seems to underline the social and popular intentions of the film, though politics are subsumed in a narrative of ambition, tolerance and male bonding. Ramsay makes different use of the dustmen's strike in *Ratcatcher*, using her child's perspective to close in on the material debris of the strike and its living consequences. She comments: 'I looked at some photographs from the time and they were quite surreal – kids pulling things from the rubbish, dressing up, finding old dolls, killing rats' (1999: viii). Ramsay has said that her experience of viewing Maya Deren's

Meshes of the Afternoon (1943–59) first inspired her to go into film-making. *Ratcatcher* bears witness to her (surrealist) interest in found objects and in the liminal states between dream and waking perversely captured on film. Part of *Ratcatcher*'s brilliance is its ability to make of the debris, the excess and refuse of the strike and its circumstances, and the very material living conditions of its protagonists, a space at once reduced, deprived, yet visually striking.

The influence of images of the period is felt in the cinematography. Ramsay says: 'I wanted the colours to be quite soft and desaturated, so we used filters to drain the colour out, and make it almost black and white at times. … In a bizarre way, the end result looks like real film from that period: we saw some stock footage from the time of the strike and we could have cut it right in' (in Spencer 1999: 18). Indeed archive news footage of the strike, watched on a black and white television fits seamlessly into the film. While confirming a kinship with film of the period, Ramsay's use of filters and drained, sometimes greenish, sometimes sepulchral light, seems also to recall the light effects of Kieślowski's *Dekalog*. (Kieślowski claimed to have been influenced by Ken Loach, who is cited by critics as a point of reference for Ramsay's viewers.)[2]

Ramsay herself trained as a fine art photographer, before attending the National Film and Television School. *Ratcatcher* has been criticised for its episodic nature and for its lack of narrative drive. I argue here that this slowness, stillness and numbness derive from two sources: on the one hand, Ramsay's concern to chart and respect the tempo and disruption of traumatic experience, its annihilation of memory and its gradual, seeping, recall; on the other, Ramsay's background in photography and her palpable experiments with the boundaries between still photography and narrative cinema. Later in this chapter, I follow up links between her work in *Ratcatcher* and contemporary photographic images of children. Throughout I suggest that *Ratcatcher*, like *La Jetée* (1963), finds in its finest moments a scintillating coincidence between its stilled, charged means of representation and its excessive, exorbitant subject.

To approach these issues, I will look further, first of all, at the opening sequences of the film, its point of reference as drama of drowning and survival. From the dream-like images of the child twisting in the curtain, the viewer is snapped into a temporal reality by his mother. The film follows an exchange between mother and son about whether he will wear his trousers tucked into his wellington boots. As we hear the mother's words, the image-track, by contrast, shows a close-up of Ryan's face, brilliantly lit, with a kitsch painting of a little boy on the wall behind him. Ryan is looking out of the window, its light reflected on his face. He is framed, pictorially, as child subject of the film. The film cuts to the image he sees: an overhead shot of his friend, James Gillespie, throwing stones into the canal.

The image out the window places on view something of the child's mind, his mental space (as windows, and the images they frame, are used recurrently as the film continues). The image Ryan sees is slightly shrouded by the blurred presence of the net curtain at the sides of the frame. This signals, arguably, that this is a fantasy space, and a pictorial space, as well as a real space (canal and wasteland) in the film. The overhead shot from the window recurs a few minutes later. We follow Ryan outside with his mother, but he gives her the slip, leaving her to look round for him in the street and find it empty. After Ryan has untucked his trousers in the tenement stairwell, the film cuts to an image of him entering the fantasy frame where he has seen James playing. We still view this scene from a flat upstairs. There is still the blur of a curtain, though now a pane cuts across the window, probably indicating that this is a different flat. As we first watch the film, it seems that this overhead shot of James and Ryan playing together is from the point of view of an anonymous observer, even perhaps that this is a disembodied point of witnessing, observation or surveillance in the film. Towards the close of the film we find that James's last exchange with Ryan, and its consequences, have been viewed by another boy, Kenny. Although it is never made explicit, in this view from the window it is likely that we see Kenny's witnessing of Ryan's death.

The shot of the boys by the canal is self-consciously artistic as framed through the window. The water of the canal is stark white, overlaid with reflections of trees and outhouses in the waste ground roundabout. The shots are reminiscent of the dripping spaces of Lars von Trier's early films or of Tarkovsky's landscapes. We cut from this muted image – where the boys' exchanges can hardly be heard – to sudden close-up images of them fighting by the canal. James pushes Ryan in and they throw mud at one another. The film cuts to Ryan's mother buying childish sandals, then back to the boys both in the water now, the sound of the waves and splashes insistent. The boys can barely be told apart.

Ryan fights James and holds him under the water. The film cuts to an underwater shot of his pale face in the greenish water, a bubble coming out of his mouth. His features have the blurred look of Ryan in the curtain, part foetus, part corpse. The soundtrack echoes with the sound of underwater breathing. The film is for an instant submerged in James's experience and at one with his fear and consciousness. He emerges from the water though, seen wet and sitting up, moving fast to push Ryan in turn under the surface. James runs fast from the scene and the film cuts to an image of the empty surface of the canal, the ripples, bubbles and noise subsiding. The new silence is the bridge to James's close-up reaction shot as he looks back to find Ryan missing. His mouth is slightly open, he seems to be listening for sound, waiting for ways to respond. He is frozen and wary. This is the film's point of (no) return:

the horror of Ryan's death reverberates through the rest of the action, but it knows of no rescue or repair. James is left solitary and surviving; his wariness, though, shows the slightest intimation that this action might be overseen, overhead, as we learn is the case towards the end of the film.

Critics have registered the shock effect for the viewer who assumes that the film's main protagonist has been drowned in its first five minutes. As Charlotte O'Sullivan says: 'we are temporarily dumbfounded, assuming our hero, our narrative centre, is dead' (1999: 50). From this moment on it becomes clear that James, not Ryan, is the film's point of focus, though memories of Ryan, and visual recall for the viewer, will play subliminally through the rest of the film. *Ratcatcher* seems to depend on a series of echoes and repetitions where we are made to think through ways in which James and Ryan are doubles of each other, and ways in which Ryan haunts James. This is signalled immediately in James's mother's response. As she comes home with her shopping, she is seen looking out a window from the tenement staircase. She is the witness to a scene where we see Ryan's drowned body on the riverbank. One of the rescuers turns him over and we see the mother's response in an extreme close-up of her eyes. James appears in the flat, his breathing cut against a sudden close-up of Ryan's pale, mud-stained lifeless face. His mother holds him close, cradling him as she says 'I thought it was you', triggering James to go limp and drop the jacket he is carrying. His mother's relief and contact come supposedly as some comfort, yet the film is not slow to register the jarring possibilities of the interchangeability of James and Ryan. It explores these through painful exchanges between James and Ryan's mother; and through a series of compulsive returns to the canal, to imagery of water and of drowning. *Ratcatcher* offers a means of thinking James's response to Ryan's death and its return in his memory. Both his relation to the grieving parent, and the film's means of contending with James's own grief and fear in returning water images, can be elucidated with reference to the work of Cathy Caruth.

In her paper, 'Parting Words: Trauma, Silence and Survival', Caruth, analysing Freud, explores what she describes as 'the surprising emergence, from within the theory of the death drive, of the drive to life, a form of survival that both witnesses and turns away from the trauma in which it originates' (2001: 7). She traces this emergence through a close reading of Freud's *Beyond the Pleasure Principle*, working in particular to understand the relation between Freud's two primary examples of trauma: the recurring nightmares of the World War One soldiers and the *fort/da* game played by the small child. Looking at these two examples in conjunction offers, for Caruth, a crucial move from 'the reformulating of life around the witness to death, to the possibility of witnessing and making history in creative acts of life' (2001: 9). Caruth reveals that her insight into Freud's text, and her sense of the emergence of the drive to life, came from her encounter with 'a real child in Atlanta, a child whose best friend had been murdered in the street and who is interviewed by the friend's mother' (*Ibid.*). Caruth places this child's death within the context of 'the contemporary history of urban violence in North America' (2001: 14). She met the child when she became familiar with a group established by Bernadette Leite to help traumatised children who had witnessed violence. Leite's own eldest son, Khalil, died when he was shot in the back one night while out with friends. Caruth explains: 'Giving the group the name "Kids Alive and Loved", whose initials – KAL – reproduce the initials of her child, Khalil Aseem Leite, Bernadette hoped to make the group not only a way of both helping the living children to get over their trauma by talking about Khalil (as well as other murders they had experienced), but also of providing a kind of living memorial to her dead son through the living children's words and lives' (2001: 15).

Caruth explores taped interviews between Bernadette and Khalil's friend Gregory. These centre around the question of mementos of Khalil. When Bernadette asks Gregory if he has any mementos of Khalil, Gregory replies: 'He has something of mine!' Khalil was buried in Gregory's shirt and watch. The exchange continues:

> B: So it made you feel good that your favorite friend was buried in your favorite shirt and your watch.
> G: (smiling again) And he has my – it's not really a hat, it's a cap. It's a little like a stocking cap, that colorful thing on his wall. Yeah, him and me and Maurice would play this game, 'left hand', where you call out what's in the person's left hand and you get to keep it. And he called that and he got it.
> B: I should give that back to you, you could take it with you as a memento.
> G: Uhuh, I would feel better if it would stay in his household. Because it's a memento of him but it's a memento of me too. (2001: 17)

Caruth is interested in the games mentioned and played here (which she sees in terms of the *fort/da* game she has analysed). She suggests that in naming the cap a memento, not of Khalil, but of himself, Greg both ties his life with Khalil's death, yet also gives up the part of himself that existed before that death. Caruth argues that this is a creative act, writing: 'he creatively transforms the language of the memento and achieves another language and another memorialization: a memorialization that takes place precisely through his separation and his own act of creation' (2001: 18). She acknowledges, however, that his refusal of Bernadette's offer to give the cap back is also a way of saying 'I will not be your dead child'. Instead of doubling his dead friend, Gregory speaks of his new-found ambition to succeed in the music business. For Caruth, Gregory finds a language of parting where he gives Khalil back to death and 'Khalil, in a sense, gives Greg back to life' (2001: 18).

This process is far less clear-cut in *Ratcatcher*. The end of the film for example seems caught between life and death, between the compulsive repetition of the death drive, and the moving, creative will to life. We see James jump into the canal himself, his body in limbo under the water. Cross-cut with this are images of the family carrying their possessions over the open field to a new house, a dream house of James's imagination. As in the end of *The Piano*, the film seems to hesitate between a dream-like death by drowning (and resistance of symbolic structures in a return to the semiotic and psychosis) and a renewed and restored order of the family, a new home. Before its equivocal close, *Ratcatcher* also leaves us in doubt as to how far James proves capable of leaving Ryan's death behind and turning himself towards a new life. Of course a major difference between James's mourning and Gregory's is that James has been responsible for Ryan's death. This needs to be taken into consideration in the discussion which follows. Nevertheless, I argue that Caruth's reading of patterns of mourning and commemoration is still instructive for interpretation of *Ratcatcher*, as in turn the film's analysis of survival of trauma may bring new resonances, and hesitations, to Caruth's argument.

Mrs Quinn, Ryan's grieving mother, is an object of wary attention in the film (reflecting the main perspective and consciousness of the film as a child's not an adult's). She is seen staring, impassive, as the funeral car drives up, then standing outside her house in the darkness, and then fighting with her husband as they try to load their furniture into a removal van. James notices her and watches her, yet always maintains a guilty distance between them. His mother shows tenderness towards Mrs Quinn, comforting her as she sits crying in the street. James is left with his mother's shopping; he is seen in a beautifully framed shot at the very edge of the image. James's mother holds her arm around Mrs Quinn, who accuses her husband of killing her boy. The film cuts to a close-up reaction shot from James, who seems to take the blame at one remove. He backs away but his mother calls him back. He fetches the shopping bags and is grasped by Mrs Quinn who wants to give him 'a wee cuddle'. We see James's pained face in close-up over Mrs Quinn's shoulder before we hear her say: 'He's the double of my Ryan.'

The identification, even confusion, of the living and dead child is extended as Mrs Quinn asks James to do her 'a wee favour': to collect the little box which is still on Ryan's bed. James seems unresponsive faced with this request; here and throughout the scene he seems unable to hear or answer Mrs Quinn's appeal. Instead he waits for and follows his own mother's promptings, as she encourages him to go upstairs and then to be grateful for the gift he has fetched. The little box contains the sandals Mrs Quinn was buying while Ryan was drowning. James's mother holds the empty shoebox while Mrs Quinn looks painfully and lovingly at James as he walks back and forwards complaining that they are 'too wee'. We see a close-up of the sandals as James finally says thanks and his mother hugs Mrs Quinn once more.

James must take the sandals as memento, forced by his mother's kindness to Mrs Quinn. In this way, as in the film's doublings and acts of identification, James is placed in some respects as Mrs Quinn's dead child. Yet once alone, with the sandals still on his feet, he deliberately scratches their brown leather with broken glass, defacing and spoiling the memento he is supposed to use and animate. The exchange is seen, like the cuddle, to bring some comfort to the grieving parent. To the guilty child, its death-bearing identification is too heavy. James has a horror of Ryan's house, running as fast as he can out of the dead child's room. His wish to leave the shoes in Ryan's household is palpable. The film cuts from the image of James scratching the shoes to a pensive shot of him staring into the canal, the dark watery space which encircles the whole of the film. The obsessive repetition of water imagery seems to say much about the draw of the death drive and the refusal of the turn to life. The reparative exchange fails in *Ratcatcher*, leaving us to question whether this failure is caused by the film's different circumstances, or whether the film offers a bleaker corrective to Caruth's tale of the pull towards life and meaning.

If *Ratcatcher* fails to confirm Caruth's intimation of the return of the life drive, the film is still usefully illuminated with reference to some of her earlier work on the temporality and disruption of trauma. In evoking a protagonist unable to witness or respond to a traumatic act, *Ratcatcher* respects thinking about the survivor (if not survival) of trauma. The film reflects in its tempo, structure and recurring motifs, the delayed and disrupted temporality of responses to trauma. This explains, I argue, the film's seeming lack of narrative drive and its numbed, almost still state (reflected too in the limbo of the dustmen's strike).

In her introduction to the volume, *Trauma: Explorations in Memory*, Caruth writes about the renewed interest in the problem of trauma in the last decades. She argues that trauma, as problem, has brought us to the boundaries of our modes of understanding: 'psychoanalysis and medically oriented psychiatry, sociology, history, and even literature all seem to be called upon to explain, to cure, or to show why it is that we can no longer simply explain or simply cure' (1995: 4). For Caruth, these disciplines are beginning to hear one another anew in the study of trauma. Her interest in the volume is in the impact of trauma on other aspects of culture, too, and she names in particular 'the construction of history in writing and film' (*Ibid.*). The major film under discussion in Caruth's volume is *Shoah* (1985), though she has written elsewhere on *Hiroshima mon amour* (see Caruth 1996). Representing a very different set of issues, a film like *Ratcatcher* can be seen to respond to trauma in its temporality and structure, as much as its excessive subject matter. Treating the film in this context necessarily aligns it with such avant-garde explorations of excess suffering, memory and mourning as found in Resnais' cinema, or indeed in the work of Chris Marker, defining the ways in which the film extends beyond British cinema.

Attempting a definition of post-traumatic stress disorder, Caruth writes:

> Most descriptions generally agree that there is a response, sometimes delayed, to an overwhelming event or events, which takes the form of repeated, intrusive hallucinations, dreams, thoughts or behaviors stemming from the event, along with numbing that may have begun during or after the experience, and possibly also increased arousal to (and avoidance of) stimuli recalling the event. (1995: 4)

Caruth specifies that the pathology of post-traumatic stress disorder cannot be defined by the event itself, but consists rather in the '*structure of its experience* or reception' (*Ibid.*). Most importantly, for my argument, the traumatic event is not assimilated or experienced fully at the time it occurs. Rather it is experienced belatedly: there is an incompletion in knowing or seeing the event. This opens the survivor up, paradoxically, to the unwilled return and recall of the event, to possession by memories of the event. These do not settle temporally or affectively but return belatedly, unpredictably. The history of the trauma remains inaccessible, while its temporality and temporal place are disturbingly disrupted. Such thinking on trauma and temporal disruption offers potential to the film-maker intent on renewing the medium's modes of representation of suffering and survival.

In *Ratcatcher* the temporal movement of the narrative is straightforward, in contradistinction to many contemporary films. Against this backbone of linear temporality, *Ratcatcher* measures the divergences and fluctuations in James's recall of Ryan's death. The film, whilst respecting and limited by its child's perspective, is also cautious about the possibility of placing James's subjective reality and experience on show. The child is to a large degree very closed from view. Ramsay reveals she chose William Eadie to play James because he was able to present an air of absence, vacancy or harshness (see Ciment 2000: 12). The viewer is left in a position to surmise James's state of mind from his numbed responses.

James's mental picture, his emotions and recall, are built out of his relation to his environment. Space and *mise-en-scène* become so many clues to his state of mind. Ramsay shows a child who does not frequently verbalise his feelings (his little sister is much more vocal and interactive). She further shows him as responsible for a traumatic death which stills his world and allows him little reprieve. Sometimes, it seems that the opening image of the child all but smothered in nylon curtain reflects the view of James's consciousness the film will offer.

Impeding our access to James's responses, delaying our understanding, *Ratcatcher* makes us look more closely at its visual and spatial evidence. While we have no mental pictures of James's brooding on Ryan's death, in some ways this death returns, and circulates in the film, in its return to images of water and in particular of the canal. The canal is a sinister, stagnant presence (the real canal on location was too polluted for Ramsay to shoot in). It is at once a real presence on the estate, yet also a prescient image of James's mind, of his depths of thought and of the reverberations of Ryan's death. Further, the watery surface appears as a mirror reflecting (mental) reality. In the returns to water imagery and the canal in particular which punctuate *Ratcatcher*, the film reflects the returns of traumatic recall. In its own structure it repeats the intrusions of recall which may dominate James's response to Ryan's death. Indeed the film returns several times to images of compulsive repeated movement: Margaret Anne rocking James's leg, James swinging in a chair, Anne-Marie swinging on the washing line. The film finds its tempo and defines its aesthetic in a reflection of its protagonist's trauma.

The first canal images come in the fight between James and Ryan. The canal becomes a point of return as James first goes back to find his shoe in the turbid water. Then it returns further in a series of scenes on the canal banks with Margaret Anne, an older girl, and a band of boys. One of the boys throws Margaret Anne's glasses into the water and they stay here through the film, just visible in the mud, a lost object in an underwater still life. After the boys have gone, Margaret Anne invites James to sit with her on a wall by the canal path. As she looks towards the canal, she says it gives her the creeps and then she asks James if he heard about the boy that drowned there. The film cuts to James saying no. Margaret Anne repeats the boy's name, 'Ryan Quinn'. Her comment, summoned by the canal's proximity, is a mental intrusion for James. While he denies knowledge of Ryan's death, it is again brought back to him. He now glances down at the open graze on Margaret Anne's knee and she lets him touch her thigh. James's first sexual experiences with Margaret Anne come in a bid for comfort and forgetting in the face of the resurgence of memories of Ryan.

The next shots of the canal come immediately after James's exchange with Mrs Quinn. He stares bleakly at the water here, only to be joined, almost ricocheting into the frame, by Kenny, a child with a mouse, Susie. Kenny becomes another double of Ryan in the film. The exchanges with him by the canal seem to allow James to repeat and recall his friendship with Ryan. The scene also reveals more of James's repression of his feelings about Ryan. He turns away from Kenny to contemplate the dark water of the canal; the film cuts to Kenny forcing Susie into the pocket of his anorak, as if James too is suddenly stifled in darkness. Kenny looks for tadpoles in the canal and the boys begin an exchange about perch in the water. While Kenny wants to collect a net from his house, James warns him that the perch would pull him under. Kenny replies that he's a great swimmer and James abruptly leaves the canal bank. In a later canal scene, Kenny is seen with his fishing net right over his head, a netted noose, making him another image of Ryan Quinn as seen in the film's opening.

In the next water scene the gang of boys is seen by the canal. One tries to push the other in 'like Ryan Quinn'. Association and recall work again to intrude for James. He falls victim to bullying. The boys threaten to throw him in the canal water, even swinging him by the arms and legs before they let him go. They then go off to Margaret Anne's house, where James has a brief encounter with her.

The film establishes the ways in which new relations with Kenny and with Margaret Anne, both associated spatially with the canal, arise after the death of Ryan Quinn. These two sets of relations are specifically juxtaposed in a scene which comes as the climax to the images of water and recall. James and his little sister have head lice; his hair is combed by his mother while Anne-Marie is scrubbed in a bath. This bathing, and cleansing is repeated in the film in a bathroom scene between James and Margaret Anne. Tenderly he combs her hair for lice, before telling her she needs to go and wash it. The film cuts to James's father asleep in bed, knocked up by Kenny's mother in distress: her son is in the canal. From the urgency of this scene, we cut to the bathroom where Margaret Anne undresses, her back to camera, while James watches from the toilet seat, catching glimpses of her body. The camera pauses on James alone as we hear the sound of the water, at once present and mnemonic, as Margaret Anne gets into the bath. In an overhead shot we see Margaret Anne going under the water to wet her hair. Her face is upside down in the frame and sinks queasily further beneath the semi-opaque, reflecting, soapy surface of the bath. Her head is completely submerged so she seems a flesh and hair shadow under the water, blurred by the soap and air bubbles. From this drowned image the film cuts to the canal and James's father dragging Kenny from the water. The images suggest and echo each other: while they represent simultaneous events, they speak too of James's painful associations, of his recalled fear as Margaret Anne slips under. Kenny is rescued, but the film cuts back to Margaret Anne now on her front, motionless, inhuman in the bath, only her hair and back visible in the frame. James is seen watching her, then looking away as she breaks through the surface and the time and sound of the shots, which had been stilled, reassert their hold. Kenny, coughing, is now sitting up in the intercut scenes; Ryan's drowning is copied and his double rescued at the moment in the film where James faces his fear of a figure drowned. The film then unfolds its most tender scene as James and Margaret Anne bath one another and play in the water.

Kenny's survival does not redeem Ryan's loss. It tells the same story differently, with a different ending. It asserts the film's ambivalence about trauma and survival, showing accidents as repeatedly urgent and haphazard, random and unrealised. James seems to find comfort, both reckoning with his fear and diverting himself from it, with Margaret Anne. Survival and optimism are intermittent in the film, rising and subsiding, with no sure basis. In this sense *Ratcatcher* is not prescriptive but patient, attentive to its child survivor, inflected by his disturbed perceptions, hesitant about whether his trauma can be adequately witnessed, remembered, represented or survived.

As mentioned above, Ramsay trained as a fine art photographer. In interview, in *Positif,* she speaks of the photographers who had a specific influence on her visual aesthetic and image construction in *Ratcatcher*: Nick Waplington, Richard Billingham and Robert Frank (see Ciment 2000: 11). She stresses that she, her director of photography Alwin Kuchler and her production designer Jane Morton looked at paintings and photographs to establish the style and visual aesthetic of her film. Rather than map these references and influences, I am interested in other dialogues which might be established between Ramsay's film-making and the photographic work of artists who have attempted to represent children within a nexus of issues about loss, transgression and sexuality.

In *Ratcatcher* Lynne Ramsay's photographing of children is painstaking and distinctive. In the scene where Margaret Anne and James bath together, lighting accentuates the pallor of their skin, their tendons and wiriness, the vertebrae of James's spine. In an earlier scene, James's little sister, Anne-Marie, played by Lynne Ramsay's niece, is also viewed bathing (again repeating water motifs in the film). She plays in the water and squirms as her mother soaps her hair. Her body, too, is pale, very skinny, visible in the frame yet not a focus of spectacle or specific attention. I want to look at the ways Ramsay escapes the type of exposure of children for which still photographer Sally Mann has been repeatedly criticised.

Anne Higonnet discusses Mann's photography in *Pictures of Innocence: The History and Crisis of Ideal Childhood*. Higonnet sums up her own general thesis as follows: 'Pictures of children are at once the most common, the most sacred, and the most controversial images of our time. They guard the cherished ideal of childhood innocence, yet they contain within them the potential to undo that ideal' (1998: 7). For Higonnet, rightly, Mann's photographs were bound to catalyse debate by virtue of their conflicting messages: childhood innocence and adult sexuality. She examines images such as 'Jessie at 5' (1987), 'Last Light' (1990) and 'The Ditch' (1987). Higonnet makes a guarded defence of Mann's work, in the first place (echoing other debates) in terms of the standing of Mann's work as art, and secondly, with more personal weight, in terms of the questions the photographs raise about maternity. Higonnet insists that the images should be seen in the context of new models of parenting which produce innovative mother-images. Conjoining Sally Mann and Courtney Love in her argument, Higonnet specifies: 'Both Sally Mann and Courtney Love turn their maternity into the vehicle of their desire. Their representations of maternity are suffused with desire, not desire in any single sexual sense, but in a much broader sense, including the need to flaunt the physical beauty of the children who are the flesh of their flesh, and the ambition to cast themselves simultaneously as mothers, as disturbingly creative artists, and as successful professionals' (1998: 199). Higonnet offers a feminist perspective, though it uneasily privileges maternal expression over childhood freedom of self negotiation.

In close readings of the images, Higonnet identifies the ways in which the mother's position is questioned in Mann's photographs. In her evocation of the birth image, 'The Ditch', for example, she writes: 'A boy, Mann's son, presses head first along a narrow channel in the sand, furrowing through the matter extending out from the photographer's, the mother's, position' (1998: 204). Reading the photograph 'Last Light', where a naked father feels the pulse in his child's neck, Higonnet writes:

> As an art historian, I think it is a modern remake of the Madonna and Child image, with the mother now the artist, and the father the parent who cradles his child against their shared knowledge of what life has in store. As a parent it seems to me the child is achingly beautiful, too precious not to dread losing – so quickly, the watch on the father's wrist and the child's pulse remind me. (1998: 202)

While some read threat more directly into the image – seeing the child strangled by the father – for Higonnet loss and fragility relate more directly to the loss in growing up and leaving childhood. Higonnet argues that 'when Mann stops ripping at old fantasies of a naturally ideal innocence, she presents startlingly novel archetypes' (1998: 204). Higonnet's argument works to open up new spaces for the viewing of Mann's work and for refusing to regard its intent as pernicious and its effect as pornographic.

One of Mann's collections of photographs is titled *Still Time* (1994). The collection opens with a quotation from Eric Ormsby's 'Childhood House' where he writes: 'Somehow I had assumed that the past stood still, in perfected effigies of itself, and that what we had once possessed remained our possession forever, and that at least the past, our past, our childhood, waited, always available, at the touch of a nerve, did not deteriorate like the untended house of an aging mother, but stood in pristine perfection, as in our remembrance' (Mann 1994: 5). Ormsby goes on to lament the passing of time and the decay of memory, eluding all recovery. The epigraph offers pause for thought in a collection entitled *Still Time*.

Still Time shows stone as friable, place as decayed, in its early black and white images. Yet this imaging of time passed and passing is transmuted into images of stillness in the polaroids from the mid-1980s. Mann photographs twining plants and petals, as if preserved below the surface of still water. The images suggest a fixing in glass or amber, a permanent sheen stretched over the delicate textures of the vegetable matter imaged. The aesthetic seems to be repeated in her later images of her children, in particular the images from *Immediate Family* and *Family Colour* collected in *Still Time*. Water returns in the image of the still surface of the lake in the menacing 'The Last Time Emmett Modeled Nude'. In other images, the glossy, reflecting colours of food dyes – raspberry pink, blood red – seem to daub the children, making them directly works of art, stilling them as aesthetic, yet messy, childish objects of beauty. Although defensively acknowledging the passing of time, Mann's photography seems to celebrate its own capacity to commemorate past moments and to still them on the photographic plate, on the glossy paper of the Aperture catalogue. She may, as Higonnet argues, radically re-view the role and sexuality of the mother as photographer. Yet in keeping with the tradition from which she is differentiated by Higonnet, Mann perpetuates a backward glance at childhood, an elegiac, if fiercely contemporary view of childish beauty. Still time is both regretted because lost and recovered nostalgically through the aesthetics of photography.

Ramsay, conversely, replaces retrospection with a cautious bid for futurity. Key here is the image of the house of childhood. In Mann's epigraph to *Still Time,* this is the past home, between preservation and decay. The image of the dream house in *Ratcatcher* is the house which James's family does not yet own. It is the house on the new estate across the fields, perfect because it is empty, still plastic wrapped, not yet inhabited. The exploration of the house in its extraordinary yellow field setting (recalling Wyeth's *Christina's World*) comes as a bid to escape the deathly pull of the canal and of the drowned child. The house is a space of transition between imagination and material reality. This is illustrated in the moment where James enters the kitchen of the dream house. Music, echoing the soundtrack of *Badlands* (1971), begins to play. Through the frame of the kitchen window the expanse of the field is visible, like a framed picture. James is seen to climb onto the draining board and then right out through the window – the glass is not yet in place – into the dream or fantasy space of the field. He rolls in the wheat, caught in the sun, in some of the most plainly beautiful and liberating shots of the film.

The house of childhood in *Ratcatcher* is an open space of the imagination and transgression where James is not held behind glass, neither fixed as ideal image or as mourned child. The stillness and still time of *Ratcatcher* speak of the stasis and circularity of trauma and traumatic response. They are imaged in the engulfing water which returns in the film. Still time is associated with the death-bearing inability to move on from the past and move out of childhood. This is the antithesis of the glazed nostalgia of Mann's childhood shots. While it is by no means certain that James will survive his ordeal and prove able to emerge from the stillness of his mourning to move into the empty space of the new house, the film nevertheless images this prospective move as progress.

The still time of childhood entraps the child in *Ratcatcher*. Ramsay shows the ways in which adult demands on the child are exorbitant; the child seeks to exit from the adult's system of exchange (embodied in its most excusable form in Mrs Quinn's mourning rituals) and from adult-orchestrated systems of representation. James may not be able to free himself from the clinging stillness – the still water – which is the immediate aftermath and after-image of Ryan's death. Yet *Ratcatcher* is finally liberating in its ability to bear witness to childhood in modes of representation which exceed and disrupt photographic and affective norms, which gesture toward a futurity in which childhood may be gladly left behind.

CHAPTER NINE

Dogme Ghosts

In his essay, 'Fathers, Fathers Everywhere', Slavoj Žižek explores the role of the father as figure of authority in Roberto Benigni's *Life Is Beautiful* (1998) and Thomas Vinterberg's *Celebration* (1998). He draws attention to the suspension of the agency of symbolic law (paternal authority) in both films. Žižek suggests that the treatment of the thematics of abuse and abusive parenthood has lost its 'innocence' (an apt concern near the end of this study); that the impact of films which treat such themes is to be found doubly in their self-consciousness as representation (postmodern pastiche) and in their revelation of the fantasies which construct paternal/filial relations (2000: 30). Looking at Dogme film-making, which reflects many of the concerns of the films discussed here, I consider the ways in which such films question paternal authority in their treatment of the missing child as subject and, more substantially in their interrogation of film (and television) as testimony.

Vinterberg's *Celebration* was released as *Dogme#1: Festen* and was the first of the Dogme films which arise out of Dogme 95, a collective of film directors founded in Copenhagen in Spring 1995. On behalf of this collective, Lars von Trier and Thomas Vinterberg drew up a series of ten rules to which a film director would need to submit for his or her film to acquire Dogme status. The rules are as follows:

1   Shooting must be done on location. Props and sets must not be brought in (if a particular prop is necessary for the story, a location must be chosen where this prop is to be found).

2   The sound must never be produced apart from the images, or vice versa. (Music must not be used unless it occurs where the scene is being shot.)

3   The camera must be hand-held. Any movement or immobility attainable in the hand is permitted. (The film must not take place where the camera is standing; shooting must take place where the film takes place.)

4   The film must be in colour. Special lighting is not acceptable. (If there is too little light for exposure the scene must be cut or a single lamp be attached to the camera.)

5   Optical work and filters are forbidden.

6   The film must not contain superficial action. (Murders, weapons, etc. must not occur.)

7   Temporal and geographical alienation are forbidden. (That is to say that the film takes place here and now.)

8   Genre movies are not acceptable.

9   The film format must be Academy 35mm.

10 The director must not be credited.[1]

These constraints, whose impact is discussed repeatedly in criticism of the Dogme films, are largely formal. They have resulted in a particular Dogme aesthetic. Less attention has been paid to the specificity of the subject matter of the Dogme films. Subject matter is partly delimited by the formal constraints, but beyond this, certain conventions seem to have arisen. In his book about the Dogme films, Richard Kelly says to Vinterberg: 'I've been wondering whether the rules inspire certain types of script, or whether certain types of script lend themselves well to the Rules.' Vinterberg replies: 'they all seem to be group portraits. They're all very melodramatic, in a way; the emotional life is very explosive' (Kelly 2000: 114). This melodramatic, emotional mood, interestingly, often manifests itself in dramas about the loss of childhood, about missing children and child abuse. Rather than seeing these subjects as necessarily suggested by the formal constraints of the Dogme rules, I suggest that their manner of treatment itself contests the dogmatism of the Rules' authority.

In the manifesto which accompanies the Rules, von Trier and Vinterberg speak against cinema as illusion. They suggest that Dogme 95 counters the film of illusion – illusions of pathos, illusions of love – by attempting to force the truth out of characters and settings. Dogme 95 has been seen to produce a new form of realism, a form of cinematic despectacularisation which has been closely associated with the development of Digital Video and the increasing breakdown of divisions between 'amateur' movie making and cinema as high art. Dogme 95 has produced in effect a new type of home movie, transferred onto 35mm for theatre presentation. In this new, stripped realist aesthetic, however, perhaps the points of greatest interest are, paradoxically, found in the last remnants and remainders of illusion.

Celebration represents a family birthday party at which a grown son accuses his father of sexual abuse of himself and his sister Linda, who has recently committed suicide. The shooting of the film, with hand-held cameras and natural lighting, is true to the realist aesthetic of Dogme 95. The very subject matter of the film – the son's revelation – becomes his attempt to force the truth out of his father, in the group family setting. His speech is even called a 'home truth' speech. Yet the difficulty of reaching a truth seems illustrated in the repetitive structure of the film, in the repeated breakdown and restructuring of the family group, in the son's need to return to and restate his revelation. As much as claiming itself as truth-bearing medium, the film is attuned to the mechanisms by which truth is denied and disavowed.

Further, *Celebration* explores the ways in which, within the constraints of the Rules, a film may work to foster illusion in recalling a past time and past experience, as it may also work to represent a psychical or dream-like reality. This is despite Rule 7 which states that temporal and geographical alienation are forbidden. Such expansion of the realist aesthetic is found notably in several scenes where the dead sister Linda supposedly returns. Helene, her sister, has been given the room where Linda died. We see it draped in dust sheets, concealed, as the family has repressed Linda's death. Although Helene says the room is spooky, like a haunted house, she decides to stay with her sister. The sister's presence is figured visually with utmost simplicity. There is a sudden change of perspective so the point of view is disembodied. We see a curtain blowing. The use of overhead shots, tentative, hovering, offers the illusion of a presence or observer.

A phantom Linda is seen further in a scene late in the film where Christian, the son, feels ill and falls to the ground. A shot of his sister is seen immediately after. The scene is dark, only candle-lit, and she flickers in and out of view. Brother and phantom sister speak of missing one another and embrace in the candlelight. Merely through its lighting and warm colours, the scene is marked out as visually distinct from others in the film. From its embedding in a psychological narrative we might see it as a hallucinatory or wish-fulfilment scene, supplementing the realist aesthetic of the film. Indeed in filming a phantom appearance with such simplicity and intimacy, with no special effects, *Celebration* seems to foster the illusion that 'truthful' film-making, with its realist aesthetic and 'home movie' values, can also sometimes capture and record moments beyond the literal visual and experiential register. As such, the film taps the desire of the viewer of home movie footage who seeks the phantom presence and animation of lost relatives and loved ones, who seeks an image of childhood, of experience, that is more than what can be recalled. *Celebration* films a moment of interference between psychical and material reality: in this respect, in its representation of the return of the phantom of the abused child, it challenges the hegemony of the rules which determine its filmic creation.

While I have begun with *Celebration* here, this chapter is mostly concerned with the films of Lars von Trier, and in particular with his television series *The Kingdom* (1994), an important aesthetic and psychological determinant of Dogme 95. Von Trier has been interested in the representation of missing children and traumatised childhood from his earliest films. *The Element of Crime* (1984) is a noir psychological thriller, narrated by a detective, Fisher, under hypnosis. Fisher is remembering his investigation of the 'Lotto' murders: little girl lottery ticket sellers have been ritually murdered and mutilated. Fisher follows the path of the killer, Harry Grey, and himself becomes the perpetrator of the last crime. He waits with a little girl who he is using as bait to catch the killer. A talisman, seen at each crime scene, slips from his pocket. The child panics, trying to smash her way out of the disused property where they wait. Fisher holds her back to restrain her and to prevent her disappearing into the night where Grey may be waiting. The child dies in the struggle. *The Element of Crime* partly recalls *M* (1931) in its treatment of child murder and criminality. Insistently here von Trier figures the pathos and purity of the child's image. The child is seen holding a doll, like a miniature image of herself. The shots are self-consciously pictorial as she is seen lying upside down and then silhouetted with the doll. Her fearful reaction to the talisman is shown in a shot/reverse shot sequence as she sees Fisher's threat and he sees her fear.

From this first film, von Trier manifests a gloating interest in suffering femininity and female sacrifice. The figures of suffering women of his later films – Bess in *Breaking the Waves* (1996) or Selma in *Dancer in the Dark* (2000) – find their forbear and model in von Trier's film-making in the image of the traumatised child. In *The Element of Crime*, the first of von Trier's so-called European trilogy (also comprising *Epidemic* (1987) and *Europa* (1991)), the suffering of children is taken as emblem within a broader post-war perspective on suffering, inhumanity and recrimination. The suffering of children is made part of a larger-scale brutalism and deterioration of moral values (as witnessed too, for example, in Michel Tournier's novel *Le Roi des aulnes*). In *The Kingdom* the suffering of children is explored more specifically within a family context, whilst the series asks larger questions about the past and phantom presences, about film and television as privileged media for the return of the unburied and the living dead.

The Kingdom, which currently runs to ten hour-long episodes, prefigures the aesthetic of Dogme 95 and its imbrication with questions of the family, abuse and truth. The opening titles' shots of *The Kingdom* bring with them the words: 'the portals of the Kingdom are opening'. While the television serial is about a modern Copenhagen hospital, this institution is built on unstable foundations, on wet marshland. The opening of the serial presages the return of the primeval, of hidden, mystical forces in the world of modern science, medicine and order. In an image reminiscent of the animations of Jan Svankmajer, we see etiolated hands growing upwards like roots. From the start of the serial von Trier recalls the subterranean and underwater imagery of his previous films, of *The Element of Crime*, of *Epidemic* and *Europa*. In this imagery, he marks his corpus as one which feeds on the unconscious, on hidden drives, on phantoms and fantasy. As manifested later in Vinterberg's *Celebration*, a realist aesthetic – hand-held camera, video footage – is exploited in the imaging of the supernatural, of images in excess of the physical world.

The return of the dead, von Trier's subject here, and the opening of the portals of the Kingdom, are channelled in the serial through the story of Mary, a ghostly child. We first become aware of Mary's presence in the hospital as Mrs Drusse, an elderly patient and mother of one of the hospital orderlies, hears crying when she is in the lift. Although she is told that the lift passes the children's ward, she understands that the crying comes from the lift shaft. This liminal space, seen as towering and limitless, is the space of interference in the serial between material reality and the spirit world. Mrs Drusse returns to the lift to hear the child crying. A tile on the roof of the lift is missing and the camera looks down on Mrs Drusse through this crevice, as if seeing her from the phantom child's perspective. Mrs Drusse reaches upwards, but she does not see Mary until the very end of the first episode, when she returns to the lift once more. Up in the lift shaft now, she sees a ghostly child ringing a bell. The image is pale and overexposed, consciously pictorial like the image of the child with her doll in *The Element of Crime*, reminiscent of a sepia photograph.

While Mary's image is the parting shot of the first episode, and her returning presence is a narrative thread in the episodes which follow, she is not the only damaged and mournful child of *The Kingdom*. Mirroring Mary, and partly reliving her story, is another small girl, Mona. Mona has brain damage as the result of a bungled operation carried out by the neurosurgeon Stig Helmer. Like Mary, alone in the lift shaft, Mona too is seen as a missing child. The first episode shows a searing overhead shot of Mona rocking back and forth. Von Trier uses a long take and still camera to draw attention to her image. Her mother berates the surgeon, 'you've taken her from me', whilst also gently tending her child. In a shot which looks forward to the pathos of the closing scenes of *The Idiots* (1998), the mother herself is rocked and comforted by Mona's nurse.

Figure 10 *The Element of Crime*

In episode two of *The Kingdom* Mary appears again and her role is now more clearly defined. In her phantom form she joins a hypnotised man who is undergoing an operation. She is invisible to the doctors and nurses in the operating theatre but visible to the suffering patient. She comforts him and strokes his hand. On awakening he testifies: 'There was a little girl'; 'I was very unsettled and she stroked my hand.' He continues: 'She tried to talk to the surgeon but he wouldn't listen.' The serial begins to insist on Mary's role as witness. She is comforter, bringing solace, as she will come to visit the pregnant woman Judith. She is also seeking expression and a means to tell her story through her insistent return. This search is shadowed by Mona's failed attempts at expression: in episode two Mona is seen surrounded by her own abstract, messy artwork. While she can neither make images or words, the red paint with which she daubs her paper and her whole room (as seen at the start of episode three) seems to express the mess and despair of her mind.

In episode three, Mrs Drusse finds more evidence of Mary's fate; it is revealed that she was ill in her father's hospital where she would be treated for free. The child is seen in a photograph with her father. She appears angelic with blond plaits and is described as 'so good and gentle'. Mrs Drusse continues to summon the ghost child and to ask her: 'Were you crying because someone hurt you?' Mary's words, 'Why must I be killed?', return towards the end of the episode. After it ends von Trier remarks: 'What we all hide away never really disappears ... a scream from the past can echo'. In episode four Mary is seen and heard screaming in the lift shaft.

Mrs Drusse determines to find out where Mary was buried. As she goes through the records looking for evidence, she makes a sickening discovery. We see Mrs Drusse's reaction shot before we see the object viewed. Her mouth is open in horror; the shot is matched by a close-up image of a child's mouth preserved in formaldehyde. Mary's scream can still be heard against the shots as the image recedes in jolts to show the full, tiny body encased in glass and viscous liquid. She is there as an oversized specimen in the pathologist's study. She stands naked in the fluid like a small nereid. Her hair is wild and her features are rudimentary. Her image would seem that of a sepia photograph, faded and rubbed, if it were not for its fearful, tactile dimensions, its monstrous presence. Seeing Mary's preserved form against an ensemble of glass specimen bottles triggers questions about science and horror, about the proximity between the images of specimens and freak-show spectacle.

The shots of Mary, even here as preserved corpse, are reminiscent of those of the girls murdered and mutilated in *The Element of Crime*. The gothic horror of *The Kingdom* makes the image one degree more unbearable as we see the child in liquid. Yet its presence also triggers meditation on the status of cinema as medium of preservation and reanimation of the dead. The image of Mary's corpse is a spectacular image in its brute horror. Its appearance behind glass signals it nevertheless as aesthetic image and as image through which von Trier both repeats and critiques the spectacularisation of suffering. This has become the signature image of *The Kingdom*, where Mary's pale dead face and open lips, reminiscent of the Medusa and Munch's *Scream*, figures in publicity material surrounding the serial. Von Trier's cinema, as the image designates, exists between testimony and spectacle.

Mrs Drusse seeks to offer Mary a proper burial. Burial is seen to be bound up with telling Mary's story. The narration of her attempts to do this trigger a sepia flashback to Mary's suffering at the hands of her father. Mary, clutching her doll, runs ahead along a rain-soaked road as she is followed by a coach and horses. She runs away from the hospital but is recaptured by her father. The child falls and cries out as her father reaches her and traps her. She is carried screaming into the vehicle. As the figure in formaldehyde is lowered into a hole in the ground, Mrs Drusse prays: 'We hope your little, troubled soul may find peace.' The camera swings round to show Mrs Drusse spooning earth onto the glass coffin. We see the face in close-up once more as it is covered over, submerged in earth. The episode ends with Mrs Drusse attempting to put together the evidence she has about Mary. Her image is superimposed on a montage sequence of shots which recall the evidence about Mary the viewer has already gleaned in the serial. It is as if we have access to Mrs Drusse's memory images, to her psychical reality, as she attempts to summon a coherent narrative of Mary's pain, of her death and her ghost's return.

Despite the burial, Mary's story returns again in episode five, 'The Living Dead'. A flashback returns us to the ambulance where Mary is carried away by her father and again she asks her question. We see her face in profile, from above; it is piteous as she weeps, wet from the falling rain. She is huddled in her suffering, as her father appears, demonic, above her. She now confronts him: 'You want to kill me with the gas'; he hits her to silence her. The camera returns to Mary, her face now very pale, though colour is in her lips. She states: 'Your crime will never be forgotten.' She names and accuses her father. The flashback cuts to Mrs Drusse, whose thought patterns the film shows, as she herself responds to the truth she has deduced. She has been carrying Mary's doll; she drops it as she makes her realisation. It is suddenly grabbed by a phantom hand reaching through the floor grating. Mary's ghost is still at large in the hospital. Mrs Drusse wrestles with the child, keeping her present and listening to her testimony. The child cries, now addressing her mother: 'I feel so ill, Mother.' The image of Mary's mother appears superimposed over the child's face, as a double exposure. The child cries, 'I miss you so, Mother.' The mother reveals the truth of her child's restless spirit: 'You must wander alone every night. No one will testify to Krüger's crime.'

As we discover Mary's fate – illegitimate child murdered by her father – we see an image of her lying curled on the floor. Her image is at once spectral – this is a double exposure – and also foetal as her head curves in on her body. Her face is outlined in light and we see her trembling in fear. It is as if we see an old photograph in animation (in keeping with the aesthetics of both the flashbacks and the ghostly, atemporal presence of Mary in the hospital). Although it is an image of the child before death, it also looks forward (or back) to the mortuary photography recalled in *Jude* or indeed in *The Others* (2001). From the ghostly child's mouth a pool of blood collects on the corridor floor. As the present blood seeps out, the image of the ghostly child fades. Blood has been seen previously in the lift; the fabric of the Kingdom is impregnated with the blood which signifies Mary's suffering. As with the images of return, harrowing and resurrection with which the serial starts, here we see the source of the returning evidence of suffering and misdeeds. The hospital bleeds for its past patients, its fabric is sentient.

Mrs Drusse, possessed of knowledge about Mary, realises that the phantom child is reliving her last day. She determines that Mary must join her mother, her spirit as well as her body must be laid to rest. Together with her son and one of the doctors, she carries out an exorcism, chasing the phantom child away through a hole in the wall to join her mother on the other side. Each of the exorcists testifies before God, 'that Age Krüger killed Mary Jensen'. Mary's story has been made a visual narrative in Mrs Drusse's thought-patterns; now the exorcists are witnesses to her suffering and offer testimony to her fate. *The Kingdom* testifies to the importance of placing trauma in narrative, visual and verbal. The series remains more equivocal, however, about whether this process can bring proper burial, symbolisation and closure.

In *Looking Awry*, Žižek argues: 'if there is a phenomenon that fully deserves to be called the "fundamental fantasy of contemporary mass culture," it is [the] fantasy of the return of the living dead: the fantasy of a person who does not want to stay dead but returns again and again to pose a threat to the living' (1991: 22). In defining this fundamental fantasy, Žižek refers first of all to popular culture, in particular to horror and slasher movies:

> The unattained archetype of a long series – from the psychotic killer in *Halloween* to Jason in *Friday the Thirteenth* – is still George Romero's *The Night of the Living Dead*, where the 'undead' are not portrayed as embodiments of pure evil, of a simple drive to kill or revenge, but as sufferers, pursuing their victims with an awkward persistence, colored by a kind of infinite sadness. (1991: 22–3)

The Kingdom has been associated by certain critics with genre horror: while describing it as a 'post-*Twin Peaks* miniseries', and comparing it to *The X-Files*, Howard Hampton comments on the familiarity of the series – it is 'as if *St. Elsewhere* were infiltrated by the restless souls of *Poltergeist*' (1995: 46). Marie-Eve Poisson mentions *The Shining* (1980) in dialogue with Lars von Trier about *The Kingdom* (1995: 120). Philip Mather compares Mary's father (Dr Krüger) to Freddy Krueger in *Nightmare on Elm Street* (1984) (1995: 17). *Variety* describes *The Kingdom* as a 'meld of black-comedy soap and Z-grade horror flick',[2] comparisons between *The Kingdom* and television series like *E.R.* and *Homicide* abound. French critic Mark Le Fanu, tapping a different vein, compares the work to other projects conceived for television which work successfully in the cinema; he names *Heimat* (1984) and *Shoah* (1985) (1995: 117). This range of comparisons and allusions is telling in the context of Žižek's argument on the living dead in *Looking Awry*.

Žižek, taking horror films more seriously than some of von Trier's critics, constructs an argument which sees the return of the living dead repeated as fantasy in both popular culture and in the history and memorialisation of mass trauma in the twentieth century: 'The two great traumatic events of the holocaust and the gulag are, of course, exemplary cases of the return of the dead in the twentieth century. The shadows of their victims will continue to chase us as "living dead" until we give them a decent burial, until we integrate the trauma of their death into our historical memory' (1991: 23). (The use of 'until' seems tactically ambiguous, the statement remaining open about whether or not this decent burial may ever be achieved.) Žižek justifies his lightning move from Romero's living dead to discussion of the holocaust by asking what he describes as 'a naïve and elementary question': why do the dead return? He contends: 'The answer offered by Lacan is the same as that found in popular culture: *because they were not properly buried*, i.e., because something went wrong with their obsequies. The return of the dead is a sign of a disturbance in the symbolic rite, in the process of symbolisation; the dead return as collectors of some unpaid symbolic debt' (*Ibid.*). The same answer seems offered too by Lars von Trier where, in *The Kingdom*, Mary is improperly buried, indeed she has not been buried at all. Further, she is seen to return again and again in an attempt to testify to her murder by her father and to allow this crime to be symbolised. (As Žižek reminds us: 'the return of the dead signifies that they cannot find their proper place in the text of tradition' (*Ibid.*).)

In the context of this broader project, my interest is in the ways in which for von Trier, the return of the living dead is figured through the fantasy of the child, Mary, who returns to the site of her death. The child has been the victim of the Father-of-Enjoyment, described by Žižek as 'this figure split between cruel revenge and crazy laughter, as, for example, the famous Freddy from *Nightmare on Elm Street*' (1991: 23). For Lars von Trier, and other contemporary film-makers, the phantom presence and recurrence of the ghosts of missing and suffering children offer a further instance of the return of the living dead. These are phantoms which return, between truth and fiction, in the complex cases of false memory syndrome; these are the photographic and video phantoms which haunt news reporting of missing children, these are the mourned and elegiac figures which return in contemporary cinema.

As Žižek has shown, popular culture has been extraordinarily reflective and expressive of the fundamental fantasies of contemporary culture. While missing and traumatised children have certainly been a staple part of contemporary horror, I have argued that this concern returns in recent independent and art film. Indeed some explanation for this can be found in the very questions which, for Žižek, the living dead seek to settle on their return: questions of symbolisation, of memory, symbolic tradition and representation.

On one level, in *The Kingdom*, Mary's ghost is exorcised and she is laid to rest, through the labour and compassion of Mrs Drusse. The events surrounding her death are quite literally symbolised as the exorcists speak the words which tell the truth of her murder by her father. Yet on another level, the series asks how film itself as medium can represent – symbolise – the suffering of children. The questions which seem to be resolved and closed in Mary's burial and exorcism are, I think, conversely opened and interrogated again through attention to Mona and the further telling of her story in the second five episodes of *The Kingdom*. Mary's story reverberates and returns more importantly throughout von Trier's later film-making to date. The return of the living dead, the phantom presence of the missing child, subtends, unsettles and dictates his Dogme films.

Dogme#2, following Vinterberg's *Celebration*, is von Trier's *The Idiots*. Comparing the film to his previous *Breaking the Waves*, von Trier has said: '*The Idiots* is a more complex, far weirder film, a film you ought to be amused and moved by, but also a bit disturbed by. The film contains a dangerousness because it juggles with the concept of normality, with the way we ought to and ought not to behave.'[3] Connected to this question of normality, of how to behave, is a history of mourning and responses to loss. On one level *The Idiots* as drama contends with inadequate responses to people with special needs and mental health problems. A group of individuals, loosely organised by a disaffected bourgeois, Stoffer, imitate the behaviour of 'idiots'. Their purpose is double: to undo social codes of behaviour in an anarchic manner, revealing in particular hidden prejudices and hypocrisy; to allow the individual to search for their 'inner idiot', finding release in a hyperbolic performance of emotion and reaction. Von Trier's strategy is relentless whereby from scene to scene the viewer's perception of differences between performance and reality, sanity and insanity is unsettled. This seems a particular effect, too, of the aesthetic created by the codes of the Dogme rules. The camera appears to capture and respond to group events or happenings, rather than record performed drama. This technique, with its riveting immediacy and responsiveness, is counterpointed by moments of withdrawal and reflection where the protagonists are 'interviewed', speaking their feelings in retrospect to camera. Although the interviewer is absent, his voice seems to be that of Lars von Trier. The technique adds to the sense of veracity and experimental film-making which *The Idiots* cultivates in its aesthetic and theme. It also marks out the role of the director, uncredited according to the Dogme rules, yet nevertheless a central presence in the very process of film-making here, coaxing performance and confessions from his cast.

A guiding thread through the film's series of rituals, events and crises is the protagonist Karen. The film begins with Karen at a fairground. She is seen from above riding along in a pony carriage, her yellow cardigan in strong contrast to the blue of the carriage. She seems dwarfed somewhat by the angle of the shot, like a child in a buggy. From these images of her loneliness in the space of the fairground, the film cuts to Karen in a restaurant. Through these initial parts of the film she is cut off from contact with others and in isolation. This is broken by Stoffer whom we encounter for the first time in this restaurant, being fed by another character, Susanne. Stoffer creates a scene as he walks about the restaurant, unsettling fellow diners and the waiter. Stoffer goes up to Karen and strokes her face. She holds his hand and offers to go outside with him, to encourage him to leave the restaurant. He firmly clasps her hand. We see them outside while Susanne tells Stoffer that he must leave Karen now. The film cuts to a shot of Karen sitting in the back of a taxi with Stoffer still holding her hand. It is as if she has been adopted and chosen for the group through her unwavering gentleness and compassion to Stoffer.

There follows one of the false documentary interview scenes. One character, speaking to camera, says: 'Karen was the last to join the group.' Another, edited in, continues: 'I think she'd have joined anything.' Why this might be is left out. The film seems to respect Karen's tentative involvement in the group's activities. In several shots she is seen from a distance, wandering outside the range of the group. In a scene where she is alone, in profile by an open window, we see her making a telephone call, but then not speaking to the voice on the line, remaining very still, silently weeping to herself. Her profile here is in close-up as, like Julie in *Three Colours: Blue*, she shrouds her face with her hand, in a gesture of comfort and denial. In a later interview another character confirms: 'It turned out that Karen really needed us badly.'

Karen's tragedy remains opaque. What she receives is unconditional comfort, in particular from Susanne, whose role is marked out in a scene between the two women. Karen is seen at the far left of the frame, standing by a window, in her black and white dress. Only her hair is visible as she looks out. The film cuts to a shot of Susanne coming closer; she is in shadow but the light, soft and hazy, highlights her face and angelic hair. She sits beside Karen at the window, their profiled faces close. Karen weeps that they are so happy there and that she has no right to be happy. Susanne comforts her and the camera moves from Susanne's face to Karen's, in close-up, weeping. Susanne's hand, like Stoffer's before, like Karen's own, is seen gently stroking Karen's hair, seeming to support her face. Susanne says: 'You're allowed to be here and you're allowed to be happy.' We see them both briefly in the frame as the camera hesitates and hovers between them. As in the tender scenes between Bess and Dodo in *Breaking the Waves*, without irony Lars von Trier shows moments of comfort between women. This fits an image of both suffering femininity and angelised maternity. The camera claims the privilege to witness these scenes, to respond to and imitate their pace and not to intrude

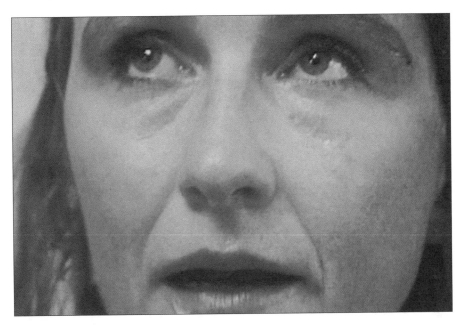

Figure 11 *The Idiots*

on their privacy (here the two women are shown entirely absorbed in their attention to each other).

If Susanne pays maternal attention to Karen, this allows Karen to begin playing (up) and to find her 'inner idiot', resulting finally in her willingness to go home and to see if she can be an 'idiot' there. She does this to prove to the other members of the group that all their activities have been worthwhile. The return home leads to the film's revelation of Karen's tragedy and grief. As she enters her family home with Susanne, the viewer is left to see her relatives' muted, unemotional responses to her. A sister explains to Susanne that they have not seen her for two weeks, since the day before the funeral. She then puts Karen's loss into words: 'Anders and Karen lost their little boy.' She continues to say that the death probably hurt Anders most. The film undercuts this as Susanne goes to find Karen and locates her looking at a photo of her baby.

The film offers a close-up of the baby photo in its silver frame held in Karen's palm. Her thumb is against the glass in a tactile image of contact between grieving mother and image of the missing child (the image is reminiscent of the mourning contact of both *Three Colours: Blue* and *The Portrait of a Lady*). Karen is seen to stroke the image lightly with her hand. We see a tiny baby, wrapped in a white hospital shift, its identification tag on its ankle. It is unclear in the image whether the baby is sleeping or whether this is a post mortem photograph taken shortly after the infant has died. As discussed in the chapter on *Jude*, such photographs serve in the long process of a parent mourning a child, commemorating the brief life and showing the presence of the beloved child. In Karen's picture there is possibly some blood or staining on the sheet beneath the child. The pathos of the image of the tiny child is fiercely enhanced by this intimation of its fragility and medical trauma. The still image which Karen holds, which we see within the frame for only a few moments, stands in stark contrast to the moving images, and hand-held camera work of von Trier's cinema. His film-making more generally, its compassion and proximity, its means of making contact, drawing links between its protagonists in continuous sweeping takes, seems an antidote to the desperate division Karen experiences in the fixity of her family home.

The camera moves from the image of the tiny child to show Karen, her head bowed, looking at the photograph, bringing her hand up to her face. Susanne, in shadow, is close beside her in the next shot. Her image is somewhat blurred, indistinct, marking her moving presence and the intensity of the emotion and feeling between the two protagonists. She says, 'My pet', and we see her wipe away Karen's tears and stroke her hair again, tending to her as if she were a grieving child. Their faces are caught together within the frame, bowing in to one another, as von Trier shows their contact with one another and Susanne's ability to find an apt response to Karen's grief. They clasp hands and Karen is seen to cry with Susanne beside her.

This interlude and Karen's small relief then lead into the arrival of Anders and the freezing of the family atmosphere once more. Karen, true to her statement to the group, breaks this as they eat tea and she begins to slobber her food, its creamy mess oozing from her mouth as she disintegrates, playing out the responses of her 'inner idiot'. Susanne watches her, patiently. The room is silent; suddenly Anders hits Karen and Susanne responds with tears, then says: 'That's enough now Karen.' Karen's mouth continues to leak, now dark liquid from the tea she has been drinking, as more tears spill over her face. Susanne and Karen decide to leave, Susanne holding Karen's hand as they walk away.

Karen's responses are explained in the context of her family: we understand why she has attached herself to the group and how their ethos offers a more viable, emotional alternative to her. The film allows us to realign how we respond to the anarchic 'idiot' performance. For Karen it seems to offer more than the numbing of emotions of her family; it offers some small sense of release and catharsis, it generates the tenderness of Susanne's non-judgemental, overarching sympathy and protection.

Von Trier has described *The Idiots* as a political film. He imagines the situation where such hyperbolic performance is at once a rational response to the horror and excess of emotion and also a soothing exorcism of pain and grief. He shows the ways in which new relations of tolerance, of tenderness, of nurturing can replace and withstand the normative functioning of the family.

Dogme film-making as pre-viewed and developed in the television series *The Kingdom* and as realised in *Celebration* and *The Idiots* turns out at least in its initial stages to be bound up with issues of the family, of loss and commemoration. Such films offer a lurid re-vision of the home movie, in their hand-held camera aesthetic and improvisation, yet also in their treatment of intimate family histories (the same might be said of Harmony Korine's 2000 film *julien donkey-boy*). In *The Kingdom* von Trier explores the possibility of film as a medium of commemoration and witnessing. He exploits the spectral, retrospective dimension of cinema in order to show the conjuring of spirits, the insistence of unfinished business. In his searing, doubly exposed images of the child who haunts the hospital, in the sounds of her cries which inflect the soundtrack, von Trier seems to mould his filming to make it adequate to respect and respond to the child as returning spectre. Hers is a drama of failed witnessing, of inadequate symbolisation. The drama raises questions about its own role in symbolising trauma and abuse, about its ability to insert these issues into cinematic tradition, to conjure them up in order to lay them to rest. These are issues which cut to the heart of questions about the role of cinema itself as witness, as testimony to current abuses and as reflector of contemporary fundamental fantasies.

As von Trier returns to the legacy of dead and mourned children in *The Idiots* he expands on an ethos and aesthetics of respect, proximity and tenderness in Susanne's attention to Karen and in the camera's feeling, mobile imitation of her moves. Cinematic adequacy and social adequacy are brought simultaneously into question as von Trier works with the medium and its interactions and interface with social reality in order to bring about new social and cinematic contact (it is no coincidence that the hand and touch should receive such privileged attention in the film, as in Jane Campion's work).

Dogme film-making works to attack social codes and symbolic structures – the law of the father – in order to re-view human inter-relation and cinematic symbolisation. It is a nice irony that discussion of Dogme film-making has been so dogged by questions of the Rules, of their enforcement or transgression in individual Dogme films. My sense is that a different understanding of the films breaks through in analysis of the inter-relation of their form and content, in an understanding of the insistence of childhood suffering, loss and mourning as subject. The Dogme brothers set up an artificial law of the father, a set of rules within and against which they work. Yet in their films they repeatedly return to re-present, pastiche and so dissolve the power of fake and faulty paternal authority, of the sexual abuser in *Celebration*, of the murderer in *The Kingdom*, of the broader paternal social and familiar structure in *The Idiots*. The drama of the missing child returns as a crucial testing ground of paternal authority, of its abuse and dismantling. Dogme films create a contestatory ethos which questions the possibility of cinema as witness to suffering and as force of social intervention. Hand-held proximity, tenderness and limitless freedom of imagination are offered as tentative responses to abuse and suffering, their possibilities of representation in cinema. Dogme films form a minimal cinema, a cinema constrained to interrogate the limits of its representational capacity. In these limits, such films also respond to the challenge of emotional extremes, of the feeling, desperate subject of the missing child.

CHAPTER TEN

Moving On: *The Son's Room*

When Nanni Moretti's film, *The Son's Room* (2001), won the Palme d'Or at Cannes it confirmed the persistence of a trend of films which, in very different ways, look at missing or dead children, malign or mourning parents and disassembled families. Interviewed in *Sight and Sound*, Moretti was asked whether he had watched other films on a similar theme. He acknowledged: 'Yes, I watched *Dekalog 1* and *Three Colours: Blue.* … But when I shoot I never think of other directors, nor do I pay homage or make direct references. Things are different when I'm working on the script – at that stage I watch films that have struck me, like *Exotica*' (in Bonsaver 2002: 30). While, as Moretti suggests, there are few direct references to these earlier films (a fleeting Kieślowski premonition aside), *The Son's Room* nevertheless bears the marks of a decade of such emotionally charged film-making, allowing the viewer to sense the impact as well as the continued interest of the topos of the missing child. *The Son's Room*, is a film about the death of a teenage son, Andrea, in a diving accident. What it tries to envisage, tentatively, is some possibility of moving on from such excessive grief. In this respect the film seems to offer a hopeful, if hesitant, point of closure to this study as a whole. Through this film we may be led to reflect on the issues which have emerged in the films of the last decade and on the innovations in film art afforded through such close attention to fear and grief.

In Moretti's career, *The Son's Room* marks a return to fiction film after a decade marked by two innovative and teasing semi-documentaries, *Dear Diary* (1993) and *Aprile* (1998). As Philip Kemp points out, there is a significant shift in tone in *The Son's Room* (2002: 56). This shift seems consciously signalled in several ways. In *The Son's Room* Moretti plays Giovanni, the missing child's psychoanalyst father. The director/actor is seen jogging by the docks in Ancona at the start of the film, tracked by the camera as he is when riding his Vespa at the start of *Dear Diary*. Yet here, in *The Son's Room*, another man on a Vespa is seen riding off into the distance, departing from Moretti's film-making. *Dear Diary* is recalled more explicitly as we see Giovanni drink a glass of water before his morning coffee (the earlier film ends deliberately with such a shot) and, in seeming imitation of Nanni of the two earlier films, watch the dance of the Hare Krishna band. *The Son's Room* passes on from such references, leaving them behind at the start of the film. As it develops, it digs more deeply into the affective material already introduced in *Dear Diary* and *Aprile*: questions of mortality, healing and cure raised in the third section of *Dear Diary*; the ties of fatherhood shown in Nanni's relation to his baby son in the intimate strand of *Aprile* which runs in parallel to the treatment of the Italian elections.

Throughout this study I have been concerned with the questions of guilt, innocence and responsibility in the treatment of parents in missing child films. Where the fathers represented in *Happiness* or *The Kingdom* imperil their children, or their relation to their children, through abuse and desire, Moretti's Giovanni is a caring, blameless father in a loving family. He recalls the benign (yet guilt-ridden) father of Kieślowski's *Dekalog 1*. In making Giovanni's responses to his son's death the primary (but not exclusive) focus of the latter part of the film, Moretti offers a cinematic treatment of a father's grief which works to match, or complement, say, Almodóvar's representation of maternal grief in *All About My Mother*.

The family which loses its son, in *The Son's Room*, is in some senses as neutral as possible (unlike many of the families represented in the films studied here). This happy normality allows the family to work as a test case for the effects of traumatic loss to be shown in greater relief. In showing these effects, *The Son's Room* is particularly expressive in its exploration of physical correlatives in the representation of grief and suffering, and further in its attention to filmic means of representing the mental replay of events. Both of these features will be discussed in more detail below. But first I consider Giovanni's profession, his work as an analyst, the one trait which sets him apart from the normal family, and yet which is key to the questions of relief and cure which *The Son's Room* will approach in its ending. If *The Son's Room* finds ways of moving on, we may wonder how this relates to Giovanni's role as analyst.

Moretti says in interview: 'The character of the psychoanalyst was the first idea for the film. I wanted to represent him as a credible character, unlike the psychoanalysts one normally sees on screen' (in Bonsaver 2002: 28). In the last section of *Dear Diary*, 'Doctors', Moretti runs through the gamut of the medical profession seeking help with the unbearable itch which is eventually recognised as a symptom of lymphoma. The prescriptions which accumulate, in the film's attention to detail, testify to the film-maker's frustration. Medicine as science will nevertheless treat his lymphoma, despite the obscure indignities of its procedures. There is ambiguity, pathos and even wry humour in Moretti's representation of the experience of the patient. Moving on from his previous treatment of doctors, in *The Son's Room* Moretti apparently crosses the doctor/patient divide, playing the analyst. The representation of the scenes with Giovanni's patients recalls the tone and structure of the scenes in the third section of *Dear Diary* and even its earlier, more humorous cutting in the second section, 'Islands'. Yet the question of the role and sense of the analyst, and of analysis in general, is brought into question more seriously. This is explored as Giovanni himself becomes the victim of traumatic loss and finds it increasingly hard to play the role of analyst.

J. Hoberman entitles an article in *Village Voice*: 'Filmmaker, Heal Thyself'. The article opens with the question: 'Can movies be overtly therapeutic? Could they minister to our needs?' (2002). Giovanni as analyst in *The Son's Room* praises a patient for going to see a film he has recommended; film and cure are curiously aligned. Anthony Lane perpetuates this link between film-viewing and analysis saying: 'You leave the film like one of Giovanni's patients rising from the couch – far from healed, but amused and pacified by the sympathy that has washed over you' (2002: 82). Moretti, like Egoyan, teases out some links between film and analysis, and *The Son's Room* follows a slow yet syncopated healing for its characters, which is strangely consoling for the viewer. Yet in his role as both film-maker and as (fictional) analyst, Moretti appears properly most willing to ask questions of both analysis as process and of film as (representation of) cure. Giovanni's mind, body and presence are the locus and focus of these questions. In the complex terms of his immediately preceding films, Moretti becomes an instrument in his own film-making (see Landy 2000: 373).

Giovanni is presented as a kind, long-suffering analyst. His words seem sympathetic and rational, while he is calm and serene. Close to the start of the film, he says to one patient: 'You always feel guilty. Responsible for what happens ... But we can't control our lives completely. We do what we can.' He faces his patients' aggression at times and allows them to play out their rejection of him in scenes where they appear to terminate analysis. He encounters the charge that he is no help to the patients (one patient speaks about the 'genius' who invented Valium: 'He knows how to help people'). Nevertheless Giovanni's own help to the patients, though questioned by the patients themselves as part of the analysis, seems not in doubt in the first half of the film. This changes in the hiatus of Andrea's death. The patients' aggression, in the playing out of transferential relations, seems less bearable after the loss of Giovanni's son. One patient retorts, 'You always come up with the same crap', and the film draws us back to Giovanni's earlier words about not being able to control our lives, words which now offer little comfort in Giovanni's new, desperate grief.

There are indeed a number of reverberations between the patients' words and Giovanni's emotions. The patient who Giovanni visited on the morning Andrea died, a patient who has been diagnosed with cancer, thinks aloud that losing a son would be too much for his aged mother. Later in the film Giovanni begins to cry when a female patient starts to talk about not being able to have children. Giovanni begins to listen to his patients in a different way, hearing inevitable echoes of his life in their narratives (as does the film viewer).[1] He questions his treatments with a mentor or colleague and says to his wife, 'I'm probably not helping them much right now', acknowledging that he no longer has any objectivity. He eventually gives up his role as analyst, saying: 'I can't do this work anymore.'

As Hoberman points out, it is striking that Giovanni, indeed none of the family members, undertake any form of therapy or counselling themselves. It is as if the death of Andrea cannot be encompassed in the psychoanalytic frame of Giovanni's profession and his family. This works not necessarily to diminish analysis as such (the film is less thorough-going than this), but to suggest that its purchase does not encompass the situation of some individuals at some moments. In that sense Giovanni ironically finds some sort of closure in leaving psychoanalysis behind; the replayed endings which have been therapeutic for his patients bring some relief to the analyst himself, when actualised, as he exits from his role as healer.

In the reading above, Giovanni's grief is seen to contaminate his work. Another reading might suggest that the role of analyst as healer, helper and protector becomes untenable for Giovanni after his son has died. He can no longer uphold a paternal law of hope, health and knowledge, the backbone which has held up his harmonious relations with his family and with his patients. Indeed the brilliance of the film seems to lie in its low-key, yet coruscating analysis of the dismantling of Giovanni's role as both father and analyst. The film avoids melodrama, instead using steadier tactics to drive its message home. Marcia Landy argues that in *Dear Diary* Moretti seeks 'a mode of expression that, in Deleuze's terms, is of "cinema, body and brain, thought"' (2000: 372). Moving from the body as instrument in *Dear Diary*, in *The Son's Room* Moretti moves on to a representation of the mind and its suffering, explored through a complex set of sensory metaphors.

In *Three Colours: Blue*, the scene following the doctor's revelation to Julie that her husband and daughter have died shows shattering glass. Literally in the film's narrative Julie smashes a window as a distraction so she can take pills to make a suicide attempt. Yet the force of the impact and the radiating shards of glass indicate her feelings, her mental buckling in response to the horror of the doctor's news. *The Son's Room* finds comparable ways of exploring and evoking the mental sensations which accompany such swingeing grief. A similar strategy of displacement is used, where the character's environment reflects the (unrepresentable) reality of his or her mind. In this displacement, the film respects the enormity and probable belatedness and indirectness of responses to traumatic loss. A relative limit of the medium (primed to represent physical and sensory, rather than psychical reality), becomes a virtue where that psychical reality is represented indirectly. Visual, aural and at times visceral effects, felt by the viewer, translate something of the horror experienced by the character. This is explored most fully in the transition from the scene at Andrea's wake to a following interior scene in the family home, after the son's burial.

More than some of the films discussed here, *The Son's Room* pays careful attention to the practical social rituals surrounding death and their material details. Giovanni is seen as he chooses a coffin for Andrea, looking through a catalogue with two undertakers. Irene's boyfriend Matteo brings clothes for the dead son to wear for the wake. There is a deeply affecting, yet understated, scene where family and friends bid farewell to Andrea as he lies in an open coffin. As Giovanni, Paola and their daughter Irene stand by the coffin, the undertakers come in with the metal cover and coffin lid. The lid is first seen carried into the frame from the left, appearing as a shadow behind the family. It is followed by the metal cover. Paola glances round and catches sight of these two objects which seem to signal the removal of Andrea and the actuality of his death. She is overcome with grief. Each family member kisses Andrea's forehead, his mother very tenderly taking his face in her hands. The undertakers then move forward to fit the metal cover. Irene asks for it to be removed once more; she looks again at her brother and then the cover is fitted. The scene has been almost silent to this point, silence broken only by the family's murmured goodbyes to Andrea. The scene is still and dignified, with plain white walls, just a few flowers in the corner and family and friends in casual but muted clothes. The film seems to stress the sombre actuality of the events, letting them be seen in a quiet, mundane idiom.

The visual unity of the scene is broken as the film cuts to a close-up of the undertaker welding the metal cover shut. The close-up shot is lit by the lurid green flare of the man's blow torch. His hands are steady as he guides the torch, moving across the frame. The viewer follows the liquid stream of metal which will close the coffin, sealing in Andrea. The undertakers' work is emotionless, methodical. What adds to the emotion and effect of the scene, however, is the sound of the blow torch which, with its flare, seems to echo the searing pain of Giovanni and Irene as they watch the scene. This effect is accentuated still further as the scene continues with the closing of the external lid.

The film cuts now to close-ups of a drill fitting the screws of the coffin. Its action seems grating and relentless, reflected in its whine and the unsettling shudder of the drill as each screw is locked firmly into place. In a continuous shot the camera follows the drill from screw to screw. Not merely the sound and action are distressing, but their insistent and rhythmic repetition. After the third screw image the film cuts to Giovanni sitting at home. The sound of the drill and screws is still heard over the shots of Giovanni at home. The status and relation of sound and image is now uncertain. Is the viewer party to Giovanni's insistent memory of the closing of his son's coffin? Does this sound grate and return in his mind? The sound, and action, seem to work more tangentially too to offer a material correlative for the repeated pain of Andrea's loss, as his absence literally sinks into Giovanni's mind, embedding itself forcefully and irrevocably into his brain. The scene cuts to an image of Paola howling on her bed. The image is in part reminiscent of the appalling grief in *Jude*. Particularly effective is the view of the moving, straightening tendons in Paola's neck, giving some sense of her physical pain and vulnerability. Words are missing and sound is used again realistically, as Paola vents her despair, but also in such a way as to render the viewing experience more painful and hence, perhaps, more sympathetic.

The second scene which again uses sensation to convey mental trauma shows Giovanni seeking some irregular distraction from or outlet for his grief. Echoing *Wonderland* he goes to a fairground, now looking to grieve his son. The scene moves the film on from the numbness and searing horror of the interior shots, the wake, the closed coffin, the empty rooms at home where both father and mother seem alone in their mourning. The scene adds sound and colour to the film, an exterior space where Giovanni, nevertheless, finds the noise and jolting pain of his mental experience played out in gaudy exaggeration. The neon and sheer light of the stands and amusement arcades clashes and dazzles on the screen. The noise of the scene comes from all directions, insistent music, the magnified sound of the stall-holders' commentaries. Speed and acceleration are accentuated too as the rides course behind Giovanni like a speeded-up film. He sits himself in front of the bumper cars, observing the shock of their contact. In the most expressive shots at the end of the scene Giovanni himself is on a ride, enclosed in a yellow metal cage as a lever lifts and falls, its mechanism again shuddering and relentless. His face

Figure 12 *The Son's Room*

in the artificial light is very pale, almost bilious. His eyes open and close as he braces himself for each lift and fall. In point of view shots we see the scene of the fairground itself rise and fall before his eyes, before we see and hear the mechanical lever of the ride turning him in his cage. Returning to shots of his face, as he looks barely able to stomach the unending ride, the film seems to reflect both his endurance in the face of grief and the irremediable physical and mental strain he is under. The scene closes more quietly with a high-angle shot of the night-time fairground scene and a fade into darkness. The following scene returns to the family home.

The fairground scene is so successful since it works both directly and indirectly. Literally Giovanni seems to find an alternative scenario in which to find some relief – he might be following one of his own suggestions to his patients. Immersion in such a strident, colourful carnivalesque scene might momentarily block the noise, expression and feeling of Giovanni's grief. Yet as the viewer watches the scene, the jolts and noise, the swinging, relentless mechanical actions of the fairground machinery, serve to reflect and illustrate the traumatised reactions of the grieving father and his heightened responses. The exterior fairground scene reflects the space of Giovanni's mind, the discordant emotions behind the face continually framed by the camera. In addition to this use of physical correlatives, *The Son's Room* also makes detailed exploration of the mental replay of events in its search to convey the feelings of the grieving parent. The interest in replay and repetition is anticipated already in the repetitive mechanism of both drill and ride. As Moretti represents replay further, the resources of cinema as medium which can restore and recall the past are used to particularly poignant effect.

The opening, fairly anodyne drama of *The Son's Room* concerns a question about whether Andrea and his friend Luciano have stolen a fossil from their school lab. This seems to bear little or no relation to the tragedy which is the film's major focus. Close to the start of the film we see Giovanni called urgently to his son's school. This and the ensuing scenes seem used partly to establish Giovanni's role as caring, fair and non-judgmental parent. We see how he deals with a minor mishap before he is called on to deal with the horror of Andrea's loss. The worry of the school and the stolen fossil feels like a rehearsal of the future drama, a rehearsal of parental worry which is dwarfed by what follows. Yet more than this, the drama of the stolen fossil already raises questions in the film about the interpretation of events and constructions which might be made. Andrea tells his parents that he and his friend Luciano are innocent. The evidence of the boy who has accused them seems less credible when he is in discussion with his parents, with Giovanni and with Luciano's father. Andrea's parents are relieved to think that he is innocent; but then he admits to his mother that indeed the boy was right, he and Luciano did take the fossil, though only as a joke. The drama calls for a re-viewing of evidence, unsettling Giovanni's certainty in his interpretation of events. This need for re-viewing and rehearsal appears to haunt him, though much more intensely, as he sets himself the task of trying to understand, and interpret Andrea's death.

The film as a whole appears to deal in rehearsals and repetitions. Structurally, scenes recur; this is particularly marked in the returning scenes of Giovanni's analytic sessions and the repeated words and scenarios of his patients. Beyond this, some scenes seem literally foreshadowed or copied in the film. This is the case with Andrea's death. Paola, like a Kieślowski heroine, is touched in the scene at the antique fair which serves as an intimation of the accident which will follow. The film cuts to shots of Irene with her friends, all on Vespas, playing about as they ride, as if the accident could befall Irene. Then it cuts further to Giovanni driving out to see his patient on narrow roads, confronting a large truck bearing down from the opposite direction. Then finally it cuts to Andrea and his friends in diving suits going out in their boat. While the film seems overdetermined and deliberate in retrospect, what it suggests in this rehearsal of events is a sense of randomness. The tragedy which befalls the family might equally have been the death of Irene or indeed of Giovanni himself. It is this randomness, this senseless ordering of events which Giovanni is shown to find unbearable. The film is particularly attentive to his attempts to master events in retrospect, through their repetition, through painful mental rehearsal and literal research. This becomes the focus of the film after the scenes which drive home the sensory reverberations of Giovanni's grief.

On the morning of the day Andrea dies there has been hesitation over the course of events. Giovanni suggests going for a run with his son. Andrea replies that he is meeting friends. Giovanni still manages to persuade him to go for a run, but then one of his patients, Oscar, calls in despair, calling Giovanni away to make a house visit. Andrea is free to meet his friends. Giovanni says to him: 'We'll do that run some other time.' The calm of the movie up to this point seems to promise infinite Sunday mornings when father and son can go running together, down to the harbour and back (Giovanni himself is seen running several times in the film). But the film works precisely to offer Giovanni literally no other time, the only future runs he can take with Andrea are imaginary, in desperate, wish-fulfilling images, virtual images which the film can make visible.

Such an image is first seen where Giovanni sits alone – his wife is in Andrea's room – and listens to a track from Michael Nyman's 'Water Dances'. Giovanni is holding the remote control to his stereo and he continually replays a few seconds of the piece, imitating and accentuating the urgent imitative patterns of Nyman's own music. The film cuts from the image of Giovanni, pensive as he listens to the music, to a shot of father and son jogging together. Giovanni is smiling here, Andrea is on his left in his red jersey. The shot seems summoned by the music, which itself reflects the stammering, halted thought patterns of Giovanni's mind. It vanishes quickly, returning us to Giovanni alone in the room. This may be a memory image or a fantasy, a projection of what might have happened differently on the Sunday morning. Some desperate escape from the present actuality of Giovanni's situation seems to be found in conjuring the fantasy.

From this reparative image the film cuts to Giovanni in a shop looking at diving equipment. He seeks information about the air cylinder and how the pressure gauge works, trying to work out whether something technical or mechanical might have gone wrong. The film cuts to a memory or fantasy image of Giovanni in the kitchen at home. He looks up and in the reverse shot Andrea, in his red jersey, meets his gaze. He says to his son: 'So, you want to go for a run?' The present enquiries in the diving shop are cross cut with the reworked memory image. The film asks both what might have happened actually and what might have happened differently. The viewer shares the psychical reality of Giovanni in these subjective shots. The film cuts then to Giovanni pensive in an analytic session, hinting thus that thoughts of his son continually return, replayed as he attempts to listen to his patients.

The first couple of reparative images of Andrea are very fleeting. But they emerge more extensively as the film continues, as if Giovanni is gradually

mastering their return in his mind or playing out his sense of guilt and wistful-
ness more fully. An analytic session (with Oscar) ends with a lengthier return
to the Sunday morning scene. In *this* replay Giovanni answers the telephone
to Oscar and is sympathetic, as before, but ends their conversation decisively
saying: 'No, I really can't today. See you tomorrow at eight.' The film cuts to
Paola who smiles at Giovanni. The film cuts again to Giovanni, now in a restaurant with Paola – the intensity of his reparative fantasies carried over from
scene to scene in his current life. In their conversation in the restaurant Paola
attempts to cut short Giovanni's obsessive return to the chance events of the
Sunday morning, to the choices he made and to the accident he sees ensuing.
She discounts his questions about the diving equipment ('It worked, they told
us that!'). She says simply: 'He went into a cave and he got lost.' She continues:
'He ran out of air while he was looking for the exit, and he took off the tank
to come back up faster.' Giovanni replies: 'Andrea, alone in a cave. It doesn't
make sense...' We see how the film, in following and respecting Giovanni's
subjective reality, has screened out incidents and evidence which we only learn
and Giovanni only acknowledges belatedly. The truth of what happened to
their son is too hard to bear, as witnessed in the scene in the restaurant where
both parents weep.

There appears to be some division between the responses of Giovanni
and Paola, as he is engrossed in replaying the past while she seems to face its
actuality. This division is subtly denied, however, in a further strand woven
into the last section of the film. Paola receives a letter addressed to Andrea,
written several weeks after his death. As in *All About My Mother*, the survival
of the son as addressee, the illusory resurrection the letter brings about, seems
to offer some comfort. Indeed Paola becomes gently obsessed with meeting
Arianna, the girl Andrea has met on a camping holiday who has not been mentioned to his parents up to this point. Giovanni stresses that they should write
to her, rather than phone her, to inform her of Andrea's death, but he hesitates
over this task, again caught in rehearsal and replay as he keeps making false
starts in his letter writing. Indeed it is in a scene where he tries to write to
Arianna that the last reparative images emerge. We catch a shot of Giovanni
and Andrea jogging together, then another where they are closer to the camera.
These punctuate the images of Giovanni in his study trying to write about his
son's death to Arianna. Giovanni appears to stop and give himself up to the
fantasy. Here Andrea says he is tired and that his friends are waiting for him
to go diving. Giovanni, in his fantasy, intervenes against fate, saying no: 'Let's
stay together, okay?' The scene ends with father and son running off together,
a painful intimation that the story could open out differently. In a following
scene where Giovanni acknowledges to his wife that he still hasn't written to
Arianna, he asks her: 'What if I'd stayed...' Paola again cuts short his des-

perate musings ('we'd have had an ice cream, we'd have seen a movie…') by saying: 'You can't turn back time!' This seems to call a halt to the reparative images, yet as Paola continues her monologue, her own ability to deal with the situation comes more into question as the film begins to pay more attention to Paola's desire to make contact with Arianna.

Giovanni seeks a return to an alternative, rewritten past in his obsessive imaginings. Paola's interest in Arianna is in parallel, I suggest, in her search to involve herself in an aspect of Andrea's life which has remained hidden for her. This is in some senses another virtual life of Andrea, conjured in the words Arianna addresses to their dead son in her letter. Paola is struck by the way Arianna describes Andrea and by the way she seems to know him. Arianna at first entirely resists any embroilment with Andrea's family, but then turns up at their apartment uninvited, offering them an image of a girl Andrea might have loved. Representing a virtual life of their son, Arianna appropriately brings with her photographs of Andrea that the family has not seen. These are images he has taken of himself with a timer in his room. These literal memory images, traces of the past, recall the living Andrea in the film, and replace the more unruly reparative images which, in their insistence, seem to disrupt Giovanni's living in the present.

Arianna is associated with the processing of the past for both Giovanni and Paola. Yet, unwittingly, she will, as her name suggests, offer them a thread to lead them out of the constant replay and enclosed space of their grief into some more possible future.

Figure 13 *The Son's Room*

In interview, Moretti comments:

> I didn't want to make it a sadistic film at the audience's expense, I
> didn't want pain to isolate the characters in their own grief. That's why
> I wanted some movement at the end, physical movement – and indeed
> there is a journey – and movement within the characters. They don't
> overcome pain, but the pain begins to transform itself into something
> else. There's a small opening towards other people, towards the outside.
> (in Bonsaver 2002: 30)

At the end of the film Giovanni and Paola appear to find some small relief in
an act of kindness towards Arianna and her new boyfriend Stefano.

Arianna tells the family that she is hitch-hiking with a friend and the
film cuts to a mobile night-time image of a road, with lights in the distance.
Giovanni, with Paola and Irene, is driving Arianna and Stefano to the next
service station so they can hitch a ride to France. They arrive at a service station and the family leave Arianna and Stefano. We see their farewells, Arianna
hugging Paola and kissing Irene. The service station is lit, but empty, slightly
misty in the night air. Several long shots show Arianna and Stefano alone waiting for a lorry to pass. The film cuts to a shot of Giovanni, Paola and Irene,
watching them through the plate glass window of the service station conve-
nience store. We next see Arianna and Stefano in the back of the car, with
Giovanni driving them on to another larger station. In its tacit editing here the
film gently begins to recall again the comedy and irony of a film such as *Dear
Diary*. There is some sense that its idiom is changing.

The journey represented has several hesitations: after the first failure
to leave Arianna and Stefano behind, Giovanni fails again to leave them at
the next service station, and then indeed at the Genoa exit. These rehearsed
and failed partings seem to repeat the rehearsed terminations in Giovanni's
analytic sessions, as well as his own failure to relinquish mental repetition of
the day of Andrea's death. Yet towards the end the mood of the film is, almost
imperceptibly, lifting. Giovanni and Paola do, at the very end, bid a final farewell to Arianna, after they have driven her not merely to Genoa but right to
the French border.

As he offers to extend the journey to Genoa, Giovanni says: 'It'll help,
right?' His desire to help Arianna appears to create a new complicity between
himself and Paola. We cut to shots of the car as it seems almost to float on the
road, the music of the soundtrack dictating the gentle rhythm and pace of the
shots. Arianna and Stefano, then Irene, are seen sleeping, protected, in the
back of the car. Forwards tracking shots and then night images of the lights
of Genoa against the darkness seem to recall the relief of Manuela's arrival in

Barcelona in *All About My Mother*. As Paola notices that they have missed the Genoa exit, Giovanni quietens her saying: 'We're almost there.' His words take on a resonance at this late stage in the film.

It is early morning when the car reaches the French border. The French flag seen flying seems a tiny illusion to Kieślowski's trilogy and its proximity to Moretti's concerns here. Now the car comes to a standstill; this journey of reparation is in some senses the reverse and repair of the calamitous driving shots and accident of the start of *Three Colours: Blue*. Giovanni and Paola walk from the car to see a view of clear blue sea and the French town in dawn sunlight beneath the mountains. Irene alone is frustrated by her parents' excessive journey; as she expresses her exasperation that they have driven her so far through the night, Giovanni and Paola laugh irresistibly at the absurdity of the situation.

The farewells are definitive as they part from Arianna and Stefano, putting them on a coach which we eventually see leaving. The last shots of the film, played against the Brian Eno song, 'By this River', show Giovanni, Paola and Irene walking on the beach. The camera recedes, pulling away from them as if we share the final point of view of Arianna, leaving on the coach, leaving this grief behind. As Philip Kemp points out: 'there's a sense that a burden may be lifting. (Quite literally they've crossed a border; the past is another country.)' He continues: 'It's a subtle, wistful closure: Moretti holds out the possibility of grief fading and lives repairing themselves, but he's too honest to offer us more than that' (2002: 56).

This end to the film, the movement out from the enclosed apartment (filled with broken objects), the sheer beauty of the early morning images of the sea and the soft, warm light over the harbour, the melancholy of the song, all bring relief and reprieve for the viewer. It seems an added subtlety that the film consciously leaves Giovanni, Paola and Irene behind at its ending. While we have seen some smoothing of their relations in this journey, some hint that, though broken, their family can refind the gentleness and humour of the time before Andrea's death, this end is still hesitant and it may be observers, rather than family members, who are leaving grief behind.

Giovanni and Paola have appeared to find relief in what might be seen as an excessive act of generosity towards Arianna. This is a strange way of doing something for Andrea and of reconfirming their role as parents and protectors, a role so deeply undermined by Andrea's death. There is relief too in the spontaneity of the act; where controlling time and avoidance of the horror of random events have been strong concerns in the duration of the movie, Giovanni here shows a new ability to act on impulse, out of kindness. Simply he finds a new way to help others. This is a way of moving on, yet, as Kemp indicates in the quotation above, *The Son's Room* does not go too far in anticipating healing, closure and release.

Offering a small opening towards the outside, Moretti still avoids sentimentality or glibness in what Deborah Young describes as the 'unforced resonance' (2001: 14) of the film's close. A departure in Moretti's film career, *The Son's Room* also offers a departure in the missing child film. While it echoes the concern to find a relation to others in the close of *Three Colours: Blue*, or the rewriting of parenting in *All About My Mother* or *Olivier, Olivier*, *The Son's Room* in its interest in endings and termination, in movement, offers thoughts on the possibility of moving on. Whilst it is modest in its claims for psychoanalysis, and does not show the family finding catharsis or protection within this frame, the film borrows one of the mechanisms of the psychoanalytic session in its ending. The family repeat their farewells to Arianna and Stefano until they seem really ready to leave them behind. Moving on, however slowly, becomes possible if grief is not denied, if the lost child is kept alive and recalled in relations to others, if loss motivates action and rare generosity.

CONCLUSION

Reflections

In Jeremy Podeswa's film *The Five Senses* (1999), the missing child, a very small girl, is recovered and reunited with her mother. Their embrace is screened on news footage which cuts through the film. Such moments of reprieve or redemption are rare within missing child films which offer, more commonly, aleatory and illusory comforts. Throughout this study I have stressed that the loss of a child knows no repair or reparation; film-makers address instead a limit subject, a subject which reaches or exceeds the bounds of representation, and normative, narrative resolution. Caution, hesitance and generosity mark the films' engagement with their subject and their refusal of (abusive) spectacle on the one hand, or of reductive cure on the other. Yet what has emerged in the echoing concerns of the separate films is a move to imagine some possible futurity, some space for moving onwards.

What the films treated come to envisage is the possibility of transforming the family, whose bases have been rocked by the loss of the child. In her study, *Antigone's Claim*, Judith Butler asks new questions about kinship relations in an era which she describes as 'a time in which the family is at once idealised in nostalgic ways within various cultural forms, a time in which the Vatican protests against homosexuality not only as an assault on the family but also on the notion of the human, where to become human, for some, requires participation in the family in its normative sense' (2000: 22). Butler points out the way family situations have changed, describing this era, as well, as:

Figure 14 *The Five Senses*

> a time in which children, because of divorce and remarriage, because
> of migration, exile, and refugee status, because of global displacements
> of various kinds, move from one family to another, move from a family
> to no family, move from no family to a family, or in which they live,
> psychically, at the crossroads of the family, or in multiply layered family
> situations, in which they may well have more than one woman who
> operates as the mother, more than one man who operates as the father,
> or no mother or no father. (*Ibid.*)

For Butler, 'this is a time in which kinship has become fragile, porous, and expansive' (2000: 23). What is salutary about the films treated is that they offer no causative correlation between these changes in family patterns and the threats to children they analyse. Indeed they offer no explanation at all of threats to children which are seen to emerge variously from the family unit itself, from family friends, from strangers, from illness, from accidents, from blind chance. In this sense the family does not simply claim its position as bastion or stronghold of family protection; this unit, this structure, does not always protect its offspring; threats do not always come from outside. Any reactionary fantasy of the normative family is dissipated.

In its concern to refuse the conservative agenda (whereby children are seen to be at risk as a result of social changes) this study has followed the

Figure 15 *The Five Senses*

lead of Henry Jenkins' work in *The Children's Culture Reader*. Exploring and defining recent scholarship on children, Jenkins draws together essays which both address what the figure of the child means to adults and offer a more complex account of children's own cultural lives. In an important political move, he is concerned to challenge the prevailing cultural myth of the innocent child and the notion of the child as victim. While the representation of child as victim is, in some senses, unavoidable in the missing child film, my aim in treating this material has been, like Jenkins, to offer a more complex interpretation of adult/child relations, of guilt and innocence. While I only touch on the issue of children's own cultural lives, debates about adult investment in the figure of the child are key to the films discussed, as are new ways of configuring parenting roles and family relations.

Instead of seeing changes to the family multiplying threats to children, the films under analysis look towards ways in which the opening of the family to other members, to other desires, works as a means (however fragile) of seeking comfort and relief. In this sense the family represented and re-imagined becomes a more open, expansive grouping of individuals; there is some possibility of expending the love for the lost child on others, other children, others in need. This expenditure may be painful or excessive, yet it also becomes a way of moving towards some new relationality, some form of commemoration in a continued nurturing role. Such generosity and liberality determine the emphasis on contact, attention and patience which I have traced in these films, in the ethos, however despairing or tentative, they ultimately share. These films do not testify to the need to survive in order to bear witness; the story of the lost child rarely figures in language. Instead, their protagonists seem to live to keep alive feelings for the missing child, and to enact those feelings through attention to others.

As form and content fold in on each other, the films themselves also consciously reflect their subject, exploiting the expressivity of the medium, imitating the disruptions of traumatic loss (through limited or filtered vision, blanks, temporal disruption and structural repetition) and intimating the possibilities of palliative attention (through allusions to mourning photography, through haptic visuality and hand-held camerawork). Their 'treatment' of the subject of missing children, as much as the subject itself, draws these films together and draws attention to their potential as reflections on cinema as a means of artistic response to personal trauma, to the fears and horrors of our (or any) era.

As mentioned above, the films studied here do not work to assign blame or explain risks to children. In parallel, I am cautious about ascribing meanings to cinema's missing children. These films offer a means of conjuring anxieties and following them through in moving forms. One of the few detailed cultural studies to approach the theme of the missing child (or in his terms 'the lost child'), Peter Pierce's excellent *Country of Lost Children* goes further than I do here to consider the child not merely as subject (in film, literature and news reporting) but also as emblem. Pierce's introduction offers a broader treatment of the theme, drawing on such diverse cultural references as the tales of the Brothers Grimm, Mahler's *Kinder-totenlieder* and Tournier's *Gilles et Jeanne*. Yet his argument throughout the book is specific to Australia, the context of his study. Pierce argues persuasively that the lost child, a recurring motif in Australian culture from the early nineteenth century, 'is the symbol of essential if never fully resolved anxieties within the white settler communities of [that] country' (1999: xi). Analysing those anxieties Pierce sees them as double-stranded. He suggests that the tales of lost children refer 'ostensibly, and poignantly' to the fear and danger of children wandering away from settled areas into the trackless bush (1999: xii). Yet, at a deeper level, for Pierce, tales of lost children represent the fears and loneliness of settlers in a new country, cut off from home.

This double intimation, that representations of lost and missing children reflect fears of real dangers to children, whilst also expressing a certain adult nostalgia and longing (for a lost childhood or home, literal or symbolic), holds true for the films studied here. Yet the contexts of the various film I analyse are relatively diverse and, unlike Pierce's material, the films do not reflect or represent one particular national and historical fear or phobia. These films do nevertheless reflect a particular era or cultural moment. This study inevitably raises questions about why missing and endangered children should emerge as an insistent subject in cinema in the last decade. How is the actuality of the theme explained within contemporary cinema?

As Joel Best suggests in the work cited in the introduction, the missing or endangered child has been a prominent concern in society and the media, in the US, from at least the 1960s. The subject itself has no novelty, though enduring pathos, as it is approached in the last decade of the twentieth century. It is certainly the case, however, as I suggest throughout, that contemporary cinema has become newly interested in the subject. Some of the critical works studied here, the work of James Kincaid or Anne Higonnet for example, argues for a specific new interest in images of childhood in contemporary culture. Such work explores the changed, sometimes disturbing investment in childhood (for Higonnet, changes in our culture's understanding of childhood may be as major as those of the eighteenth century). While changing perceptions of and investments in childhood are crucial to the context of this study, the subject of the missing child stands apart from other images of childhood in certain ways. In particular, in the ways in which the missing child necessarily raises questions about grief and traumatic loss (which, though they may be managed in different ways in different eras are surely constant).

I suggest that it is not in society or the state of the world that we find an answer for the persistence of the theme of the missing child in contemporary cinema. Rather I think answers lie in cinema itself. In the most direct sense, the power and emotion of films such as *Three Colours: Blue* or *Exotica* have, as in the case of *The Son's Room*, influenced other directors; this is not to suggest necessarily a return to this theme as tribute or as resolution of an anxiety of influence, but as evidence of the productive enmeshing of the concerns of contemporary films. Not merely are contemporary films, like *Code Unknown* (2000), *Amores Perros* (2000), *Lantana* (2001) (with its own missing child thread), themselves self-consciously braided from a number of narrative strands, such films are also ever-increasingly intertextual and interconnected with each other. Coterminous with this awareness of interconnection, and equally important for this study, is the attempt witnessed in such independent and art cinema (seen also, say, in the work of Larry Clark, Catherine Breillat, Gaspard Noé and countless others) to push cinematic representations to new limits in thinking and showing extremes of fear and desire.

The suffering of children appears a limit or absolute in ethical thinking; the grief of mourning parents is popularly reckoned an ultimate horror (witness the words of Almodóvar quoted above). Cinema of the end of the twentieth century and of the first part of the twenty-first century has newly contended with such senseless (and timeless) fear and horror. Just treatment of such material is a peculiar challenge to the contemporary film-maker. In treating the subject of the missing child, directors have remained ambivalent about the specificity of its relevance to the current period. While directors such as Todd Solondz or Atom Egoyan are acutely attentive to markers of period and era – and as such make their representations of missing and endangered children reflective of the contemporary period shown – this topos is not seen as only specific to the present moment, as witnessed in references to earlier works such as *M* and *Don't Look Now*. This sense is further corroborated by the period dramas discussed here which, though showing a different historical context, work retrospectively to establish a continuity in the experience of grief and pain. The insistence of the subject in contemporary cinema comes, if anything, in the accumulation of representations and their cross-contamination.

These films are typified by the directors' reluctance to let the missing child become an emblem of innocence, nostalgia or indeed of childhood itself (and this again marks out these films from the works studied by Pierce). Instead the missing child is, in such contemporary film, more properly a vanishing point, an absence around which the narrative is elaborated. But I would argue that if the missing child, rather than the lady who vanishes, has become the lost object of contemporary cinema, this says more about advances in the representation of women in the cinema, and in the figuring of elusuive femininity in both films and film theory, than it does about the specificity of our culture's investment in childhood as subject. This suggests that the theme of the missing child is interesting precisely in its conjuring of an absence. Indeed it becomes a condition of many of these films that the child is missing in the film itself rather than represented as emblem, that the film-maker too contends with the challenge of showing the child as absent, or only virtually present in photographs, memory and fantasy images. The lost child may be represented, as in Australian paintings or fairytales, wandering in the bush or woods; the missing child might never be literally present again though seen with desperate pathos in last photographic images (as in the recurring pictures of Holly Wells and Jessica Chapman in the summer of 2002).

While I suggest, then, that film-makers are seeking an aesthetic challenge and charge in their treatment of this excessive subject, it might be asked what distinguishes the missing child as subject from other extreme topics in recent cinema. As I have stressed throughout, the missing child affords particular, emotive opportunities for thinking mourning and commemoration. The child, missing, requires a pained reckoning with the possibilities of managing loss, loss of the loved one, loss of identity. Indeed questions of the management of loss and possibilities of survival have emerged repeatedly in discussion of these films. In the Introduction I suggested that possibilities of survival remain hesitant, and I would argue that loss, rather than survival, is the dominant subject of the films studied. Nevertheless the films are also linked in their concern to debate, imagine or refute possibilities for the management of loss; in this these films reveal something of the cultural specificity of their period. Missing children and bereaved parents are shockingly immemorial subjects. Late twentieth and early twenty-first-century society testify more generally, however, to a new drive towards memorialisation (in memory books, spontaneous memorials, more elaborate graves and inscriptions)[1] and towards the management of loss, primarily through counselling. While the films discussed here do not explicitly reflect these changed social mores or expressions of grief, they might be seen to intersect with and intervene in a contemporary Western culture and media which has a new investment in exploring pathos. This is what makes their treatment of the subject of the missing child a contemporary concern; it is not particular to this period, but this period has a particular interest in observing, managing and testifying to such losses. And contemporary film, in response, offers at times a stark reminder of the unmanageability of such loss.

Some twentieth-century returns to the Victorian theme of the death-bound or endangered child have favoured the gothic and blackly-comic: Edward Gorey's *The Gashlycrumb Tinies*, for example, or The Tiger Lillies' 'Junk Opera' adaptation of *Shockheaded Peter*. By contrast, the films under analysis here, whether they revisit the past or reanimate its interest in child mortality and misadventure, favour elegy as mode. These films are haunted by spectral visions, glassy and watery reflections, video and photographic prostheses, which barely screen or hide the fissure left by the loss of the child. In contrast to the popular media, the demands they make on the viewer are extreme as they return to us compulsive images of bodily distortion, of emesis and evisceration, and sheer sounds of horror outside language. Responses shadow one another, as concerns reverberate and images seep from film to film. Yet this familiarity does not lessen the films' effect. Instead the viewer faces 'a bracing of nerves/For something that has already happened' (Hughes 1998: 134). In the impact of their continued return to pay attention to missing children, these films open a space for reflection in the viewer and for (feeling) contact with their subject.

NOTES

Introduction

1   See also James N. Tedisco & Michele A. Paludi (1996) *Missing Children: A Psychological Approach to Understanding the Causes and Consequences of Stranger and Non-stranger Abduction of Children* (Albany, New York: State University of New York Press).

2   See Liliane Binard & Jean-Luc Clouard (1997) *Le Drame de la pédophilie: Etat des lieux; Protection des enfants* (Paris: Albin Michel), pp. 104–6 on the Dutroux affair. The volume also details other notorious recent cases in France and Belgium.

3   See http://www.missingkids.com and http://www.namca.com

4   See http://perso.club-internet.fr/apev

5   See http://interpol.int

6   It has nevertheless been very informative to read such books as Elisabeth Kübler-Ross's compassionate study *On Children and Death: How children and their parents can and do cope with death* (New York: Simon and Schuster, 1983), and a number of testimonial and fictional accounts of the experience of losing a child.

7   Berlant refers here to the work of Roland Barthes and Pierre Bourdieu.

Chapter 1

1   See the following critical discussions of *Three Colours: Blue*: Geoffrey

Macnab (1993) 'Trois Couleurs: Bleu', Sight and Sound, 3, 11, pp. 54–5; Dave Kehr (1994) 'To Save the World: Kieślowski's Three Colours Trilogy', Film Comment, 30, 6, pp. 10–20; Michel Estève (1994) 'Trois Couleurs: Bleu ou l'apprentissage de la liberté', in Michel Estève (ed.) Krzysztof Kieślowski (Paris: Lettres Modernes/Etudes Cinématographiques), pp. 121–7; Vincent Amiel (1995) Kieślowski (Paris: Rivages/Cinéma), p. 134; Sean Portnoy (1997) 'Unmasking Sound: Music and Representation in The Shout and Three Colours: Blue', Spectator, 17, 2, pp. 50–9; and Geoff Andrew (1998) The 'Three Colours' Trilogy (London: British Film Institute), pp. 25–37. (Translations are my own unless stated otherwise.)

2 The screenplay tells us that she frames the image with her hand in such a way that she can only see the small coffin. Krzysztof Kieślowski & Krzysztof Piesiewicz (1997) Trois Couleurs: Bleu (Paris: Arte Editions/ Hachette), p. 13.

3 Emma Robinson offered this reading of the pool scenes in her paper, 'Memory, nostalgia and the cinematic postmodern', at the 1996 Screen Studies Conference in Glasgow.

4 See Dave Kehr (1994) 'To Save the World: Kieślowski's Three Colours trilogy', for a broader exploration of rebirth and resurrection in the trilogy.

5 These are scenes 38, 44 and 59 in the screenplay.

6 In interview Kieślowski reveals that it was his assistant's idea to include the ultrasound image. See '"La liberté est impossible", an interview with Krzysztof Kieślowski by Michel Ciment & Hubert Niogret', in Vincent Amiel (ed.) (1997) Krzysztof Kieślowski (Paris: Jean Michel Place/Positif), p. 129.

7 For a reading which goes further to explore questions of the semiotic in Three Colours: Blue, see my 'Three Colours: Blue': Kieślowski, colour and the postmodern subject', Screen, 39, 4 (Winter 1998), pp. 349–62.

8 See André Bazin (1967) What is Cinema?, trans. Hugh Gray (Berkeley and Los Angeles: University of California Press); Roland Barthes (1981) Camera Lucida: Reflections on Photography, trans. Richard Howard (New York: Hill and Wang); Christian Metz (1982) Psychoanalysis and Cinema: The Imaginary Signifier, trans. Celia Britton, Annwyl Williams, Ben Brewster & Alfred Guzzetti (London: Macmillan).

Chapter 2

1 Jackie Stacey (1987) 'Desperately Seeking Difference', Screen, 28, 1, pp. 48–61; Teresa de Lauretis (1994) The Practice of Love: Lesbian Sexuality and Perverse Desire (Bloomington and Indianapolis: Indiana University

Press), pp. 116–23.

2 Laura Marks comments similarly: 'Egoyan has made a number of feature films devoted to the question of how technological reproductions of images are used as prostheses for memory and for sex'. 'Deterritorialized Film-making: a Deleuzian politics of hybrid cinema', *Screen*, 35, 3 (Autumn 1994), p. 252.

3 Geoffrey Macnab speaks of Mitchell Stephens (Ian Holm), in Egoyan's *The Sweet Hereafter* (1997), as 'yet another "adjuster" to set alongside the insurance loss assessors, taxmen, censors, photographers, voyeurs and gigolos who pass for heroes in his work'. 'The Inscrutable in pursuit of the Unspeakable', *The Independent, The Eye on Friday* (19 September 1997), p. 12.

4 Jonathan Romney warns in an article on *Exotica*: 'there's a perilous borderline between alluding to exploitation, and exploitation period'. 'Exploitations', *Sight and Sound*, 5, 5 (May 1995), p. 7.

5 Amanda Lipman suggests: 'Zoe plays the part of dispassionate matriarch', in a review of *Exotica, Sight and Sound*, 5, 5 (May 1995), p. 45.

6 See Sigmund Freud (1991) 'Mourning and Melancholia', The Penguin Freud Library, vol. 11, *On Metapsychology: The Theory of Psychoanalysis* (Harmondsworth: Penguin), pp. 245–68. See also Judith Butler's re-reading of this essay in 'Imitation and Gender Insubordination', in Diana Fuss (ed.) (1991) *Inside/Out: Lesbian Theories, Gay Theories* (New York and London: Routledge), pp. 13–31.

7 See Judith Butler, *Gender Trouble: Feminism and the Subversion of Identity* (New York and London: Routledge, 1990); *Bodies that Matter* (New York and London: Routledge, 1993). Diana Fuss's *Essentially Speaking; Feminism, Nature and Difference* (New York and London: Routledge, 1990) also raises particularly relevant questions about the multiple and contradictory nature of identity.

8 hooks comments importantly: 'we have all been socialized to learn in parts – to see only fragments. This fractured mode of seeing leads most critics in the United States to see a film like Atom Egoyan's *Exotica* and never notice the way it raises issues of race, class, nationality. Looking through a narrow lens, they see the film as exclusively about sexuality' (1996: 27).

Chapter 3

1 See Kimberley Cooper (1999) 'Beyond the Clean and Proper', *Vertigo*, 9, pp. 45–6. Sophie Grassin also refers to *Seul Contre Tous* in '*Happiness* de Todd Solondz', *L'Express*, 11 February 1999 (BIFI press dossier).

2 See Anne Higonnet (1998) *Pictures of Innocence: The History and Crisis of Ideal Childhood* (London: Thames and Hudson) and Marianne

Hirsch (1997) *Family Frames: Photography, Narrative and Postmemory* (Cambridge, Mass. and London: Harvard University Press).

Chapter 4

1 Agnieszka Holland, in an interview cited on Tartan video slipcase.

Chapter 5

1 See discussion of Penley's work in Lucy Fischer (1996) *Cinematernity: Film, Motherhood, Genre* (Princeton, NJ: Princeton University Press), p. 22.

Chapter 6

1 See her quoted comments in Mary Cantwell, 'Jane Campion's Lunatic Women', in Wright Wexman (ed.) (1999) *Jane Campion: Interviews* (Jackson, Mississippi: University Press of Mississippi), pp. 153–63.
2 See Stella Bruzzi (1997) 'Desire and the costume film', *Undressing Cinema* (London: Routledge), pp. 35–63.

Chapter 7

1 Quoted from Emanuel Lewis (1983) 'Stillbirth: Psychological Consequences and Strategies of Management', in A. Miunsku, E. Friedman & L. Gluck (eds) *Advances in Prenatal Medicine*, 3, (New York: Plenum), pp. 205–45.

Chapter 8

1 See Derek Malcom, '*Ratcatcher*', *The Guardian*, 16 August 1999. Available at: http://film.guardian.co.uk/edinburgh/story/o,4135,74289,00.html
2 See Danusia Stok (1993) *Kieślowski on Kieślowski* (London: Faber and Faber), p. 32. (Kieślowski makes particular reference to *Kes*.)

Chapter 9

1 See Richard Kelly (2000) *The Name of this Book is Dogme 95* (London: Faber and Faber), pp. 226–8. See also Stig Björkman (2000) *Lars von Trier: Conversations avec Stig Björkman* (Paris: Cahiers du cinéma), pp. 161–2.
2 *Variety* cited in the entry on *The Kingdom* in John Walker (ed.) (1998)

Halliwell's Film and Video Guide 1999 (London: HarperCollins), p. 443.

3   Lars von Trier, in interview, quoted on the Tartan Metro DVD of *The Idiots*.

Chapter 10

1   For Kemp, Giovanni, in contrast to his wife and daughter, closes his grief away, 'letting it poison his relation to his family and his patients' (2002: 56).

Conclusion

1   See many examples in Elizabeth Hallam & Jenny Hockey (2001) *Death, Memory and Material Culture* (Oxford and New York: Berg).

BIBLIOGRAPHY

Ahmed, Sara & Jackie Stacey (eds) (2001) *Testimonial Cultures, Cultural Values*, 5, 1.

Almodóvar, Pedro (1999) *Tout sur ma mère* (Scénario bilingue). Paris: Cahiers du cinéma.

Amiel, Vincent (1994) 'Plongées dans la passion', *Positif*, 403, 24–5.

____ (1995) *Kieślowski*. Paris: Rivages/Cinéma.

____ (1996) 'Kieślowski et la méfiance du visible', *Positif*, 423, 73–4.

____ (ed.) (1997) *Krzysztof Kieślowski*. Paris: Jean Michel Place/Positif.

Amini, Hossein (1996) *Jude: The Shooting Script*. London: Nick Hern Books.

Andrew, Geoff (1998) *The 'Three Colours' Trilogy*. London: British Film Institute.

Angot, Christine (1990) *Vu du ciel*. Paris: Gallimard.

Ariès, Philippe (1983) *The Hour of Our Death*, trans. Helen Weaver. Harmondsworth: Penguin.

Arroyo, José (1999) '*All About My Mother*', *Sight and Sound*, 9, 9, 40.

Artus, Jacqueline (1992) 'L'enfant fantôme: Un entretien avec Agnieszka Holland', *Le Nouvel Observateur*, 29 October (BIFI press dossier).

Atkinson, Michael (1998) 'Michael Winterbottom: Cinema as Heart Attack', *Film Comment*, 34, 1, 44–7.

Aumont, Jacques (1992) *Du Visage au cinéma*. Paris: Cahier du Cinéma.

Axelrad, Catherine (1996) '*Portrait de femme*: La femme peintre et son modèle', *Positif*, 430, 9–10.

167

S.B. (1996) *'Jude'*, *Cahiers du cinéma*, 508, 82.

S.B. (1999) *'Happiness'*, *Cahiers du cinéma*, 532, 79.

O.D.B. (2000) *'Ratcatcher'*, *Le Point*, 7 January (BIFI press dossier).

Baignères, Claude (1992) 'La logique du malheur', *Le Figaro*, 23 October (BIFI press dossier).

Bal, Mieke (1999) *Quoting Caravaggio: Contemporary Art, Preposterous History.* Chicago and London: The University of Chicago Press.

Bal, Mieke, Jonathan Crewe & Leo Spitzer (eds) (1999) *Acts of Memory: Cultural Recall in the Present.* Hanover and London: Dartmouth College/University Press of New England.

Barthes, Roland (1981) *Camera Lucida: Reflections on Photography*, trans. Richard Howard. New York: Hill and Wang.

Bazin, André (1967) *What is Cinema?*, trans. Hugh Gray. Berkeley and Los Angeles: University of California Press.

Baudelaire, Charles (1961) *Les Fleurs du mal.* Paris: Garnier.

Beaucage, Paul (1998a) 'Lars von Trier, cinéaste des limites', *Cinébulles*, 17, 2, 31–5.

_____ (1998b) *'Le Royaume II'*, *Cinébulles*, 17, 3, 53–5.

Berlant, Lauren (1997) *The Queen of America goes to Washington City: Essays on Sex and Citizenship.* Durham, North Carolina and London: Duke University Press.

_____ (2001) 'Trauma and Ineloquence', in Sara Ahmed & Jackie Stacey (eds) *Testimonial Cultures, Cultural Values*, 5, 1, 41–58.

Bernstein, Nina (2001) *The Lost Children of Wilder.* New York: Random House.

Bescos, José Maria (1992) *'Olivier, Olivier'*, *Pariscope*, 28 October, 83.

Best, Joel (1990) *Threatened Children: Rhetoric and Concern about Child-Victims.* Chicago and London: University of Chicago Press.

Berthomieu, Pierre (1996) *'Jude*: Vivantes couleurs', *Positif*, 430, 17–18.

Binard, Liliane & Jean-Luc Clouard (1997) *Le Drame de la pédophilie: Etat des lieux; Protection des enfants.* Paris: Albin Michel.

Birch, Helen (ed.) (1993) *Moving Targets: Women, Murder and Representation.* London: Virago Press.

Björkman, Stig (2000) *Lars von Trier: Conversations avec Stig Björkman.* Paris: Cahiers du cinéma.

Blumenfeld, Samuel (2000) *'Ratcatcher'*, *Le Monde*, 12 January (BIFI press dossier).

Bonsaver, Guido (2002) 'Three Colours Italian', *Sight and Sound*, 12, 2, 28–30.

Boyer, Marie-France (2000) *The Cult of the Virgin: Offerings, Ornaments and Festivals.* London: Thames and Hudson.

Boym, Svetlana (2000) *The Future of Nostalgia*. New York: Basic Books.

Bratton, Jackie, Jim Cook & Christine Gledhill (eds) (1994) *Melodrama: Stage, Picture, Screen*. London: BFI Publishing.

Brooks, Xan (1999) 'Happiness', *Sight and Sound*, 9, 4, 4.

Burnett, Ron (1990) 'Speaking of Parts', in Atom Egoyan, *Speaking Parts*. Toronto: Coach House Press, 9–22.

Butler, Judith (1990) *Gender Trouble: Feminism and the Subversion of Identity*. New York and London: Routledge.

____ (1991) 'Imitation and Gender Insubordination', in Diana Fuss (ed.) *Inside/Out: Lesbian Theories, Gay Theories*. New York and London: Routledge, 13–31.

____ (1993) *Bodies that Matter*. New York and London: Routledge.

A.C. (2000) 'Une Enfance à Glasgow', *Les Echos*, 12 January (BIFI press dossier).

Carrère, Emmanuel (1985) 'L'Europe après la pluie: sur *The Element of Crime*', *Positif*, 288, 45–6.

____ (1996) *La Classe de neige*. Paris: Gallimard.

Caruth, Cathy (ed.) (1995) *Trauma: Explorations in Memory*. Baltimore and London: Johns Hopkins University Press.

____ (1996) *Unclaimed Experience: Trauma, Narrative, and History*. Baltimore, Maryland and London: Johns Hopkins University Press.

____ (2000) 'Parting Words: Trauma, Silence and Survival', in Sara Ahmed & Jackie Stacey (eds) *Testimonial Cultures, Cultural Values*, 5, 1, 7–27.

Cavell, Stanley (1996) *Contesting Tears: The Hollywood Melodrama of the Unknown Woman*. Chicago and London: University of Chicago Press.

Charville, Christopher (1998) *Erick Zonca*. Paris: Editions Scope.

Cheshire, Ellen (2000) *Jane Campion*. Harpenden: Pocket Essentials.

Chevalier, Jacques (1986) *Kids: 50 films autour de l'enfance*. Paris: Centre National de Documentation Pédagogique.

____ (1988) *Kids: 51 films autour de l'enfance*. Paris: Centre National de Documentation Pédagogique.

Church Gibson, Pamela (2000) 'Fewer Weddings and More Funerals: Changes in the Heritage Film', in Robert Murphy (ed.) *British Cinema in the 1990s*. London: British Film Institute, 115–24.

Ciment, Michel & Hubert Niogret (1985) 'Entretien avec Lars von Trier', *Positif*, 288, 47–50.

Ciment, Michel & Yann Tobin (1996) '"Des personnages auxquels on refuse l'accès à la société": Entretien avec Michael Winterbottom', *Positif*, 430, 23–8.

Ciment, Michel (2000) 'Entretien: Lynne Ramsay, "Je préfère les stratégies obliques"', *Positif*, 467, 8–12.

Codelli, Lorenzo (2001) 'Entretien: Nanni Moretti', *Positif,* 483, 8–13.

Conn, Andrew Lewis (1999) 'The Bad Review *Happiness* Deserves', *Film Comment,* 35, 1, 70–2.

Cook, Pam (1996) *Fashioning the Nation: Costume and Identity in British Cinema.* London: British Film Institute.

Cooper, Kimberley (1999) 'Beyond the Clean and Proper', *Vertigo,* 9, 45–6.

Coppermann, Annie (1992) 'Le retour de l'enfant prodigue: *Olivier, Olivier,* d'Agnieszka Holland', *Les Echos,* 28 October (BIFI press dossier).

Creed, Barbara (1993) *The Monstrous-Feminine: Film, Feminism, Psychoanalysis.* London and New York: Routledge.

G.D. (2000) 'Un premier film pour Lynne Ramsay', *Le Figaroscope,* 12 January (BIFI press dossier).

Davis, Colin (2000) *Ethical Issues in French Fiction: Killing the Other.* London: Macmillan.

Deleuze, Gilles (1983) *Cinéma 1: L'Image-mouvement.* Paris: Minuit.

_____ (1985) *Cinéma 2: L'Image-temps.* Paris: Minuit.

Deleuze, Gilles & Claire Parnet (1996) *Dialogues.* Paris: Flammarion.

Desbarats, Carole, Daniele Riviere, Jacinto Lageira & Paul Virilio (1993) *Atom Egoyan.* Paris: Editions Dis Voir.

Egoyan, Atom (1993) *Speaking Parts.* Toronto: Coach House Press.

_____ (1995) *Exotica.* Toronto: Coach House Press.

Errigo, Angie (1996) *'Jude',* *Première,* 4, 9, 15.

Estève, Michel (ed.) (1994) *Krzysztof Kieślowski.* Paris: Lettres Modernes/ Etudes Cinématographiques.

J-M.F. (1992) 'Perdu: *Olivier, Olivier',* *Le Monde,* 31 October (BIFI press dossier).

Feinstein, Howard (1996) 'Heroine Chic', *Vanity Fair,* 436, December, 90–7.

Ferenczi, Aurélien (1992) 'Show Devant: Pascale Breugnot contre Agnieszka Holland', *7 à Paris,* 28 October, 20–3.

Films in Review (1997) 'FIR chats with director Michael Winterbottom', 48, 1–2, 73–4.

Fischer, Lucy (1989) *Shot/Countershot: Film Tradition and Women's Cinema.* Princeton, NJ: Princeton University Press.

_____ (1996) *Cinematernity: Film, Motherhood, Genre.* Princeton, NJ: Princeton University Press.

Francke, Lizzie (1996) 'On the Brink', *Sight and Sound,* 6, 11, 6–9.

Freud, Sigmund (1985a) *The Interpretation of Dreams, The Penguin Freud Library 4.* Harmondsworth: Penguin, 652–783.

_____ (1985b) 'The "Uncanny"', *The Penguin Freud Library 14, Art and Literature.* Harmondsworth: Penguin, 335–76.

_____ (1991a) 'Mourning and Melancholia', *The Penguin Freud Library 11,*

On Metapsychology: The Theory of Psychoanalysis. Harmondsworth: Penguin, 245–68.

____ (1991b) 'Beyond the Pleasure Principle', *The Penguin Freud Library 11, On Metapsychology: The Theory of Psychoanalysis.* Harmondsworth: Penguin, 269–338.

Frois, Emmanuèle (1992) 'La réalisatrice d'*Europa, Europa* abandonne les méandres de l'histoire pour raconter un authentique fait divers', *Le Figaro,* 23 October (BIFI press dossier).

Fuss, Diana (1990) *Essentially Speaking; Feminism, Nature and Difference.* New York and London: Routledge.

____ (1995) *Identification Papers.* New York and London: Routledge.

Garber, Marjorie, Beatrice Hansson & Rebecca L. Walkowitz (eds) (2000) *The Turn to Ethics.* New York and London: Routledge.

Gelder, Ken (2000) 'Jane Campion: Limits of Literary Cinema', in Deborah Cartmell & Imelda Whelehan (eds) *Adaptations: From Text to Screen, Screen to Text.* London and New York: Routledge, 157–71.

Gentry, Ric (1997) 'Painterly Touches', *American Cinematographer,* 78, 1, 50–7.

Gili, Jean A. (2001) '*La Chambre du fils*: La force du destin', *Positif,* 483, 6–7.

Gledhill, Christine (ed.) (1987) *Home is Where the Heart is: Studies in Melodrama and the Woman's Film.* London: BFI.

Goldstein, Ruth M. & Edith Zornow (1980) *The Screen Image of Youth: Movies about Children and Adolescents.* Metuchen, NJ and London: The Scarecrow Press.

Gomez, Carlos (1992) 'Frissons d'une mère et fascinants faits divers', *Le Journal du dimanche,* 25 October (BIFI press dossier).

Goodhew, Philip (1997) 'It was grim, I was happy', *Sight and Sound,* 7, 7, 61.

Grassin, Sophie (1999) '*Happiness* de Todd Solondz', *L'Express,* 11 February (BIFI press dossier).

Guthke, Karl S. (1999) *The Gender of Death: A Cultural History in Art and Literature.* Cambridge: Cambridge University Press.

Hallam, Elizabeth & Jenny Hockey (2001) *Death, Memory and Material Culture.* Oxford and New York: Berg.

Hampton, Howard (1995) 'Wetlands: *The Kingdom* of Lars von Trier', *Film Comment,* 31, 6, 40–7.

Haskell, Molly (1974) *From Reverance to Rape: The Treatment of Women in the Movies.* Baltimore: Penguin.

Hearty, Kitty Bowe (1998) 'Suburban Shocker', *Interview,* 34–6.

Herman, Judith (1994) *Trauma and Recovery.* London: Pandora.

Herpe, Noël (2000) '*Ratcatcher*: La pesanteur ou la grâce?', *Positif,* 467, 6–7.

Higonnet, Anne (1998) *Pictures of Innocence: The History and Crisis of Ideal Childhood*. London: Thames and Hudson.

Higson, Andrew (1996) *Dissolving Views: Key Writings on British Cinema*. London: Cassell.

Hirsch, Marianne (1997) *Family Frames: Photography, Narrative and Postmemory*. Cambridge, MA and London: Harvard University Press.

Hoberman, J. (2000) 'Filmmaker, Heal Thyself', *Village Voice*. Available at: http://www.villagevoice.com.

Holland, Agnieszka (1996) (in collaboration with Régis Debray and Yves Lapointe) *Olivier, Olivier*, trans. Gaile Sarma. Portsmouth, NH: Heinemann.

Homes, A. M. (1997) *The End of Alice*. London: Anchor.

hooks, bell (1996) *reel to real: race, sex and class at the movies*. London: Routledge.

Hughes, Ted (1998) *Birthday Letters*. London: Faber.

Huston, Nancy (1995) *Désirs et réalités: Textes choisis 1978–1994*. Montréal: Leméac.

Jacobson, Harlan (2002) 'Knock Before You Enter', *Film Comment*, 38, 1, 59.

James, Henry (1985) *Novels 1881–1886*. New York: The Library of America.

Jarman, Derek (1994) *Blue*. Woodstock: The Overlook Press.

Jeancolas, Jean-Pierre (1999) '*Tout sur ma mère*: Le corps est une enveloppe modifiable', *Positif*, 460, 12–25.

Johnson, Barbara (1987) *A World of Difference*. Baltimore and London: Johns Hopkins University Press.

____ (1998) *The Feminist Difference*. Cambridge, MA and London: Harvard University Press.

Jonquet, François (2000) '*Ratcatcher*', *L'Evenement du Jeudi*, 13 January (BIFI press dossier).

Kandinsky, Wassily (1977) *Concerning the Spiritual in Art*, trans. M. T. H. Sadler. New York: Dover Publications.

Kaplan, E. Ann (ed.) (1978) *Women in Film Noir*. London: BFI.

____ (ed.) Psychoanalysis and Cinema. New York and London: Routledge.

Kaufman, Anthony (1998) 'October Drops *Happiness*', *Independent Film and Video Monthly*, 21, 8, 8–10.

Kehr, Dave (1994) 'To Save the World: Kieślowski's *Three Colours Trilogy*', *Film Comment*, 30, 6, 10–20.

Kelly, Richard (2000) *The Name of this Book is Dogme 95*. London: Faber.

Kemp, Philip (2002) '*The Son's Room*', *Sight and Sound*, 12, 3, 56.

Kennedy, Harlan (2000) '*Ratcatcher*', *Film Comment*, 36, 1, 6–9.

Kieślowski, Krzysztof & Krzysztof Piesiewicz (1997) *Trois Couleurs: Bleu*. Paris: Arte Editions/Hachette.

Kincaid, James (1992) *Child-Loving: The Erotic Child and Victorian Culture.* New York: Routledge.

____ (1998) *Erotic Innocence: The Culture of Child Molesting.* Durham and London: Duke University Press.

Kinder, Marsha (1992) 'High Heels', *Film Quarterly,* 45, 3, 39–44.

Klass, Perri (1991) *Other Women's Children.* London: Mandarin Paperbacks.

Klinger, Barbara (1994) *Melodrama and Meaning: History, Culture, and the Films of Douglas Sirk.* Bloomington and Indianapolis: Indiana University Press.

Kristeva, Julia (1980) 'Giotto's Joy', *Desire in Language: a Semiotic Approach to Literature and Art,* trans. Leon S. Roudiez. New York: Columbia University Press, 210–36.

____ (1983) 'Stabat Mater', *Histoires d'amour.* Paris: Denoël, 295–327.

Kübler-Ross, Elisabeth (1983) *On Children and Death: How children and their parents can and do cope with death.* New York: Simon and Schuster.

Kuhn, Annette (1995) *Family Secrets: Acts of Memory and Imagination.* London and New York: Verso.

Lacan, Jacques (1994) *The Four Fundamental Concepts of Psycho-analysis,* trans. Alan Sheridan. London: Penguin.

Lalanne, Jean-Marc (1999) 'La nouvelle Eve', *Cahiers du cinéma,* 535, 34–5.

Landrot, Marine (2000) 'Ratcatcher', *Télérama,* 12 January (BIFI press dossier).

Landy, Marcia (2000) *Italian Film.* Cambridge and New York: Cambridge University Press.

Lane, Anthony (2002) Review of *The Son's Room, The New Yorker.* 4 February, 82. Available at: http://www.metacritic.com.

De Lauretis, Teresa (1994) *The Practice of Love: Lesbian Sexuality and Perverse Desire.* Bloomington and Indianapolis: Indiana University Press.

Le Fanu, Mark (1995) '*The Kingdom*: Esprit des étangs de blanchiment', *Positif,* 413/414, 115–17.

Lerner, Laurence (1997) *Angels and Absences: Child Deaths in the Nineteenth Century.* Nashville and London: Vanderbilt University Press.

Lipman, Amanda (1995) 'Exotica', *Sight and Sound,* 5, 5, 45.

Loiseau, Jean-Claude (1999) 'Pedro Almodóvar: *Tout sur ma mère*', *Télérama,* 2575, 28–34.

Lucia, Cynthia & Ed Kelleher (1999) 'Happiness', *Cinéaste,* 24, 2–3, 80–3.

J.-L. M. (1992) 'Abondance de thème: *Olivier, Olivier* d'Agnieszka Holland', *La Croix,* 31 October (BIFI press dossier).

J. M. (1992) '*Olivier, Olivier*', *Cahiers du cinéma,* 461, 72–3.

P. M. (2000) 'Ratcatcher', *Le Nouvel Observateur,* 13 January (BIFI press dossier).

Macnab, Geoffrey (1993) '*Trois Couleurs: Bleu*', *Sight and Sound*, 3, 11, 54–5.

____ (1996a) '*The Kingdom (Riget)*', *Sight and Sound*, 6, 1, 43–4.

____ (1996b) '*Jude*', *Sight and Sound*, 6, 10, 45–6.

____ (1997) 'The Inscrutable in pursuit of the Unspeakable', *The Independent*, *The Eye on Friday*, 19 September, 12–13.

Malcolm, Derek (1997) 'Review of *Jude*', *Moving Pictures International*, 23, 13.

____ (1999) '*Ratcatcher*', *The Guardian*, 16 August 1999. Available at: http://film.guardian.co.uk/edinburgh/story/o,4135,74289,00.htmL

Mann, Sally (1994) *Still Time*. New York: Aperture.

Margolis, Harriet (ed.) (2000) *Jane Campion's The Piano*. Cambridge: Cambridge University Press.

Marks, Laura (1994) 'Deterritorialized Film-making: a Deleuzian politics of hybrid cinema', *Screen*, 35, 3, 244–64.

____ (2000) *The Skin of the Film: Intercultural Cinema, Embodiment and the Senses*. Durham, North Carolina and London: Duke University Press.

Marshall, Lee (2001) '*La Stanza del figlio*', *Screen International*, 16 March, 22.

Mather, Philippe (1995) 'Un hôpital fantastique', *Cinébulles*, 14, 4, 16–17.

Maurer, Monika (2000) *Krzysztof Kieślowski*. Harpenden: Pocket Essentials.

Mayne, Judith (1992) 'Paradoxes of Spectatorship', in Linda Williams (ed.) *Viewing Positions*, 155–83.

____ (1993) *Cinema and Spectatorship*. New York and London: Routledge.

McFarlane, Brian (1996) '*Jude*', *Cinema Papers*, 113, 53–4.

____ (1997) '*The Portrait of a Lady*', *Cinema Papers*, 115, April, 35–7.

Metz, Christian (1982) *Psychoanalysis and Cinema: The Imaginary Signifier*. trans. Celia Britton, Annwyl Williams, Ben Brewster & Alfred Guzzetti. London: Macmillan.

Modleski, Tania (1988) *The Women Who Knew Too Much*. New York and London: Methuen.

Mottet, Jean (ed.) (1999) *Les Paysages du cinéma*. Seyssel: Editions Champ Vallon.

Mueller, Matt (1997) 'Kidman Forever', *Première*, 5, 2, 44–51.

Mulvey, Laura (1988) 'Visual Pleasure and Narrative Cinema', in Constance Penley (ed.) *Feminism and Film Theory*. New York: Routledge, 57–68.

Nicholls, Mark (1997) 'She Who Gets Slapped: Jane Campion's *Portrait of a Lady*', *Metro*, 111, 43–7.

O'Neill, Eithne (1998) '*The Kingdom II*: vérité monstrueuse', *Positif*, 452, 58–9.

O'Shea, Sinead (2002) '*The Son's Room/La Stanza del figlio*, *Film Ireland*,

86, 33.

O'Sullivan, Charlotte (1999) *'Ratcatcher'*, *Sight and Sound*, 9, 11, 50–1.

Ozick, Cynthia (2000) 'Cinematic James', *Quarrel and Quandary*. New York: Alfred A. Knopf, 148–54.

Parish, James Robert (1994) *Ghosts and Angels in Hollywood Films*. Jefferson, NC and London: McFarland.

Penley, Constance (1989) *The Future of an Illusion: Film, Feminism, and Psychoanalysis*. Minneapolis: University of Minnesota Press.

Pevere, Geoff (1995) 'No Place Like Home: The films of Atom Egoyan', Atom Egoyan, *Exotica*, 9–41.

Phelan, Peggy (2001) 'Converging glances: A Response to Cathy Caruth's "Parting Words"', in Sara Ahmed & Jackie Stacey (eds), *Testimonial Cultures, Cultural Values*, 5, 1, 27–40.

Piégay, Baptiste (2000) *'Ratcatcher'*, *Cahiers du cinéma*, 542, 70.

Pierce, Peter (1999) *The Country of Lost Children: An Australian Anxiety*. Cambridge: Cambridge University Press.

Pincus, Adam (1999) 'Mommie Dearest', *Filmmaker*, 8, 1, 46–9.

Poisson, Marie-Eve (1995) 'Entretien avec Lars von Trier', *Positif*, 413/414, 118–22.

Porte, Joel (ed.) (1990) *New Essays on The Portrait of a Lady*. Cambridge: Cambridge University Press.

Portnoy, Sean (1997) 'Unmasking Sound: Music and Representation in The Shout and Blue', *Spectator*, 17, 2, 50–9.

Radstone, Susannah (2001) 'Social Bonds and Psychical Order: Testimonies', in Sara Ahmed & Jackie Stacey (eds) *Testimonial Cultures, Cultural Values*, 5, 1, 59–78.

Rae, Graham (2000) 'Striking Gold in Glasgow's Trash-Strewn Streets', *American Cinematographer*, 81, 4, 14–17.

Ramsay, Lynne (1999) *Ratcatcher*. London: Faber.

Richard, Frédéric (1992) *'Olivier, Olivier*: Détournement mineur', *Positif*, 381, 40–1.

Rodier, Melanie (2001) 'Case Study: *The Son's Room*', *Screen International*, 8 June, 17.

Rohrer, Trish Deitch (1998) 'Sexual Perversity in New Jersey', *Première*, 12, 3, 61–4.

Romney, Jonathan (1993) *'Olivier, Olivier'*, *Sight and Sound*, 3, 2, 53–4.

_____ (1995) 'Exploitations', *Sight and Sound*, 5, 5, 6–8.

Rooney, David (2001) *'The Son's Room'*, *Variety*, 19 March, 30.

Roy, Jean (1992) 'Campagne et gros sabots', *L'Humanité*, 5 September (BIFI press dossier).

_____ (2000) 'L'Espoir sous la fange', *L'Humanité*, 12 January (BIFI press dossier).

Ruby, Jay (1995) *Secure the Shadow: Death and Photography in America.* Cambridge, Massachusetts and London: The MIT Press.

Sanderson, Mark (1996) *Don't Look Now.* London: BFI.

Silverman, Kaja (1988) *The Acoustic Mirror: The Female Voice in Psycho-analysis and Cinema.* Bloomington and Indianapolis: Indiana University Press.

_____ (1992) *Male Subjectivity at the Margins.* New York and London: Routledge.

Simonelli, Rocco (1997) 'Jude', *Films in Review,* 48, 1–2, 73–4.

Smith, Paul Julian (1994) *Desire Unlimited: The Cinema of Pedro Almodóvar.* London: Verso.

_____ (1996) *Vision Machines: Cinema, Literature and Sexuality in Spain and Cuba.* London: Verso.

_____ (1999) 'Silicone and Sentiment', *Sight and Sound,* 9, 9, 28–30.

Soila, Tytti, Astrid Söderbergh & Gunnar Iversen (1998) *Nordic National Cinemas.* London and New York: Routledge.

Solondz, Todd (1998) *Happiness.* London: Faber.

Spencer, Liese (1999) 'What are you looking at?', *Sight and Sound,* 9, 10, 16–19.

O.St (2000) 'L'Enfance mal traitée', *Libération,* 12 January (BIFI press dossier).

Stacey, Jackie (1987) 'Desperately Seeking Difference', *Screen,* 28, 1, 48–61.

_____ (1994) *Star Gazing: Hollywood Cinema and Female Spectatorship.* London and New York: Routledge.

Strauss, Frédéric (1994) *Pedro Almodóvar: Conversations avec Frédéric Strauss.* Paris: Cahiers du cinéma.

_____ (1996) *Almodóvar on Almodóvar,* trans. Yves Baignères. London: Faber and Faber.

_____ (1999) 'A coeur ouvert: Entretien avec Pedro Almodóvar', *Cahiers du cinéma,* 535, 36–40.

_____ (2000) *Conversations avec Pedro Almodóvar.* Paris: Cahiers du cinéma.

Tanner, Tony (1985) *Henry James: The Writer and his Work.* Amherst: University of Massachusetts Press.

Taylor, Charles (2000) 'Dream On', *Sight and Sound,* 10, 7, 36–7.

Tedisco, James N. & Michele A. Paludi (1996) *Missing Children: A Psychological Approach to Understanding the Causes and Consequences of Stranger and Non-stranger Abduction of Children.* Albany: State University of New York Press.

Tesson, Charles (2001) 'Où sont passées les découvertes?', *Cahiers du cinéma,* 558, 12–14.

Thomson, Patricia (1998) 'Rechristening *The Kingdom*', *American Cinematographer*, 79, 6, 24–8.

Toscan du Plantier, Daniel (1992) 'Holland: La Pologne en France', *Le Figaro* magazine, 31 October (BIFI press dossier).

Tranchant, Marie-Noëlle (2000) 'Lynne Ramsay, l'enfance retrouvée', *Le Figaro*, 13 January 2000 (BIFI press dossier).

Trémois, Claude-Marie (1992) *'Olivier, Olivier'*, Télérama, 2233, 28 October, 38–9.

Vallet, François (1991) *L'Image de l'enfant au cinéma*. Paris: Les Editions du Cerf.

Vierne, Maïté (1995) *La Figure de l'ange au cinéma*. Paris: Les Editions du Cerf.

Viviani, Christian (1996) *'Portrait de femme*: L'art d'un portrait', *Positif*, 430, 6–8.

Warner, Marina (1978) *Alone of all her Sex: The Myth and Cult of the Virgin Mary*. London: Quartet.

Wenders, Wim (1989) *Emotion Pictures*. London: Faber.

Wright Wexman, Virginia (1999) (ed.) *Jane Campion: Interviews*. Jackson, Mississippi: University Press of Mississippi.

Williams, Linda (1990) *Hard Core*. London: Pandora.

_____ (ed.) (1994) *Viewing Positions: Ways of Seeing Film*. New Brunswick, New Jersey: Rutgers University Press.

Wood, Robin (1999) *The Wings of the Dove: Henry James in the 1990s*. London: BFI Modern Classics.

Deborah Young (2001) 'First Look: *The Son's Room*', *Film Comment*, 37, 3, 14–15.

_____ (2002) 'Me, Myself, and Italy', *Film Comment*, 38, 1, 56–8; 60–1.

Žižek, Slavoj (1989) *The Sublime Object of Ideology*. London: Verso.

_____ (1991) *Looking Awry: An Introduction to Jacques Lacan through Popular Culture*. Cambridge, Mass: The MIT Press.

_____ (1997) *The Plague of Fantasies*. London: Verso.

_____ (2000) *The Art of the Ridiculous Sublime: On David Lynch's Lost Highway*. Seattle: University of Washington [Walter Chapin Simpson Center for the Humanities Occasional Papers 1].

Zweig, Stefan (1999) *Twenty-Four Hours in the Life of a Woman*, trans. Eden and Cedar Paul. London: Pushkin Press.

INDEX